The Business Organisation
and its
Environment

The Business Organisation
and its
Environment

BOOK 1

Matthew Glew

Michael Watts

Ronald Wells

Heinemann Educational Books

Heinemann Educational Books Ltd
22 Bedford Square, London WC1B 3HH

LONDON EDINBURGH MELBOURNE AUCKLAND
HONG KONG SINGAPORE KUALA LUMPUR NEW DELHI
IBADAN NAIROBI JOHANNESBURG
EXETER (NH) KINGSTON PORT OF SPAIN

First published 1979
Reprinted 1979
Reprinted with amendments 1980, 1983

British Library Cataloguing in Publication Data

Glew, Matthew
    The business organisation and its environment.
    1. Corporations
    I. Title   II. Watts, Michael, b.1943
    III. Wells, Ronald
    338.7   HD2731

    ISBN 0–435–45899–X

Printed in Great Britain by Butler & Tanner Ltd,
Frome and London

Contents

Preface

The two volumes of this book and their respective workbooks are specifically designed to assist students studying Common Core Modules 3 and 4 entitled 'The Organisation in its Environment' which represents an integral part of the Business Education Council National Award. The contents and its format closely follow the National Award Course Specification.

The book seeks to guide students towards an understanding of their roles within the business environment. Consequently it provides them with a basis for analysing the economic, legal, social and political problems that effect the business world. The material has been presented in such a way that it is in accordance with the underlying BEC philosophy of an interdisciplinary approach to business studies courses. A balance has been maintained throughout the book between the disciplines of economics, law, government and sociology, thus providing a complete view of the operations of the business organisation.

The book will also prove valuable for students requiring an introduction or conversion course to the BEC Higher National Award. In addition, students engaged upon professional and managerial courses will find that the wide perspective which it provides on the business environment can successfully augment their studies.

Matthew T. Glew
Michael G. Watts
Ronald M. Wells
November 1978

1. The Reasons for Different Forms of Organisation

Reasons why organisations are formed

The discovery of oil off the UK coastline has undoubtedly been one of the most exciting and economically significant events of this century. However, its successful exploitation has required one of the most expensive, highly technical and complex operations ever undertaken. For example, the exploration of the famous Forties oil field in the North Sea has involved working over 2000 metres below the sea-bed in water as deep as 130 metres. The complexity of the operation is even more apparent when it is realised that a single rig on a nine-day exploration of the North Sea requires around 3000 tonnes of equipment in order to operate. Supplies of casing, fuel, mud, and cement as well as the necessary spare parts, food and clothing must all be transported from a supply base which might be located over 100 miles away.

How can these technical and physical problems be overcome in order to make the best or optimum use of the oil available? The solution has been found in the development of appropriate organisations or systems of arrangements. These are capable of co-ordinating the discovery, drilling, refining and distribution stages of the oil operation. They are also able to employ a variety of specialists from all over the world, such as civil engineers, surveyors and geologists, and delegating authority to them in such a manner as to ensure that the task is carried out efficiently. This responsibility has been shouldered by a combination of state-controlled and multinational organisations.

It is possible to generalise from the particular case of North Sea oil to say that if man is to make the optimum use of any of the natural resources which are available to him then this may only be achieved through the development of an appropriate organisation. Consequently, this may be considered as the basic reason for the forming of any organisation, as its creation provides for the co-ordination of the operation, the employment of specialists and the appropriate delegation of authority to achieve the required overall objective.

The specific objectives of the organisation will determine whether it is established in the public or private sector. The **public sector** is that part of the economic system controlled by the government. Organisations created in this sector are generally concerned with the **maximisation of national welfare**. The **private sector** is that part of the economic system which is completely independent of government control. The specific objective leading to the creation of organisations in this sector is the **maximisation of profit**. A third type of organisation may be identified whose specific objective is the making of decisions as economically as possible. This type of organisation may operate in the public or private sectors, and is essentially an administrative body.

The reasons that have been put forward for the formation of an organisation are those which explain its initial conception. However, the continued existence of organisations and their growth is generally due to market forces, and economic and social pressures, which provide advantages for expansion. These will be explored in detail in Chapter 2.

Characteristics common to all forms of organisation

All organisations, whether in the public or private sectors, whether large or small, whether operating in a business or administrative environment have certain common features. These are illustrated in Fig. 1.1 (overleaf).

1. *All organisations are governed by certain rules and regulations*, which are either written down, verbally passed on, or assumed to be known. These provide guidance for those who are charged with the responsibility of ensuring the organisation's

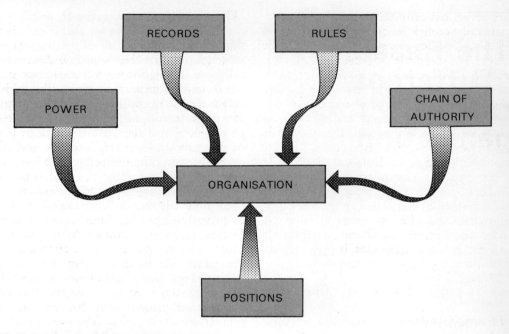

Fig. 1.1: Characteristics of organisations

future and adherence to certain required standards or procedures. For example, in the case of a small retailer these may merely be a question of handing down through the family the attitudes towards the business and the approach towards the customers that has been found to be most successful, whereas for a large manufacturing company the rules and regulations may be more formally expressed in the form of the Memorandum and Articles of Association, the organisation's manuals, the annual reports, or the employee's rulebooks.

2. *All organisations share a system of positions through which their work is actually carried out.* This means that everyone within an organisation has a role to perform. Obviously, large organisations will require many specialist roles, whereas small organisations will have individuals who are responsible for two or three functions. For instance, in a large company there would probably be a marketing department in which one individual might have the responsibility for export sales, whereas in a smaller concern one individual might have to combine the role of export manager with those of responsibility for advertising, market research, product planning and general domestic sales, under the umbrella title of marketing manager. Chapter 2 will investigate in detail the variety of different positions within the company.

3. *All organisations require some sort of recognised chain of authority* regarding the carrying out of certain jobs or functions. Basically, there must be someone at the head of any organisation with ultimate responsibility for its relative success or failure. This person should then be able to delegate certain functions and tasks to other individuals beneath him, who in turn should be able to do the same. The size of this structure will depend on the size of the organisation concerned. For example, the sole trader running a shop may be ultimately responsible for his business and only be able to delegate some of the service in the shop to his wife, whereas in a large company the managing director may take ultimate control, and he may then delegate to his directors the functions of marketing, finance, company secretary, production and personnel. They in turn will delegate to their subordinates, who in turn will delegate to the people beneath them, and so on.

4. The *power and authority within an organisation is vested in the hands of those who are capable of making decisions which ensure the achievement of the objectives of the organisation.* For example, in the case of a nationalised industry such as the Coal Board, ultimate power is in the hands of Parliament, the Minister for Energy, the Board and the chairman, who all influence the policy of the industry in various ways to ensure that it meets its objectives.

Authority refers basically to legalised authority, which generally comes from the owners of any business as they provide the resources to create the organisation. For example, legalised authority is vested in the shareholders of a company, who therefore earn a right to a say in how the company is run and attempts to achieve its objectives.

5. *All organisations have some system of recording information relating to their activities, which provides guidance for future action.* For instance, in the case of organisations working in the North Sea regular records are required relating to such matters as geological structures, drilling operations, refining, equipment, transport, personnel, costs and sales. This information is vital in order to develop appropriate production, purchasing, personnel, financial and marketing strategies. It is also necessary for fulfilling legal requirements such as taxation, VAT and so on.

Types of organisations

The diagram (Fig. 1.2) shows the major types of organisation operating in the United Kingdom. This section is to be devoted to a description of the nature and functions of the private and public sector business organisations. An examination will also be included of their different legal forms, and the social and economic implications of their activities. The public sector administrative organisation will be examined in depth in Book 2.

Fig. 1.2: Main types of organisations

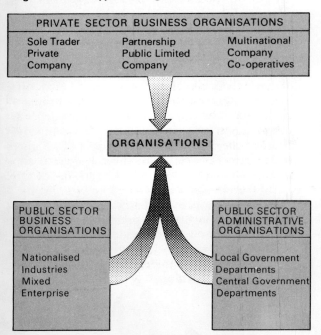

The Private sector

The Sole Trader

The sole trader is the simplest and, hence numerically, by far the most commonly occurring form of business organisation in the United Kingdom. Basically, a single person provides the capital, takes the decisions and assumes the risks of the business. It is a type of organisation particularly well suited to local retail outlets, and small local services such as hairdressers and window cleaners, where customers value personal attention.

Legally the sole trader has unlimited liability so that he is personally liable for all of the debts of his business up to the limit of his or her personal estate. This may mean that in the case of insolvency even the sole trader's house and car could be taken in order to settle his debts. There are no formal legal procedures to go through when setting up as a sole trader unless the business is being run under a name other than that of the owner. Then under the 1981 *Companies Act* the name of the business must be disclosed. For example, if Mr Jones was to run a window cleaning business called 'Sparkle' then he would need to disclose this name so that those dealing with his business are aware of his true identity. The affairs of the sole trader's business are completely private other than for the information that he has to reveal to the Inland Revenue for taxation purposes, and to Customs and Excise for the payment of Value Added Tax if his turnover is greater than £17,000 per annum.

The social and economic implications of sole traders are rather mixed. They epitomise the old idea of the free enterprise economy whereby the individual relied upon himself to make a living. He is his own boss, capable of implementing policies when he sees fit, and is answerable to no one apart from his consumers. This last point means that he tends to survive against the competition from his larger rivals by building up very good personal relationships with his customers, and trying to ensure that his service is of the highest standard. Another method of survival has been sought by many sole traders battling with the great multiples in the retail trade. By grouping together they have been able to enjoy some of the economies of scale associated with bulk purchasing. For example, 'Spar' (Society for the Protection of the Average Retailer) have formed their own purchasing and distribution system. These associations are able to benefit from some of the other advantages of large-scale organisations such as advertising and packaging.

Economically the sole trader suffers from a lack of finance. This is because he is largely dependent upon borrowing from the commercial banking system and is unable to command the same sort of credit as a larger organisation. Unfortunately, this means that any expansion or modernisation which might lead to greater consumer choice or lower prices is very difficult to achieve.

Finally, it should be remembered that it is often within very small simple organisations like that of the sole trader that new ideas may be nurtured, new industries bred and future industrial leaders trained.

The Partnership

A partnership may consist of any number between two and twenty persons. However, as a result of the 1967 *Companies Act* there is no restriction on the number of partners making up a firm of solicitors, accountants or members of a recognised stock exchange. The partners provide the capital for the business and share the resulting profit or loss. This is an ideal form of organisation for a relatively small business requiring more capital than one man can provide. It is particularly suitable for professional men such as doctors, dentists, accountants, architects and solicitors.

There are two types of partnership. The **'ordinary'** or **general partnership** was established by the 1890 *Partnership Act*. The basis of this type of partnership is that, in the absence of any statement to the contrary, all partners should share profits and losses equally; all partners are subject to unlimited liability; and all partners have equal rights in the running of the firm. The ordinary partnership is dissolved either compulsorily or voluntarily in the event of:

1. the termination of the agreed period of its duration;
2. the completion of the venture for which the firm was founded;
3. the general agreement of the partners;
4. the death or bankruptcy of any partner;
5. the order of a court.

The second type of partnership is the **'limited' partnership** which was established by the act of the same name in 1907. The advantage of this type of partnership is that it allows for the formation of a partnership between an active partner and one or more 'sleeping' partners, who are not partners in the fullest sense as they take no part in the management of the firm. However, they do enjoy the privilege of limited liability, which means that they are only liable for the debts of the business up to the extent of the capital they have put into the venture. Such partners are desired not for their expertise but rather for the capital they are prepared to put into the business.

Just as with the sole trader, the affairs of the partnership do not have to be revealed apart from to the Inland Revenue and Customs and Excise. The main significance of this type of organisation is that its structure allows for the taking on of specialists, and the provision of extra capital to finance an expansion where it is felt to be necessary. Like the sole trader, it is a sufficiently small and flexible type of organisation to encourage the development of new ideas, processes and initiatives.

The Private Joint Stock Company

The private joint stock company is one which has not stated in its Memorandum of Association that it is a public company. It consists of an association of not less than two people who contribute towards a joint stock of capital through the ownership of shares for the purpose of carrying on business for profit. The term **'joint stock'** refers to the total assets of the company and includes such items as plant, machinery, raw materials and stocks of finished goods. The ownership of these assets is vested in the shareholders who have put forward the finance with which the assets were acquired. In the case of many private firms the majority of shares may be held by the members of one family or one or two key directors in the business.

There are two main types of shares, which are referred to as **'preference'** and **'ordinary'**. The difference between these two types lies in the degree of risk associated with them. The ordinary share is the most risky, in that its return depends entirely upon the fortunes of the company. Although there is always the prospect of a higher dividend to compensate for the risk there is also the danger of a nil return. As the fortunes of this type of shareholder are so bound up with the fortunes of the company he has a right to elect the directors to manage it. The preference share is less risky as it carries a fixed dividend which is paid before the ordinary dividend is established. However, even these shareholders may receive nothing if the company has done very badly. Many preference shares are issued with 'cumulative' rights by which unpaid dividends may be carried forward to future years when the company's fortunes might have improved. Due to the smaller amount of risk involved in the holding of this type of share they very rarely carry any voting rights or say in the running of the company. In all cases the transfer and taking up of shares must be conducted through private channels. The private company is an ideal form of business enterprise for family concerns and the launching of new ideas or ventures and is often a natural development from the partnership or sole trader.

There are a number of legal requirements based on the *Companies Acts* of 1948, 1967, 1976, 1980 and 1981 that organisations must satisfy before they are able to operate as a company. Under these it is necessary for the company to submit certain documents.

1. The *Memorandum of Association* must state the company's name, address of its registered office, objectives, amount of authorised capital and that the liability of its members is limited. This document must be signed by at least two people who must declare that they wish to be formed into a company and promise to pay for the shares they have agreed to take.

2. The *Articles of Association* provide information on the proposed internal organisation of the company. They give details on such areas as the rights of shareholders, the procedure for private share transfer, and the manner in which meetings are to be held.

3. A statement has to be made concerning the company's nominal capital.

4. Particulars have to be given concerning the nature of the directors and secretary.

5. A declaration has to be made that the Company Acts have been complied with.

Once these documents have been approved, the company will be issued by the Registrar of Companies with a *Certificate of Incorporation*. This means that it is accepted as a separate legal entity which gives its members the privilege of limited liability. The shareholders are therefore only liable up to the extent of the size of their holding in the company. The company also has continuity while there are shareholders alive and able to trade. The affairs of this type of organisation are more public than those of the partnership and sole trader because it is required to file its accounts with the Registrar of Companies.

The overall control and management of the private company is generally in the hands of the **directors.** They are elected by the shareholders, and exercise their powers through a chief executive who may be a managing director or general manager. A private company need only have one director, and its directors may continue in office irrespective of their age. These factors combine to make it an attractive form of organisation for small family businesses. The voting powers of the company's shareholders at company meetings is generally proportionate to the number of shares that they hold.

The most important implication of the formation of a private joint stock company is that *it confers limited liability on its owners*. This principle of limited liability means that the degree of risk associated with any venture has been clearly expressed and so individuals may be more willing to invest in the enterprise. This means that many sole traders or partnerships are able, by forming themselves into private companies, to attract the type and amount of finance necessary to pursue new ventures, expand or modernise, which otherwise might have been impossible.

The Public Limited Joint Stock Company

This form of business organisation is essentially an extension of the private company. The main difference is that the public limited company must state in its Memorandum of Association that it is a public company. Also it may appeal to the general public for capital, and it must use in its name the words 'public limited company' or plc. There must be a minimum authorised share capital of £50,000. The rules concerning directors are different. A public company must have at least two directors, and the directors of a public company must retire at seventy unless continuance in office is approved by the shareholders. Finally, in the private company, many of the shareholders might be directly involved in the running and management of the business, whereas in the public company there is an apparent divorce between ownership and management. Although the shareholders own the company, they have little opportunity of directly influencing company policy, with the possible exception of annual general meetings or extraordinary meetings. Their control is exercised through the elected board of directors which then appoints the officials to run the business. This division is increased by the fact that people holding shares are always able to relinquish their ownership by freely selling them. When the shares are listed on the stock exchange the specialist facilities of this market may be used.

This form of organisation is especially suitable for large-scale activities where a great deal of capital is required. Consequently it tends to dominate in such areas as car production, the chemical and petro-chemical industries and the tobacco industry.

In a similar manner to the private company, the public company has to fulfil certain legal requirements and issue similar documents in order to qualify for a certificate of incorporation. But then it has the added power to issue a prospectus in an attempt to persuade the public to invest in the firm. The prospectus must be drawn up in accordance with the 1948 Companies Act giving details of the company's operations, history, financial position and directors. The actual sale of the shares will generally be handled by an Issuing House.

The activities of public joint stock companies in the United Kingdom have some very far reaching implications. As a form of business organisation they are relatively small in number, and yet they command a very significant portion of economic activity. The Annual Abstract of Statistics for 1982 reveals that in 1977 there were 975 quoted companies in the United Kingdom. They had a combined gross trading income of £11,522m, and each employed on average 5,564 people, with a combined employment representing just under 21 per cent of the total working population. Consequently their fortunes may be said to govern the livelihoods of many people in the United Kingdom.

The economic advantage they enjoy from being able to raise finance from the public means that the scope and scale of their operations may be very large. They are able to achieve all the benefits of economies of scale, and move towards a size at which they are making the optimum use of resources. It also suggests that where this sector raises finance on the open market, resources should be allocated towards those projects which are economically most sound.

Probably one of the most significant implications of the existence of this type of organisation is that due to the ease of the transfer of the ownership of shares; many financial institutions— for instance insurance companies, private pension funds and unit trusts—have been able to participate on behalf of their investors in the ownership of United Kingdom industry. This was revealed in the 1975 Royal Commission on Income and Wealth, Report No. 2 (Cmnd 6172) which showed that over 50 per cent of the ordinary shares of the top thirty public companies in the United Kingdom were held by institutions. This indicates that the ownership of industry is spread very far, because the institutions themselves have two million shareholders; some of the institutions are pensions funds with a total of thirteen and a quarter million members of occupational pension schemes, and other institutions are assurance companies with fourteen million savers through life assurance. Therefore, the true ownership of public companies is effectively in the hands of people who in many cases have little knowledge of the fact as they rely upon the financial institutions to handle their interests. This means that, quite apart from the significance of this type of organisation as an employer, the nation as a whole has a tremendous vested financial interest in its affairs.

Finally, as a result of the ease with which the shares of the public company may be transferred, another form of business organisation has grown up. This is referred to as a **holding company**, which has achieved financial control over other companies through the acquisition of shares. In some cases these subsidiary companies, as they are termed, may provide the holding company's only source of income. Financial control is achieved by the acquisition of 51 per cent of the ordinary shares of the subsidiary though often a holding of less than 50 per cent may give effective control. Each subsidiary retains its original name and continues to function as a separate entity. However, due to the majority shareholding of the holding company it may direct the policy of the subsidiary to fulfil its overall strategy.

Multinational Companies

A multinational could be defined as an organisation in which all considerations related to its growth processes and survival are based wholly on the interests of the organisation itself, national pressures having no influence except in so far as constraints are imposed on it by any country in which it functions. In addition a multinational is defined as an enterprise which owns or controls producing facilities (i.e. factories, mines, oil refineries, distribution outlets, offices, etc.) in more than one country. Taken together these two definitions conjure up a picture of a large world-wide organisation controlling many companies and outlets, whose pursuit of its own objectives comes before any national or even international considerations. This is, in fact, a fairly accurate description of some of the really large multinationals, such as Royal Dutch Shell, Unilever or General Motors. They are truly internationally based organisations with a management team including many different nationalities. They have world-wide interests, often highly diversified, and in some cases they control larger resources than some of the governments with which they deal, even in northern Europe let alone those of developing countries. Table 1.1 shows the world's leading multinationals. Their relative size may be appreciated when it is realised that Exxon's sales for 1978 of $280,076m. were equivalent to approximately 23 per cent of the United Kingdom's GNP.

Multinationals operating in the United Kingdom are obviously subject to the normal company acts, and are expected to abide by national economic, social, and political policies. However, it is not always possible to make them fully accountable; for instance, due to their international nature, they may not reveal information on their operations abroad. This international nature may be appreciated by considering the activities of British Petroleum which is the largest multinational concern in the United Kingdom. It operates in over 70 countries through 650 subsidiaries and associated companies.

Multinationals are undoubtedly the most significant of all the forms of business organisation.

It is predicted that by the turn of the century the largest two hundred and fifty multinationals will account for roughly half the world's output. The social and economic implications of their operations are considerable. They may help to stimulate growth in a country by injecting capital, skill, enterprise and expertise into their operations in its economy. For example, the North Sea oil programme benefited from the experience and expertise that the large multinationals were able to bring in from abroad. Due to their size, the multinationals are able to spend a great deal on research and development, which has meant that they have contributed a considerable amount to the world's technological development.

Multinationals have been criticised on the grounds that their activities may pose a serious threat to a country's national sovereignty. This is because, as they act internationally, they may switch resources between countries to secure the best labour, location and tax advantages and in so doing it may become beyond the power of any one government to control them. Also, by a system of internal transfer pricing, they may minimise their tax burden. This may be achieved by adjusting the price at which a product is transferred from a subsidiary in one country to that in another. By doing this the profits made on the product may be declared in the country with the most favourable tax rates. Such a situation is portrayed in Fig. 1.3 (p.8) which shows the advantage to the multinational of declaring its profits in country B, thus minimising its total tax burden. Multinationals may undermine national sovereignty still further

Table 1.1: The world's leading multinationals

Company	Country of origin	Main activity	Sales 1978 ($ million)
Exxon	USA	Petroleum products, gas, chemicals	64,000
General Motors	USA	Automobiles	63,000
Royal Dutch Shell	UK/Neth.	Petroleum products, gas, chemicals	45,000
Ford Motor Company	USA	Automobiles	43,000
Mobil Oil	USA	Petroleum products, gas	37,000
Texaco	USA	Petroleum products, gas, chemicals	29,000
British Petroleum	UK	Petroleum products, gas, chemicals	27,000
Standard Oil of California	USA	Petroleum products, gas, chemicals	24,000
International Business Machines	USA	Office equipment, computers	21,000
Gulf Oil	USA	Petroleum products, gas, chemicals	20,000

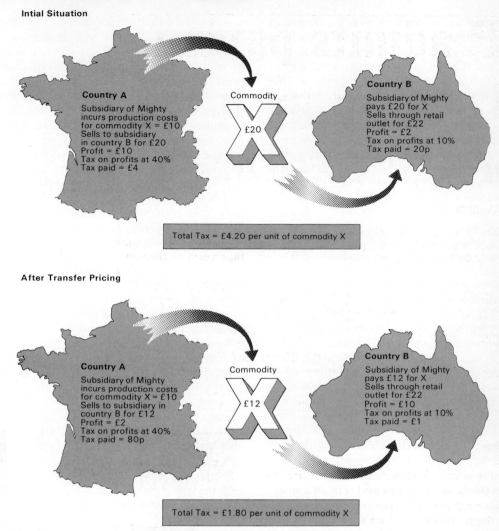

Intial Situation

Country A
Subsidiary of Mighty
incurs production costs
for commodity X = £10,
Sells to subsidiary
in country B for £20
Profit = £10
Tax on profits at 40%
Tax paid = £4

Commodity
X
£20

Country B
Subsidiary of Mighty
pays £20 for X
Sells through retail
outlet for £22
Profit = £2
Tax on profits at 10%
Tax paid = 20p

Total Tax = £4.20 per unit of commodity X

After Transfer Pricing

Country A
Subsidiary of Mighty
incurs production costs
for commodity X = £10
Sells to subsidiary in
country B for £12
Profit = £2
Tax on profits at 40%
Tax paid = 80p

Commodity
X
£12

Country B
Subsidiary of Mighty
pays £12 for X
Sells through retail
outlet for £22
Profit = £10
Tax on profits at 10%
Tax paid = £1

Total Tax = £1.80 per unit of commodity X

**Fig. 1.3: Transfer pricing between subsidiaries of
'Mighty' multinational company**

by switching sums of money from one country to another in anticipation of a devaluation or revaluation of the currency thus contributing to exchange rate instability. As about one-eighth of world trade is internal to multinationals it means that their activities may have a serious effect on the ability of a particular country to control its balance of payments. To a certain extent multi-nationals are able to ignore a country's financial, monetary, fiscal or prices and incomes policies because many of their activities take place abroad. Finally, they may even attempt to influence a country's internal politics as is shown by the news-paper article (Fig. 1.4) revealing some of the activi-ties of British Petroleum and Shell.

Co-operatives

A co-operative is basically a 'self-help' organisa-tion. It is a voluntary association of independent economic units such as households, workers, busi-nesses or farms who join together to control and share the profits of production, or to achieve economies in buying or selling products, or for finance or insurance. The main types of co-opera-tives operating in the United Kingdom are shown in Fig. 1.5.

The retail co-operative societies are the ones with which most people are familiar. They have to be registered as self-governing bodies under the *Industrial and Provident Societies Acts*. The members of these societies are also the customers

BP admits paying £1.3m. to push foreign contracts

BY KEVIN DONE

British Petroleum admitted yesterday that it paid out more than £1.3m. in contributions to political parties, payments to Government officials and commissions to potential customers' employees during the four years to the end of 1975.

The payments are disclosed in a report lodged by the company with the U.S. Securities and Exchange Commission drawn up after 12 months of internal investigations into more than 140 companies of the BP Group operating in more than 70 countries.

The investigations began after it was disclosed last year that BP and Shell had contributed £3.3m. to Italian political parties in the five years between 1969 and 1973. Of this total about

£800,000 came from BP.

During the four years of the latest investigations, 1972-75, £503,000 was paid out to political parties in Italy, and political contributions totalling £139,000 were made in six other countries.

Breaking established company rules, BP kept off-the-book funds in four countries totalling some £126,000.

Of this, about £56,000 was paid out to minor Government officials, and the remaining funds

were used for such diverse purposes as paying "commissions" to employees of customers without the customers' knowledge and reimbursing employees for expenses incurred by them abroad in excess of their foreign currency allowances.

A further £25,000 paid to Government officials and customers' employees were booked as commissions or distribution expenses and two payments totalling £2,600 went through as "repairs" and "car hire."

Fig. 1.4
Source: *Financial Times*, 4 June 1977.

who use the shops. The society's shares are not quoted on the stock exchange and remain constant in value. Any number of shares may be issued. The return to the members on their shares is normally in the form of a payment of fixed interest on capital and a dividend on purchases, either in the form of cash or trading stamps. The shareholders have only one vote each irrespective of the size of their investment in the society. This prevents any one member or group of members from taking control of the society. They elect a board of directors, or a Committee of Management, who in turn employ officials to manage the day-to-day running of the business, and are responsible for its overall policy. The retail societies are members of the Co-operative Wholesale Society (CWS) from whom they may purchase their stock. The CWS is managed by representatives elected from the retail societies and helps to provide, for the smaller societies in particular, some of the advantages of bulk purchasing which they would not otherwise have been able to enjoy.

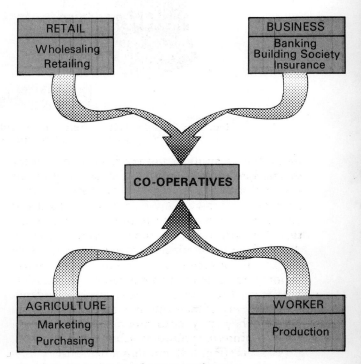

Fig. 1.5: Main types of co-operatives

During the past twenty years the retail societies have tended to suffer as a result of the competition from the larger supermarkets such as Tesco, Sainsburys and Fine Fare. Their share of the total retail business fell from 10·9 per cent to 7·0 per cent between 1961 and 1979, whereas that of the larger multiples rose from 29·2 per cent to 46 per cent. This decline in business has contributed towards the creation of a smaller number of larger co-operative units since the war. For example, after the Second World War there were well over 1000 separate societies in operation, whereas now there are less than 200, plus 30 branches of the Co-operative Retail Services Limited. This is the largest society with over two million members.

The main implication of the existence of this type of organisation in retailing concerns the aspect of 'self help'. By combining to form a retail co-operative, households should be capable of protecting themselves from unfair and dishonest trade practices and ensuring their needs as consumers are satisfied. This was the purpose of the first retail co-operative set up in Lancashire in 1844 by the 'Rochdale Pioneers'. They jointly provided the capital to open a small grocery warehouse to supply their needs. This was in order to fight against profiteering in the retail sector.

Apart from the retail societies there are a number of other co-operatives operating in the United Kingdom. In the field of commerce there is the Co-operative Bank, the Nationwide Building Society and Co-operative Insurance Society. In agriculture, marketing and purchasing co-operatives are formed. For example, farmers might find it advantageous to establish a co-operative for the purchase of fertilisers and foodstuffs, or for the marketing of fruit, livestock and grain. In each case larger quantities might be handled and consequently economies of scale enjoyed. In the field of production, a number of co-operatives exist producing such items as boots, shoes and clothing. The Labour Government of 1974–9 lent its support to the creation of more productive worker co-operatives where the purpose of establishing the co-operative was to save jobs. This was the case with Kirkby Manufacturing and Engineering, the Meriden Motor Cycle operation and the *Scottish Daily News*, all of which were threatened with closure and a resultant loss of jobs until the workers took over.

This type of organisation has tremendous social and economic implications, because in theory the wages of workers should be related to profits, which should encourage hard work and a raising of productivity. Also, as each worker is on equal terms with his counterpart, there should be very few industrial disputes. Certainly in the case of Meriden and Kirkby this seems to have been true as there was a noticeable change in shop floor attitudes and a significantly higher level of productivity after they became co-operatives.

Following the publication in October 1977 of a White Paper entitled 'Report of the Working Group on a Co-operative Development Agency' (Cmnd 6972) the last Labour Government set up a new Co-operative Development Agency. Its function was to identify, promote and encourage viable projects to be undertaken on a co-operative basis.

The public sector

The Nationalised Industries

A nationalised industry may be described as an organisation created by Act of Parliament, owned by the general public, but directed by the government. The major nationalised industries are shown in Table 1.2. Their relative size and significance as employers of labour may be appreciated when it is considered that Imperial Chemical Industries, which is the fourth largest private sector industrial company in the UK, employed 143,200 people in 1980 and had a turnover of £5,715,000,000.

Legally this type of organisation is vested not in a company but in a **public corporation**, which has been created by statute. The statute grants each

Table 1.2: The main nationalised industries, 1976–77

Industry	Turnover (£'000)	Employees
Electricity Council and Boards	6,093,700	158,780
Post Office	5,193,300	422,902
National Coal Board	3,740,400	297,000
British Gas Corporation	3,502,700	104,100
British Steel Corporation	3,105,000	181,000
British Railways Board	2,644,900	239,680
British Airways	1,919,600	56,866
British Shipbuilders	869,638	72,700
South of Scotland Electricity Board	625,437	13,624
National Bus Company	581,907	58,379

Source: '*The Times* 1000, 1981–82'

corporation certain fixed financial and economic rights and duties. The corporation is created as a separate legal entity which can sue and be sued in the courts, and which can hire and fire its staff. Therefore, with the exception of matters specified in the statutes, a public corporation is free to conduct its business as it sees fit, and even its finances are treated separately from those of the Government. Finally, the nationalised industries have no shareholders as such, as their equity is said to belong to the nation.

The nationalised industries are organised, controlled and run by four groups. First, *Parliament* which is responsible for general policy. Secondly, the *Minister* assigned to the industry who represents its interests in Parliament and is responsible for ensuring that its activities reflect the public interest. Thirdly, each nationalised industry has a *Board* or *Council* which is responsible for the day-to-day running of the industry. Finally, the activities of the nationalised industry are observed by the *Consumer Consultative Council*. It acts as a watchdog for the consumer and also as a sounding board for new ideas or proposed changes put forward by the Minister or Board.

The majority of nationalised industries were created as a result of the compulsory purchase by the Government on behalf of the nation of the assets and ownership of an industry which had previously been in the private sector. Obviously, such action has tremendous social, legal and economic implications. The recognition of these has depended to a large degree upon whether an individual is a supporter or opponent of nationalisation. The supporters see the process of nationalisation as the realisation of a natural monopoly. They claim that the very nature of such operations as rail, electricity and gas lend themselves to a large-scale form of organisation. This is because they have the potential to enjoy extensive economies of scale, and competition is deterred by the heavy initial costs of capital, research and advertising. Consequently they form a natural monopoly, and in order to reduce any danger of consumer exploitation, supporters feel that this should be operated in the public sector. Supporters also feel that nationalisation provides the state with the opportunity to control the allocation of some of the nation's key resources such as coal and steel. This is felt to be desirable because it is considered that the private sector sometimes fails through the market mechanism to recognise a particular need of society. Advocates of nationalisation also point out that it provides the state with the opportunity to control for strategic reasons those areas of economic activity, for instance transport, power and basic raw materials, which are crucial to national security. The case favouring the nationalised industries is also made on the basis that they are responsible for 10 per cent of GDP in Britain, and so it is possible for the Government to use them as a balancing factor in the economy. For example, during periods of high unemployment, jobs may be maintained in the nationalised sector. During perods of inflation their prices and costs, especially incomes, can be carefully controlled. Many western countries combine the nationalisation of certain basic industries with free enterprise in the rest of the economy. It is this mixture which leads to such economies being termed **mixed economies.**

Those opposed to nationalisation feel that it has rather different implications. The greatest complaint is that the nationalised industry is totally insensitive to the needs of its consumers due to its centralised form of administration. The fact that it is a state-run monopoly is felt to aggravate the situation still further. This is because it is considered that, as the industry has been effectively removed from the discipline of market forces, there is no way in which it can accurately gauge the needs of the consumer. Another major criticism often levelled at the nationalised industry concerns the way in which it is controlled and administered. It is felt that the administration of an individual industry or service requires an approach which is totally different from that employed in government administration. It is claimed, therefore, that the Government personnel involved in running the nationalised industry are incapable of carrying out the task efficiently. Added to this is the point that the public sector lacks the spur to efficiency of the profit motive, which dominates in the private sector. Finally, some opponents of nationalisation feel that it will lead to an extension of state activities which will result in an infringement of private rights in that private property is compulsorily taken into public control.

The Mixed Enterprise and the National Enterprise Board

The mixed enterprise might be described as a sort of mixed joint stock company. Basically, it is an ordinary joint stock company created under the normal company acts in which the state participates as a shareholder. The balance of the shares are held privately. Where the state is the dominant shareholder it is able to control the policies of the company. On the other hand, if the state is merely a significant shareholder, then the company will continue to operate in a similar way to any other public or private company.

The **National Enterprise Board** (NEB) which was set up under the 1975 *Industry Act*, controls these new mixed enterprises. The Board acts as a kind of holding company to which the Government entrusts its shares in the various mixed enterprises. The principle interests of the National Enterprise Board in these mixed enterprises are shown in Table 1.3. The subsidiary companies are those in which the Government has a controlling interest. The associated companies and other investments are those with which

the Board has become generally involved in order to provide finance for expansion and technological innovation and development.

The National Enterprise Board is answerable to the Secretary of State in the same way as the nationalised industries. Although the Secretary of State is responsible for appointing the Board, all the appointments in the mixed enterprises are its responsibility.

When the National Enterprise Board was originally created under a Labour Government in 1975 its wider long-term role had the greatest significance, because it suggested a fundamental restructuring of British industry around a larger public sector. The Board had been given the task of creating a more competitive industrial economy, and of providing or safeguarding employ-

Table 1.3: Principle Interests of the National Enterprise Board, 1981

	Main Activity	Shareholding		Percentage held by the NEB
In subsidiary companies				
Aregon Group Ltd	View data software	2,500,000	Ord	75.8
		2,500,000	Pref	100
British Underwater Engineering Ltd	Underwater engineering equipment	2,388,714	Ord	73·5
		5,430,286	Pref Voting	70·9
Data Recording Instrument Co Ltd	Computer peripherals	14,290,000	Ord	100
		1,000,000	Pref	100
INMOS International PLC	Integrated circuits	1,850,000	Ord	56
		2,500,000	Pref	100
INSAC Group Ltd	Software marketing	9,100,000	Ord	100
NEXOS Office Systems Ltd	Electronic office systems	155,990	Ord	52·5
		28,257,000	Pref Voting	100
Wholesale Vehicle Finance	Motor distributor finance	7,246,250	Ord	75
In associated companies				
Celltech Ltd	Bioengineering	5,060,000	Pref Ord ⎫	44
		220,000	Ord ⎭	
George P Brown (Holdings) Ltd	Welding and metal forming equipment	14,700	Ord	49
		27,551	Pref	100
Monotype Holdings Ltd	Typesetting equipment	22,785,430	Ord	49·8
Systems Programming Holdings Ltd	Software services	200,000	Ord	40
		1,200,300	Non-Voting Ord	40
Systime Ltd	EDP systems marketing	92,900	Ord ⎫	29·5
		47,600	Voting Pref ⎭	
		1,350,000	Pref	50
In other investments				
Francis Shaw PLC	Process machinery	1,400,000	Pref Ord	100
Quest Automation PLC	Computer aided design	490,815	Ord	3.5
		2,250,000	Pref	100

Source: National Enterprise Board, *Annual Report and Accounts 1981*

ment. It was to attempt to do this by assisting firms with investments, reorganising industry where necessary through the extension of public ownership into both ailing and profitable companies, and promoting industrial democracy in the undertakings it controlled.

There were fundamental changes to this long-term role when a Conservative Government came to power in 1979. Under some of the provisions of the 1980 *Industry Act* the Conservative Government considerably reduced the powers of the NEB. It was directed by the Government to concentrate on providing help to high technology companies, firms in the assisted areas and small businesses. As part of the Conservative Government's general policy of *privatisation* the NEB's subsidiaries had to be returned to private ownership once they had become viable; for example, in 1981 the NEB's interests in System Designers International Ltd were sold for £1·19m. Also before acquiring shares in companies or making loans, the NEB had to demonstrate that the companies involved could not acquire finance from the private sector.

In September 1981 the position of the NEB was altered still further when it was combined with the National Research Development Corporation (NRDC) to operate under the title of the British Technology Group. The NRDC had originally been set up in 1949 in order to provide support for the exploitation of inventions and finance for innovation by industrial companies. Under the new framework both organizations were to retain their existing statutory functions and purposes and were to be separately accountable to parliament. However, by linking the technical expertise of the NRDC with the commercial experience of the NEB it was hoped that the British Technology Group would:

1. encourage investment in technical innovation;

2. exploit technology derived from UK public sector sources such as the universities, polytechnics and various research bodies;

3. provide finance for small companies with growth and innovative potential;

4. encourage investment in high technology industries in the English Assisted Areas.

2. The Organisation—its Objectives and Policies

The maximisation of profits and conflicting objectives in the private sector

In order to assess the success of a company, it is necessary first to discover its broad **objectives**, then to examine the business decisions taken by the company, and to appraise them in the light of its objectives. In short, the success of an organisation will be measured against the extent to which its aims are secured. To conduct such an analysis it is necessary to identify the range of objectives which may be open to a firm.

The Importance of Profits
It is often assumed that in a capitalist economy, or within the market sector of a mixed economy, the sole pursuit of a firm is the maximisation of profits. Indeed this is an important assumption in that part of micro-economic analysis which seeks to demonstrate how a firm, under varying degrees of competition, will decide upon a level output when this objective of maximum profits is secured. Such theory deals not only with the desire of the firm to achieve maximum profits but also with the aim of securing at least 'normal profits'.

A firm may be making profits after deducting the costs associated with production, but there is also a certain level of profit which is necessary in order to produce a return on capital which compensates the owners for the risks which they have taken. The theory then suggests that this minimum return which owners are prepared to accept would be regarded as a 'normal' profit, and if such a return is not forthcoming then capital will eventually be withdrawn from the enterprise and invested elsewhere. What is regarded as a 'normal' profit will of course according to this definition differ between industries, as the degree of risk will depend upon the type of activity the enterprise is engaged in. If a firm is operating in a highly competitive and uncertain market, this normal profit will have to be far greater than the normal profit acceptable from a business venture in a more secure market. This normal profit is in fact likened to a cost, in that it must be covered, and any profits in excess of this level are regarded as 'pure' profit and are seen as an additional return to the owners of capital which more than compensates for the risks involved.

The Gap Between Ownership and Control
The development of the joint stock company as a type of business unit has made possible the growth of major firms, ownership of which is in some cases spread over many thousands of **shareholders**. The powers to decide upon the policies which the company should follow have been vested in the **board of directors**, while the more detailed running of the business, implementing company policies, will be largely left to **salaried managers**. A growing characteristic therefore of major firms is the widening gap that exists between ownership and control, and whereas the main concern of shareholders as owners may be the maximisation of the return on their investment, those who actually exert influence over the control of the company may see the need to subordinate the objective of maximising profits to other policy aims. A conflict may arise therefore between what the shareholders see as the main objectives of the company, and what the board of directors and the professional management of the concern regard as priorities. If shareholders regard the maximisation of profits as the primary objective, and manage to organise themselves effectively so that their views are eventually communicated to those responsible for taking business decisions, there is no guarantee that the shareholders will possess the business expertise to ensure that future decisions comply with their objective. Their review of the company's activities would have to be both detailed and ongoing and would present them with formidable problems of organisation and might even hinder the running of the business itself. The very size of company which the joint stock venture has promoted has produced a highly complex business unit which the average shareholder will have great difficulty in understanding.

Status and Prestige
The objectives of the company, which are not necessarily compatible with the maximisation of

profits, will perhaps reflect the aims of those holding directorships and management positions. This situation may not arise if those holding such positions of influence also have a substantial capital stake in the business. A company may, for example, have started as a relatively small family concern and the desire to secure profitable expansion may have obliged the owners to seek additional funds via the transformation to a joint stock company. In this case, the retention of large capital stakes by the original owners and their appointment to top management or directorships will ensure that their profit motive remains dominant.

If, however, such a large and direct influence does not exist, then other objectives can be pursued. Once a profit level has been reached which directors and managers believe will satisfy shareholders, chances arise to pursue other aims. The board of directors may be dominated by personalities who seek to identify themselves with a very large company, and they may see the appropriate yardstick as being the extent to which the company expands in terms of the volume of sales or turnover. This may help to secure greater prestige for these people themselves, but the result may not be a maximisation of profits. The extra units of output may add more to costs than to the firm's revenue, but as long as a 'normal' profit is produced the directors may be satisfying shareholders while still being able to enhance their reputations with status and prestige.

This non-monetary objective may also be furthered by emphasising the importance of product development and improved techniques which, although impressive from the purely technological point of view, may not be directly geared to maximising profits. Research and development projects involve substantial sums of money and may be undertaken even though they yield a lower return than if the funds had been spent on less prestigious but more practical projects.

Security and Power

Security may be another objective. Directors and managers may feel that their security of tenure is greater if they operate the business to ensure a secure profit, although perhaps a lower one than could be achieved. Maximising profits may involve risks that threaten their positions if a new aspect of the business should prove unsuccessful.

These objectives can be furthered by seeking to expand the volume of sales and so securing a larger share of the market. This increase in sales and more powerful position in the market may be seen as a means of reducing the threat from both existing and potential competitors. Again this may result in the company extending its volume of sales to a level that would not be justified if profit was the sole motive. Such an expansion of the firm may also widen the power and area of responsibility of managers and directors and earn them a salary in excess of those in smaller but more profitable concerns.

The Influence of Government Policy

The objectives of the firm may also be influenced by pressures originating from outside sources and in particular from governments seeking to achieve certain political, social and economic objectives through the activities of businesses. The environment within which the firm operates will be partly a reflection of the current government's policies in these areas, and the firm will be obliged to take account of them in formulating its objectives. The pursuit of profit, security, prestige or power may involve business decisions which may have to be tempered by taking account of their impact upon employment levels, either national or local, the implications for industrial relations, the effect upon the environment, consumer safety, and the extent to which they comply with the government's interpretation of competition and monopoly. At the same time pressure may be exerted upon employers to consider the repercussions of their decisions upon the general economic climate and the course of economic events which such decisions may influence. It has been suggested that firms are beginning to display a social conscience in that they may prove amenable to external pressures and act within a code of business conduct that takes account of wider non-commercial issues.

The Reconciliation of Conflicting Objectives

The degree to which profit maximisation is subordinated to other objectives involves an analysis of the firm's policies in the light of different time periods. It may well be that what at first seem to be the conflicting objectives of shareholders and those who actually control the business, can in fact be more closely reconciled when short-term and long-term effects of decisions are assessed. The following discussion of the means by which a firm can secure its objectives may help to throw some additional light upon this debate.

Policies to secure the organisation's objectives

A feature of the last decade is the rapid concentration of industrial and commercial activities so that the output of many goods and services now lies under the control of a few major companies. The reasons behind such concentration will depend upon the objectives of the firms involved, and one can again identify the motive of increased profits as a major influence.

Horizontal Integration and the Reduction in Unit Costs

A firm is said to expand horizontally when it increases the scale of its operations while continuing to specialise in its existing range of output. As its output rises it can expect to benefit from **economies of scale** in that for a given proportionate increase in output the firm can expect to incur a less than proportionate increase in its costs. The result of such an expansion would then be a fall in the unit costs of production, and on the assumption that the market was able to absorb the increased output without a major reduction in price, the firm could expect to increase its profits. Horizontal expansion may take the form of a simple amalgamation of enterprises producing the same product or providing the same service, and this is likely to guard against a fall in the market price of the good or service, as the total supply to the market may remain virtually unchanged. The more efficient output from a single but now larger concern will replace the separate supplies from the original firms which took part in the amalgamation. Once this breakthrough into lower unit costs is achieved, and profits increased, the process may indeed become cumulative. The improvement in efficiency and lower unit costs will enable the firm to become more competitive by lowering its prices below that of its remaining competitors and so securing a further increase in its market share. At the same time the increased profits will enable the firm to invest in the productive capacity to meet this increased demand, and this additional expansion may produce further economies of scale which will again strengthen its competitive position. It is possible that economies of scale will be derived in the following areas:

1. *The larger a firm becomes, the greater the opportunities for taking advantage of the increased specialisation or division of labour.* As the volume of output expands, an employee can be kept fully occupied on a narrow range of tasks and consequently become more skilled. The breaking down of a complicated job into a series of what may become routine operations allows the employment of relatively unskilled labour and allows more specialised skills to be used in aspects of production that use these skills more fully. Training periods can be shorter and therefore the worker becomes more productive at an earlier stage and an easily acquired skill will reduce wastage during the learning period. The splitting up of a complex task into easily identified operations is likely to hasten the introduction of increased mechanisation. A single worker will need only the equipment relevant to his own specialist task and time is saved in that he does not have to move around between operations to use different items of plant and equipment.

2. *There will also be economies associated with purchasing and marketing.* Raw materials, components and other inputs can be obtain at a lower unit cost if bought in bulk. The supplier will offer a discount because he in turn will benefit from the economies of scale associated with a long production run and bulk distribution. Purchasing staff will not have to be increased in the same proportion, particularly if the expansion of output produces increased orders placed with existing suppliers, and the staff may also be organised to deal with specialist areas of purchasing. When sales increase, the costs incurred in marketing will not rise in the same proportion, especially if increased sales are mainly to existing customers where again distribution economies may arise.

3. *Small firms suffer from the existence of the indivisibility of plant and machinery and other items of fixed capital in that they are generally available only in a limited range of working capacities.* A small firm will be forced to operate such items below full capacity but the maximum utilisation of capacity will be necessary to keep unit costs to a minimum and develop a strong competitive advantage. Only an increase in output may make this possible. If a larger item of capital is then required it will not cost proportionately more to purchase, operate and maintain.

4. *Financial economies will be open to a large, well-established firm which can raise funds on more favourable terms than a small firm.* The former can offer greater security and has a proven record of success, while the latter will be regarded as a more risky venture and accordingly be obliged to pay a higher rate of interest. The costs of floating a large

public issue of shares does not increase in the same proportion as the size of the issue.

5. *The position of a large firm will be further strengthened by the availability of funds for research and development and the employment of specialist staff in this department.* New products and techniques can then be put to profitable use and make it progressively more difficult for the small firm to close the competitive gap that exists between them and the large concerns.

Diseconomies of Scale as Constraints upon Horizontal Integration

Horizontal integration may be partly motivated by the firm's desire to gain a greater share of the market for reasons of security of profits, while also ensuring the survival of the organisation. A firm may therefore continue to expand despite the fact that its unit costs show a tendency to increase as it experiences diseconomies of scale. Its most profitable level of output may have been passed and the increasing size of the business brings organisational problems that may outweigh economies from the areas already described.

The sources of such diseconomies tend to be human in nature, whether at management level or shop floor. A very large and complex organisation will make demands upon management skills that cannot readily be met, because the supply of such skilled personnel at any one moment will be limited. The firm may grow at a rate which exceeds the improvement in managerial techniques required to guarantee the smooth and successful running of the business and to take advantage of potential economies of scale. The decision-taking procedure may be slowed down and sections within the organisation may sense a feeling of remoteness from each other. The process of expansion may have involved a greater degree of specialisation among workers which in turn may produce a deterioration in industrial relations. A disadvantage of the specialisation of labour is that workers become dissatisfied with the continuous repetition of a single routine operation and a consequent loss of job satisfaction. They may seek a higher monetary reward as compensation, and at the same time the greater bargaining strength which results from increased specialisation will make the threat of industrial action all the more serious for the firm, as the whole productive process may come to a halt if certain workers use strike action.

Horizontal Integration and other Objectives and Constraints

The striving for greater security of profits rather than their maximisation would also suggest policies designed to strengthen the firm's control over the market through a **merger** or **take-over**. This would help to dissipate some of the risks inherent in a competitive market and also accord with the objective of status and prestige. The merger may be promoted by a mutual interest in pooling resources to withstand the growing strength of an overseas producer who is attempting to make inroads into the domestic market. Survival may also be the motive for a merger during a recession, as neither firm may be sure which has the greatest potential to ride out the recession.

As far as potential competition is concerned, a firm may seek to stifle newcomers by price-cutting, which its greater financial strength may make possible, or by establishing subsidiary companies to undertake this operation on its behalf. The firm may sense a threat from a new technology that could produce a strong competitor, and here again the reaction may be to secure the company which is in the process of developing the new product or technique and obtain any patent rights. The patent may not necessarily be exploited, but the firm will feel more secure if it is obtained. At the same time a firm may hesitate to undertake its own investment programme, as such schemes often involve expenditure totalling many millions of pounds, and a greater control over a large part of the market may be a prerequisite for new projects if they are to produce an acceptable return. A long period often exists between the start of such developments and when they actually come into operation and make a contribution to revenue that covers the initial outlay. A secure position in the market will help to reduce some of the risks involved.

The successful development and application of a new technology can also be seen as a means of promoting security itself in that it can be likened to a 'barrier' to entry for potential competitors. They may not be willing to accept the risk of failing to gain a sufficiently large share of the market to enable them to reach the minimum level of output necessary for such technology to be commercially viable. This may indeed prevent them at the outset from raising the initial capital, and investors will be aware of the existing dominance of well-established firms.

The possibility always exists that the horizontal integration of a firm may produce such a strong hold over the market that, feeling protected from competition, it gradually increases its prices and profits and generally uses its position of power narrowly to pursue its own interests. Policies designed to achieve a more secure position in the market could then be interpreted as a means of obtaining much larger long-run profits. The extent to which a firm can reap such profits will depend upon the degree of vigilance exercised by the Monopolies Commission and used in implementing measures, passed by the government to prevent or control monopoly situations, such as the Restrictive Trade Practices Acts and the Monopolies and Mergers Act. Even if intervention is not forthcoming, the profits derived from the market in question may reach those levels which make technical 'barriers' to entry more readily surmountable, as the anticipated return may make the development of previously uneconomic substitutes more attractive.

Such monopoly profits and the subsequent adverse publicity may harm the company's public image and detract from the possible objectives of prestige and status. Similarly an organisation may pass over the possibility of making large profits out of a sudden and temporary shortage of a product, such as a foodstuff, where output is very susceptible to outside influence. The firm may place a value upon the resultant loss of goodwill and the impact upon future customer loyalty. A further discipline may also be the state of the labour market. During a period of recession a firm may hesitate to make its workers redundant as this may jeopardize its situation in the event of an upturn in the market. To lay off skilled workers and break up successful research units involves the risk of being unable to recruit them when demand recovers. Such decisions however will rely heavily upon the firm's interpretation of future market trends. It may even be prepared to produce output to add to its stock of finished goods and this will also ensure links with suppliers. Other short-term measures may include providing its customers with extended credit facilities to protect its sales outlets. It will have a vested interest in extending trade credit, without which those firms which constitute its customers cannot survive. These short-term objectives will, however, be constantly reviewed in the light of the anticipated duration of the downturn, and the extent to which they will contribute to longer-term objectives.

Vertical Integration and Possible Objectives

The objectives of the firm may point to expansion in a vertical direction whereby the firm involves itself in additional stages of production or distribution. An enterprise may seek to engage in *either* more of the processes undertaken before it receives a product as a raw material or component, *or* those which contribute to the end-product before it is purchased by the consumer. A brewery, for example, may expand horizontally via amalgamations with other breweries and then expand vertically towards the market by securing more retail outlets in the form of public houses and off-licences. The same brewery may then decide to expand vertically backwards towards the source of its raw materials by securing its own hop fields and bottle-manufacturing plant. This type of expansion may also allow a firm to achieve those objectives associated with increasing profits through greater efficiency, as well as increasing its power over the market, thus making it more secure and ensuring its survival. Vertical expansion is likely to benefit the firm in the following areas:

1. *By securing the sources of its raw materials and other inputs, such as components, the firm will make supplies more secure.* This will prove particularly advantageous when the market demand is rising rapidly, as the firm might otherwise experience shortages and delays when, for example, component manufacturers do not possess the capacity to deal with an increase in both the size and number of orders.

2. *Adjustments in the productive capacities necessary to cope with changes in demand may be more quickly and accurately achieved if more of the processes are under the control of a firm.* Market trends will be more readily transmitted down the line and help reduce the problem of either an excess or a shortage of capacity as independent firms would not co-ordinate their investment plans. This will assist the integrated firm in developing a more effective investment programme.

3. *Some industrial processes are more efficiently undertaken if they are conducted in close proximity to each other.* Several processes may, for example, require that each of them is carried out at very high temperatures. If they were undertaken by separate firms, then the need to reheat the inputs would result in much higher production costs. This would be the case, for example, with the production of metals, oil products and chemicals.

4. *The firm would also have greater control over the quality and design of its inputs and from the very begin-*

ning they can be geared to suit the firm's individual requirements. An independent component manufacturer, for example, may produce a standard product with certain features which are superfluous to a particular firm's need, yet in other ways it may have certain limitations. The supplying firm may not consider it worth while introducing improvements which do not coincide with the needs of a sufficiently large number of its customers. A user firm may be particularly interested in developments in the areas of heat resistance, electrical conductivity and a longer life for its components, and such improvements are more likely to occur if the firm can control the manufacture of its own components.

5. *The firm may believe that it has now reached a size where it becomes viable to enter into the field of distribution.* The first move may be to introduce its own transport fleet which will make it independent of outside hauliers and the public transport system. The size of its business may not only make this commercially viable but will allow greater flexibility in delivery dates and times, as well as reducing the impact of outside influence which may restrict deliveries.

6. *Rather than deal with an independent wholesaler, the firm may absorb this role itself if retail outlets or customers place sufficiently large orders.* The manufacturer may therefore deal directly with retail units or users, and the next move may be the opening up of his own retail outlets if he is producing consumer goods. This movement towards the market may be to increase the presence of his goods in the market itself particularly during a period of recession. Having direct contact with the consumer will also give the firm first-hand knowledge of changes in tastes and preferences and enable it to act accordingly.

The vertical integration of a firm will mean in some cases that the advantages derived from specialising in a narrower range of activities will have to be sacrificed to a certain extent. The firm may believe, however, that the increased security and power which such vertical expansion brings, more than compensates for the tendency for some costs to increase.

Lateral Integration
Diversification of a firm's activities is also a feature of lateral integration whereby a firm increases the range of its output. A pharmaceutical company, for example, may have recognised in the course of its development that additional products could be

produced with very little adjustment. The process involved, the skills and inputs, may readily lend themselves to multi-product growth; it may be possible to utilise a by-product; and the same retail outlets can be used to sell additional products. Diversification may also be motivated by the desire to reduce the firm's reliance upon a single product for its revenue, and to enable it to spread risks over a wider range of products and markets, and this reduction in risks may outweigh any advantage lost by moving away from a specialised output.

International Expansion
The firm's expansion plans may go beyond its home market and seek to expand its sales in overseas markets, and this may be the case when the domestic market shows a lack of sustained growth or is experiencing a prolonged recession. A rapid rise in the size of overseas markets may see a firm seeking to enter the export field by establishing a specialist department to promote its product abroad. It may, however, be entering a highly competitive market and its position and sales contacts might be improved by setting up production units in the overseas market itself. This objective could also be secured by take-overs or mergers involving a company which is already resident in the overseas market. This will also help the firm overcome any restrictions in the form of tariffs or quotas which have been placed upon goods entering the particular overseas market concerned.

For example, a motor vehicle manufacturer may face a heavy import duty on its exported vehicles and so decide to set up an assembly plant in the overseas market itself. This pattern of expansion has led to the growth of **multinational companies** such as Ford, Philips, ITT and ICI, which have production units in several countries. They have been motivated by several factors, such as possessing the ability to switch production from plant to plant when external events in a particular economy are mitigating against efficiency. This type of expansion also allows them to move into those areas where they can take advantage of relatively abundant and cheap supplies of labour. They may select a location where they can minimise their tax burden and they have the power to decide where, within their organisation, their profits should accrue. As far as possible, they will ensure that profits are allocated to the subsidiary which is resident in a country where the tax laws are most favourable to them. This quest for overseas operations, whether in selling or actual production, can also perhaps be interpreted as a desire to extend the power and influence of the firm beyond the boundaries of the country of origin.

Political Influence as an Objective

As the organisation grows, the possibility arises that the power which it develops can be used to influence the overall political and economic environment in which it operates. It may seek to reduce the risks which it sees arising out of an environment by exerting pressure upon governments to follow a policy which is in their own commercial interest. This practice of political lobbying is not restricted to the multinational corporation, but can be pursued by smaller companies who form their own trade and manufacturers' associations to communicate their opinions to the government. They will concern themselves with such issues as import duties, company taxation, prices and incomes policies and industrial relations.

The extent to which a government is susceptible to such pressures will depend greatly upon its integrity and the extent to which it can accommodate the industry's aims within the broader context of its economic, social and political programme. Increasingly, governments are obliged to make reference to the views of both organised labour and employers' associations in an effort to formulate their overall strategy.

Nevertheless, this is a two-way process in that governments will also seek to use organisations as a means of implementing their policies. Not only will a government adopt measures which influence the overall economic climate within which a firm operates, but it may attempt to use firms as a means of securing political, economic and social objectives in a more direct way. The objectives of the firm and the means of achieving them may therefore be partly guided by the need to comply with the government's aims in the fields of investment, wages and pricing policies, employment and the location of its activities.

Failure to take account of such issues may even threaten the independent survival of the organisation and promote more direct state intervention in its operations. A firm may place a 'cost' upon the effects of ignoring the government's aims, and compliance with them may be seen as ensuring the continued independent existence of the firm to pursue its longer-term objectives.

The Eventual Importance of Profits

It is therefore possible to identify several objectives and the means by which an organisation may seek to pursue them to a greater or lesser extent. Nevertheless, one should not underestimate the role of profits as a measurement of the company's success, as profits will be a vital precondition for creating the scope for the alternative objectives. Profits are an important source of funds for investment purposes, and without new and improved techniques the competitive position of the organisation will deteriorate and result in a failure to achieve even normal profits. A discipline will be imposed by the need to ensure a dividend that reduces the likelihood of a take-over bid. If insufficient profits are made and this is reflected in a fall in the value of its shares, it may render itself open to a take-over bid by another organisation which may believe that the shares undervalue the company's assets and potential earning power. A further discipline may be imposed by the large shareholders and financial institutions with a sizeable involvement threatening to withdraw their support, particularly when a comparison is drawn with a firm in the same industry which has produced a higher return. The firm may attempt to give as good an impression of its performance and future prospects as it possibly can, but in the long run comparisons will be drawn with others in its field. This will influence those who have an active role in directing and managing the organisation.

The objectives of nationalised industries

The reasons why some major industries have been nationalised have already been outlined in Chapter 1. These reasons were essentially based upon the desire to fulfil the practical expression of a particular socialist ideology, whereby the means of production and the distribution of the resultant output should be brought under the control of the state. Economic motives were generally concerned with the aim of securing economies of scale, avoiding the wasteful duplication of effort, reducing the threat of exploitation of consumers by monopoly suppliers, and using investment expenditure in such undertakings as a means of maintaining employment levels in the economy as a whole and in depressed areas in particular. Nationalisation stemmed from the recognition that the traditional private enterprise organisation had to be replaced in some sectors by state control and ownership if these objectives were to be achieved.

Nationalised Industries and their Non-commercial Objectives

From their very conception the industries were never given a very clear indication as to what their objectives should be, and the framework within which they had to operate was constructed as a result of equally inconsistent references to various commercial, economic and social criteria. The relative importance of such criteria not only changes with the government in power, but also over the life-span of the same government. Major decisions regarding the size, timing and location of investment, and pricing policies, can only be taken if clear guidelines concerning the industries' objectives are laid down.

An investment project, for example by British Rail, will have a purely commercial objective if it is concentrated upon those routes where it is likely to produce the highest return. Wider economic repercussions of the project, however, may have to be taken into account if a fuller analysis is made of the expenditure in the light of the current economic climate and the extent to which the economy can cope with such an increase in expenditure without meeting a shortage of resources and the build-up of inflationary pressures. Again, investment plans would have to be modified if a board was responsible for considering the social effects of its decision upon regional employment levels. Investment funds are after all limited, and investment by the National Coal Board, for example, in certain pits may be at the expense of other areas where high unemployment is of concern to the government. Similarly, a purely commercial decision by British Rail may involve the closure of certain routes, or drastic reductions in the frequency of some services if losses are to be reduced and further investment programmes concentrated upon the more lucrative routes. They may, however, be obliged to take heed of the effect upon rural areas where alternative means of transport may be limited and where cuts may reduce job opportunities for residents in rural areas. This may also conflict with the government's desire to reduce the pressures in certain urban areas, as firms will not be enthusiastic about moving there if the work force finds its transport facilities seriously limited. At the same time rail closures will attract more people into what may be congested urban areas. A closure of certain lines may also create the need to expand road-building programmes, which will place an additional call upon the economy's limited resources as well as increasing social problems closely connected with road traffic, such as accidents, congestion and pollution, and the impact upon the rural landscape.

An improved commercial return could be achieved by raising the price of the product or service in question, but this will involve questions of social justice if items like electricity, gas, coal and public passenger fares are increased, particularly if they are important items of expenditure for those on lower incomes. The respective boards may be obliged to follow government directives concerning price stability as an important economic aim may be to take some of the pressure out of inflation. Moderating price increases in the public sector may be seen as a means of helping this anti-inflationary policy, since items such as energy, transport, communications and steel may be important costs for many firms in the private sector.

The First Approach to Nationalised Industries

In the period following the first major nationalisations the industries concerned were directed to 'pay their way', and this was taken as meaning that revenues on average over a number of years should cover costs, and these latter costs were to include interest, depreciation, capital redemption and a provision for reserves. At the same time they had to pay due regard to the 'public interest', though what this latter obligation actually meant was never clearly defined. They were, however, instructed not to discriminate between consumers where prices were concerned, and this often meant that the industries adopted an averaging process where costs were concerned to retain uniform prices. The important issues regarding what actually constituted the national interest and who was to meet any resultant losses remained ill defined. Thus pricing and investment decisions had to be taken, which allowed the industries to meet their commercial obligations taking one year with another. Conflicts, however, were bound to arise as pursuit of this commercial objective involved them in decisions which might not comply with a particular interpretation of the public interest, such as closing uneconomic coal mines or railway lines, and burning coal in power stations rather than oil. The boards were being expected to take what were in many cases political decisions. They may also have been under pressure to buy capital goods from UK suppliers to assist employment in the capital goods industries and reduce the UK import bill, when they would have preferred to buy from overseas producers.

A pricing policy which was socially and politically acceptable would not necessarily be compatible with a system of prices which sought to bring about more rational investment decisions. Resources which can be devoted to investment at any one moment are limited, and in order to ensure that they are allocated to achieve the greatest return to the economy as a whole a rational pricing policy is required. If a product or service is priced below the true costs incurred, this can artificially stimulate demand (compared with that for a possible substitute), and it will in fact be provided at a much higher cost in terms of all the resources used. The ensuing increase in demand may then result in investment to cater for it, and this will perpetuate the output of the good or service provided at an artificially high cost. The substitute may be priced at a higher level but represent a closer reflection of its true costs. Investment decisions may therefore be based upon distorted prices and lead to an incorrect allocation of investment and new capacity.

The National Coal Board, for example, does not price coal according to its source of origin but adopts an average so that the more efficient pits subsidise the less productive ones. However, this complies with the government objective of maintaining employment in certain areas of the country where coal-mining is the main source of employment. Within the energy industry as a whole, prices do not reflect the costs of supplying consumers in different locations at different times of the day, and investment plans are not a rational reflection of which industry has a superiority in a particular area. Public policy towards transport has tended to emphasise, rather than close, the gap between relative prices and costs where rail and road transport are concerned. Meeting the national interest has meant maintaining uneconomic routes which are subsidised to a certain extent by lines where the railways face less competition from road transport.

Road hauliers, on the contrary, have had more freedom and have not been subject to a pricing policy which takes account of all the costs incurred by the economy as a whole in providing both passenger and freight movement. This also applies to the private motorist, as road transport is not priced according to the resources devoted to the provision of roads and their maintenance. There are also some costs which may not be quantifiable in terms of those resources which are consumed as a result of accidents, policing and those costs upon which society as a whole may place a value. This covers intangibles such as congestion, pollution and noise. If road transport had been subject to a system of pricing that reflected the costs incurred by different types of users in different parts of the country, and British Rail had been given greater freedom in a pricing policy that reflected its superiority in certain types of freight and passenger transport, then a policy might have been formulated which prevented the present artificial imbalance.

The Government White Paper on Nationalised Industries 1961

This period of confusion, arising primarily from a variety of ill-defined objectives and criteria for governing decision-making, led to mounting deficits in the early years, for British Rail in particular. This led in 1961 to the publication of a White Paper on 'The Financial and Economic Objectives of the Nationalised Industries', which showed a marked emphasis on a commercial approach. The main points of this White Paper were as follows:

1. The time period over which nationalised industries were supposed to pay their way was to be five years and the need to avoid making a loss was regarded as a minimum objective.

2. Each industry was now given a specific target as a return and this rate of return was measured as income, before interest and depreciation had been allowed for, as a percentage of net assets. The depreciation, moreover, was to be calculated on the basis of what the item of plant was likely to cost when it had to be replaced, as this would take account of inflated price levels. The White Paper continued the practice of requiring the industries to build up reserves and funds for capital investment.

3. The White Paper struck a more direct tone when it stated that 'there are powerful grounds in the national interest for requiring these undertakings to make a substantial contribution towards the cost of their capital development out of their own earnings, and to reduce their claims on the nation's savings and the burden upon the exchequer'. This may have compelled them to discover more accurately where their losses were being incurred and to consider the necessary adjustments to their prices and scale of operations.

4. The government also recognised 'that the industries must have greater freedom to make upward price adjustments especially where their

prices are artificially low,' and they accepted the difficulties in measuring the success of the industries because of the complexity of their objectives.

5. The White Paper also took account of any unprofitable activities which the industries were expected to undertake as part of the government's overall social and economic policies. This could have made a contribution to morale in the industries, as they could now possibly specify the reasons for certain loss-making activities or expected shortfall in their target.

6. The White Paper concentrated on financial matters but still gave no clear guidelines as to what would be an acceptable means of achieving these objectives. In particular, pricing policy was not clarified, as higher prices could increase returns where little competition existed, but how would this comply with the public interest?

7. This White Paper also failed to give a clear indication as to who was responsible for deciding which loss-making activities should continue in the public interest, and led to the practice of cross-subsidisation or overall deficits that did little to enhance the image of the industries or improve their general morale.

The Government White Paper on Nationalised Industries 1967

A further White Paper was published in 1967 entitled 'Nationalised Industries—A Review of Economic and Financial Objectives'.

1. This again contained a commercial directive in that 'investment projects must normally show a satisfactory return in commercial terms', but the rate of return was reduced in importance when it came to decisions relating to prices and investments. Increasingly, the rate of return was to 'reflect different statutory and social obligations, conditions of demand, domestic costs and other factors peculiar to the individual undertaking'.

2. The paper stressed the importance of taking into account the impact of its investment intentions upon the economy as a whole, in that costs and benefits may arise which were not likely to be included in the investment appraisal conducted by the industry itself.

3. The use of cost–benefit techniques was a recognition that projects should be judged by their respective contributions to total welfare in the community. An investment in the public transport network should not be considered solely in terms of the direct costs involved in providing an additional or improved service and likely monetary income, but should also take into account the likely costs and benefits which may arise elsewhere as a direct result of the project.

4. This new approach would involve a cost–benefit analysis, whereby the more obvious costs and benefits to the industry are considered in conjunction with the costs and benefits to society as a whole, although these latter calculations were to be left to the government. This was to be the case where costs and benefits were not readily quantifiable and value judgements were required. It was, in fact, an attempt to introduce a more sophisticated means of estimating the non-commercial consideration that for too long had been left to the boards. It also coincided with improved techniques of conducting cost–benefit analyses that sought to take account of the effects of economic decisions.

5. It was hoped that a cost–benefit approach would contribute to a more efficient allocation of resources in terms of improving general welfare. Such an analysis was undertaken before it was finally decided to build the new Victoria Line on the London Underground. Estimates of the financial implications for the London Transport Board indicated that the new line would lose £2 million per year and other lines would lose £1 million as passengers would be lost to the Victoria Line. A return on the project of 11 per cent was however estimated when wider social costs and benefits were considered, and in particular benefits were expected to accrue in the form of less congestion on surface routes. It was felt that this would speed the flow of traffic and also produce fewer accidents. Value judgements also had to be made regarding the benefits to communities that would otherwise be disrupted by the need to extend road facilities, the lessening of pollution and the easing of urban stress upon themselves. Admittedly the latter are difficult to quantify, but they do affect general welfare.

Similarly, the Central Electricity Board's choice between coal or oil-fired power stations has implications for the coal-mining industry and its importance as a source of employment in a particular region of the country, as well as effects upon the country's import bill. The growth and means by which nuclear energy is to be generated is to be decided after potential environmental effects have been taken into account. Consideration of such non-commercial criteria is now the responsibility of the government, as is the decision from where the capital goods will be purchased.

6. The 1967 White Paper also recognised the importance of a pricing policy that would contribute to this more efficient allocation of resources, and where possible the boards should move in this direction by adopting prices that more closely reflected the total consumption of resources used in providing the goods or services. The charges for rail transport and electricity, for example, do now reflect to some extent the higher costs of meeting peak-hour demand which arise out of the level of capital investment required to meet the peak demand.

The Approach to the Nationalised Industries in the Early 1980s

The policy of the Conservative Government which came to power in 1979 was based upon the view that returning whole or parts of such industries to the private sector wherever practicable would be the best spur to efficiency and a more productive use of the nation's resources.

The Government believed that the discipline of free market forces would in the long run bring benefits to both consumers and user industries in the form of more competitive prices and better services. One of the original justifications for nationalisation was that economies of scale would bring increased efficiency but the new Government held the view that monopoly power and the lack of market discipline had produced the opposite effect. Using the nationalised industries as a means of achieving certain objectives in employment and reducing inflation had produced serious side effects so that these industries were no longer serving the long-term interest of the nation as a whole.

The Government had seen the private sector respond to the growing recession and stricter financial climate by rationalisation programmes that sought to exert a greater control over costs and offer more competitive prices. Thus to help ensure that the nationalised industries paid greater attention to costs the Government made it clear that they could no longer rely upon financial assistance from the Exchequer to support excessive increases in their labour costs and the losses resulting from a lack of competitiveness. The combined losses of the nationalised industries had also made a significant contribution to the renewed growth of the PSBR. It was also held that nationalisation had increased the scope for the politicisation of business decisions especially where closures or redundancies were contemplated as part of rationalisation programmes.

The Government saw no benefit in public ownership of industries, such as British Airways, in a competitive environment, and also questioned public ownership of firms in monopoly positions, such as gas and electricity. Its aim was to bring in private capital after restoring to profitability the ones that were unprofitable. British Telecom, for example, was to be allowed to issue a bond to raise capital and this reflected the Government's wish to see such industries compete fairly with the private sector for funds. In other cases this move towards privatisation was to take the form of direct asset sales, for example, the sale of British Rail hotel properties. Joint ventures were also to be encouraged, such as the one that involved British Telecom, Marconi and British Aerospace to launch a British satellite.

By May 1982 four public sector firms had been returned to the private sector, the largest of which was British Aerospace. The Government also had plans to seek private sector participation in another five industries, either in whole or in part. These included British Airways, the British Gas Corporation (BGC) and the British National Oil Corporation (BNOC). The intention was to transfer the oil exploration and production business of the BNOC to the private sector, sell off the BGC's interests in North Sea Oil while also opening this organisation to more competition in both the buying and supplying of gas and gas appliances. A further example of the Government's desire to see the nationalised industries operate in a more competitive climate were Acts that liberalised parts of the postal and telecommunications monopolies and relaxed the licensing laws governing the operation of long-distance buses.

The main departments within an organisation and their functions

As an organisation expands the scale of its operations, it can take advantage not only of the specialisation of labour, but employees can be combined to form specialist departments. Each will tend to concentrate upon a particular aspect of the activities which must be undertaken to produce the good or service and its eventual supply on to the market. The establishment of specialist departments will depend upon the extent to which the size of the firm makes such a structure viable. The relative importance of the departments within this structure will in turn be largely influenced by the type of activity with which the firm is concerned. It is possible to identify several functions which

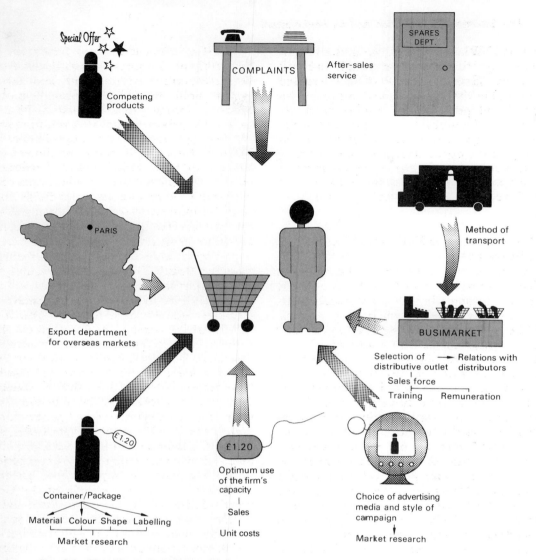

Fig. 2.1: The Marketing Department

Within the figure:

Special Offer

Competing products

COMPLAINTS

After-sales service

SPARES DEPT.

Method of transport

PARIS

Export department for overseas markets

BUSIMARKET

Selection of distributive outlet → Relations with distributors

Sales force

Training — Remuneration

£1.20

Container/Package

Material Colour Shape Labelling

Market research

£1.20

Optimum use of the firm's capacity
|
Sales
|
Unit costs

Choice of advertising media and style of campaign

Market research

---

will be of varying degrees of importance, though even here the size of the firm and its main activity may require specialist sections within these broad departmental functions which make up the organisation itself. Liaison between departments and sections will also be an important factor in an organisation so that the whole operation can be conducted as efficiently as possible. Effective communication within the firm will be an essential precondition for successful business.

Marketing

This overall function can often be expected to embrace the following policies and activities working towards the successful sale of the good or service. (Fig. 2.1.)

(a) *The whole marketing philosophy should be customer orientated* in that it seeks to establish what prospective consumers want, to satisfy this by producing a product which will lead the buyer to repeat a purchase, and to establish a reputation in the eyes of the customer which will lead to the product being recommended to others.

(b) *The level of sales should be sufficient to enable the firm to make optimum use of its productive capacity* and any increase in sales should be of a level and a period of duration which makes the introduction of new and perhaps improved capacity a profitable proposition, or assists in achieving other objectives which the firm may regard as important.

(c) *In a competitive market it will be essential to keep up to date with the activities of its competitors.* The firm must be aware of possible inroads being made into its own sales, and what policies it should adopt in both the short term and long term either to defend itself or to gain an advantage over such competitors. Accordingly, consideration should be given to the main areas upon which the firm believes it has scope to operate. It should examine such areas as price, quality and other non-price techniques which may retain customers or attract sales. Such non-price factors may include, over a limited period of time, gifts, competitions or special offers which entail the collection of coupons, box tops or wrappers, and the use of indirect price cuts on discount multi-packs. These measures can be used as a short-term response to competitive pressures and they avoid the necessity of restoring a price cut if long-term policy dictates an alternative strategy. Price cuts are more readily forgotten compared with price increases and the latter will be particularly important to regular customers.

(*d*) *Close contact should be maintained with market trends.* Shifts in consumers' tastes and preferences must be analysed with a view to amending products or introducing new lines that may justify any additional expenditure by the firm. This may involve the use of a market research unit to study consumer demand from the point of view of expanding existing sales or the possible openings for new products. Market research must identify the type of person who is likely to constitute the market and what factors are likely to influence a consumer's final choice.

(*e*) *The market research unit will work in close contact with the advertising section.* The result of market research will help the framing of an advertising campaign that selects appropriate media for reaching the prospective market, and highlights those features which the research shows are likely to be the main selling points. The unit will build up a valuable indication of the type of person at whom the campaign should primarily be aimed, and the 'message' will be designed to attract this prospective buyer.

(*f*) *The choice of distributive outlets may have to be periodically reviewed and in the case of a new product a decision will have to be taken regarding the most suitable means of distribution.* For example, the firm may perhaps consider direct contact with the customer via mail order, its own retail units, or whether a wholesaler should be used as a means of getting the product on to the market. The factors considered before a means of distribution is finally decided upon are discussed in greater detail in Chapter 7.

(*g*) *If independent outlets are used, the policy should be to secure good business relationships with those who own or manage them.* Keeping a good working relationship with shopkeepers and buying staff in other distributive outlets is a vital factor in sales promotion. This will be necessary if a sales promotion campaign involves the co-operation of such people in using part of their area for a special display unit or other sales promotion aids. Special awards for reaching certain sales levels may be another way of gaining their co-operation. Such people must be given a status which reflects their importance to the organisation using them as distributive outlets.

(*h*) *A non-price factor in sales may be to ensure that adequate after-sales services are provided.* This will be particularly important in the case of durable goods and those of a technical nature, because over their useful life they can expect to require servicing or replacement of parts. This covers items such as motor cars, domestic appliances, office equipment and machinery. Some of these obligations may be provided under the terms of a guarantee, but the continued success of a product will depend heavily upon maintaining a good reputation for providing an efficient back-up service.

(*i*) *Sales forecasting will also indicate the extent to which the current sales force can cope with any changes.* This may involve the department's co-operation in training programmes for new sales personnel or drawing up the main features of a retraining scheme, if the firm is to cope with additional and new products. There may also be a need to review the factors determining sales staff's earnings, such as bonus and commission schemes, in order to maintain an effective and enthusiastic sales force.

(*j*) *An organisation may seek to expand its sales by entering overseas markets.* This will involve the choice of the most appropriate distributive outlet for supplying overseas markets. Possibilities involve the use of an overseas agent, working on commission; an export merchant house buying from the supplier and using its own knowledge of overseas markets and selling facilities; or the firm may decide to establish an overseas subsidiary to handle its own trade in certain regions. The export section will need to familiarise itself with all the documentation associated with both the export and import of goods. It will have to take account of laws in the importing country which may involve changes in the product itself, permitted ingredients and additives, safety regulations, environmental safeguards and standard sizes and capacities; such alterations to a mass-pro-duced, standardised product may affect the profit-ability of the project. Exporting staff can seek expert advice from the **Department of Trade and Industry** which also provides regular infor-mation on events such as overseas trade fairs. If the exporter gives his overseas buyer credit as a means of obtaining export orders, the **Export Credits Guarantee Department** will provide financial guarantees to the commercial banks, so that exporters themselves can secure credit from the banks at a more reasonable rate of interest until they receive payment from overseas. The same de-partment will also, on receipt of a premium, insure the credit which the exporter has provided to his overseas customer. This will reduce some of the risks associated with a failure on the part of the foreign customer to meet his financial com-mitments. Assistance can also be obtained from the organisation's own trade or employer association, the Confederation of British Industry, local chambers of commerce and services to exporters provided by the commercial banks.

(*k*) *Successful marketing can also be aided by an attractive container or package.* The market research, advertising and design teams will co-operate to produce a container or package. Varying degrees of importance are attached to shape, material, colour, labelling and requirements such as ease of handling, stability, visibility of contents, type of stopper or lid, and its ability to keep contents fresh.

(*1*) *Arrangements will have to be made to deal with the transport of the finished products to the distributive outlet or customer.* The appropriate section may use the transport facilities offered by an independent firm, or an organisation may decide to invest in its own transport facilities if the size of its con-signments and the location of its customers make this worth while. Vehicle capacity will need to be fully utilised on outward journeys and if possible also on return journeys. Time, bulk, security, value and weight will be considered in selecting the most suitable means of transport. If this means the use of a highly specialised type of vehicle, it may prove more economic to use the services of an independent specialist company which will be able to operate on a larger scale, as otherwise unit transport costs may prove very high. The transport section may find that its output and eventual market make it possible to use unit loads, such as those used for standard **containers,** which can be readily transferred between road, rail, sea and air transport.

Production

Production includes those activities which com-mence with the receipt of raw materials and even-tually give rise to an end product. Production management in an organisation will concentrate primarily upon the planning and control of all the various stages of production so that the most efficient use is made of the company's productive capacity. The nature of the production processes will vary according to the size of the organisation, the initial state of raw materials and components, the extent to which they must be worked upon, and the size of the production run which the firm can expect. The way in which production is organised and likely areas of concern will differ widely between organisations, as can be seen if a manufacturer producing mass-produced pass-enger cars is compared with one producing cus-tom-built vehicles. Similarly, different techno-logies will of course be employed in different in-dustries.

Production is as much in evidence in service in-dustries as in manufacturing industries. A car-hire firm, an insurance company or a financial institu-tion must organise themselves in such a way that their service is provided to clients as efficiently as possible. Competitive pressures upon them can be just as great as those experienced by manufactur-ing enterprises. Whatever the nature of the under-taking, the aims of production planning and con-trol will be to decide upon the physical means by which the end product is to be achieved, where the activities should be located, the timetable for various stages and the personnel to be involved in such stages. The production plan will then seek to ensure that once established the programme is adhered to, and that any departures from it, in-tended or otherwise, are accorded the same degree of attention. (Fig. 2.2, p. 28.)

(*a*) *At some stage or other, one would expect the pro-duction department to be in close and continuous contact with the research and development staff.* In particular, they will need to be involved in the design stages of a basic product as this will give an early indica-tion of the extent to which existing production techniques can cope with the processes involved, and thus assess the area where changes must be made either in the design of the product itself or in the firm's production facilities. The product must be designed to meet the customer's re-quirements, but at the same time efficient and profitable production must be organised.

Drawings and specifications including as much

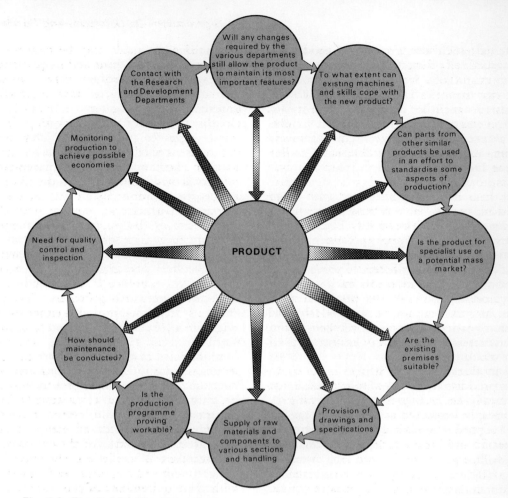

Fig. 2.2: The Production Department

The circles in the figure contain the following text:

- Will any changes required by the various departments still allow the product to maintain its most important features?
- Contact with the Research and Development Departments
- To what extent can existing machines and skills cope with the new product?
- Monitoring production to achieve possible economies
- Can parts from other similar products be used in an effort to standardise some aspects of production?
- Need for quality control and inspection
- PRODUCT
- Is the product for specialist use or a potential mass market?
- How should maintenance be conducted?
- Are the existing premises suitable?
- Is the production programme proving workable?
- Supply of raw materials and components to various sections and handling
- Provision of drawings and specifications

detail as possible will be compiled so that the end product can be reproduced as exactly as possible. The specifications will include a description and directions relating to the various processes involved, together with a parts list which may require its own drawings and specifications. Tolerances which allow the design team to achieve their objectives and still remain within the limits necessary for efficient production, will be designated so that both machines and operatives can work within the tolerances permitted.

Cost control will be instituted from the initial stages to consider the implications for the number of operations, the materials and the assembly work involved. Effort may then be directed towards securing further standardisation, such as the extent to which components can be drawn from other products or used in other lines. Design may be simplified to keep within a minimum variety of separate components or operations, and in con-

junction with a decision on standard sizes and capacities for the end product, this will allow the firm to take advantage of long production runs.

When the design has been fully developed, a few prototypes may be produced for experimental and test purposes. This may be followed by a larger pre-production run to gauge the performance of the production facilities. An opportunity then arises to make alterations to the production plan, such as those concerned with equipment, tools, factory lay-out and communications between different sections.

(b) *A dominant factor in determining the way in which production will be planned and controlled, is whether a small number of individual products or various levels of standardised products are required.* This will affect the type of manual skills required, capability of machines, and the factory lay-out itself, including intermediate handling and eventual storage.

At one extreme there is a unit of production which is specifically designed to meet the individual requirements of a particular customer. In this case, the raw materials and components will not necessarily be available from stocks, nor will stocks of the end product be maintained. Unit production also requires that labour, equipment and factory lay-out must be of a flexible nature to deal with these individual orders or relatively short production runs.

Longer runs are usually associated with **batch production**, which is repetitive though not necessarily continuous. The size of a batch will depend upon an economic quantity considering the changes which may be necessary before moving over to a different type of batch. If production is organised so as to lend itself to a variety of processes or products, this will be of particular use to a firm seeking to even out the work-load which particular operations impose upon other sections in the production department or in the organisation as a whole.

Flow production occurs when the demand is such that products are required to provide a continuous supply, and both production planning and control must be organised accordingly. This type and level of production is usually characterised by more specific and longer-term arrangements regarding skills, equipment, lay-out and communications, so that a flow of output can be maintained. Investment in this type of single-purpose capacity can often involve very large sums of money, and the work of the sales forecasting unit will be vital in ensuring that optimum use is made of the capacity, since its inflexible nature may not readily lend itself to alternative uses if the market does not live up to expectations. If British Leyland, for example, are to invest in capacity specifically designed to produce a new Mini, then an expenditure of over £200 million on plant and equipment must be justified by sufficient output and sales to make the proposition commercially viable.

(*c*) *Production planning will give a strong indication as to what extent the existing design of premises, specific site and general location will contribute towards the efficient and profitable conduct of the organisation's activities.* In conjunction with the findings of the market research unit, purchasing and personnel departments, a decision will have to be made concerning the most appropriate design and location of the premises. Many factors have to be considered in deciding upon the location of the organisation's productive units. For example, the personnel department may be concerned about the availability of labour and its particular skills. The purchasing department may be interested in the economic supply of raw materials, components, and necessary services to aid production. On the other hand, the marketing department may be supporting a location which suits the market to be supplied and the extent to which local transport facilities meet these requirements, while the provision of communications will be of varying degrees of importance to all the departments within the organisation. A more detailed account of the location of industrial and commercial activities is given in Chapter 5.

Once the eventual location of the premises has been decided upon then the production department will be involved in the design of premises to suit its particular requirements. The provision of floor space can be provided either by extensive single-storey facilities or by a multi-storey building. The existing premises may be unsuitable both from the point of view of location and also of construction. The production department will consider such matters as the degree to which various building designs meet requirements concerning the efficient provision of internal power sources, the internal movement of materials and components and personnel, and the provision of lighting, heating and ventilation. The overall working environment and conditions will have to comply with the requirements of the Factories Acts and those factors which produce a contented work force.

(*d*) *Production planning will be undertaken to organise the product through its various manufacturing stages, starting perhaps with the initial treatment of raw materials, the manufacture of components, their assembly and final finishing and packaging.* The whole of this exercise must be carefully planned so that the sections involved are operating at optimum levels, and the various activities sufficiently co-ordinated to avoid both bottle-necks and idle capacity.

The production planning department must liaise with the marketing department to transform the latter's requirements into detailed instructions, so that the actual departments involved in production can achieve a smooth and efficient manufacturing process. This will result in production programmes or schedules dealing with the timetabling of the processes and the quantities involved to achieve suitable targets.

Once these schedules have been formulated a

works order will be issued to authorise production to fulfil an order to the firm. This works order will contain details such as the code and job numbers allocated to it, the description of the product and its quantity, the materials required and the operations to be performed upon the product, their sequence and the time allowed for each of these operations.

(*e*) *To keep these schedules up to date and to trace the progress of works orders a section will be allocated the task of ensuring that the production departments are meeting their targets and adhering to the timetable.* This progress control allows information to be fed back to reveal the actual progress compared to the planned timetable, and to give details of any discrepancies. Any shortcomings can then be investigated to prevent the situation from deteriorating into more serious departures from the production schedule, and this possibility may then be minimised by rescheduling.

(*f*) *A further aspect of production control is achieved by materials control, which contributes to production by ensuring that materials are provided in the stipulated quality and quantity in the correct places and at the appropriate time.* This materials control section will need to keep in close contact with the other departments and sections whose areas of work include such matters as the purchase of materials and other items, their receipt, storage, and allocation from stores. Internally produced components will require that the materials control section works closely with the inspection and quality control sections.

(*g*) *Successful production control will also require details of the current stock position in the stores, so that supplies can be replenished to avoid hold-ups in production.* Stores control must seek to strike a balance between ensuring that sufficient stocks are held of various items to enable production to proceed smoothly, and ensuring against too much capital being tied up in stocks. Other factors to be considered concerning stocks would include the availability of storage space, their likely price fluctuations, perishability and possible obsolescence, the time lags between ordering and delivery, and the quantities of stocks constituting the most economic orders. This control will have to be exerted not only over the direct stores used for raw materials, components and finished parts, but also over the indirect stores including tools for manual use or in machinery. There may also be a need for a maintenance store for items to service and repair plant and equipment.

(*h*) *Adequate maintenance of plant, equipment and buildings will always be vital, as their failures and shortcomings can lead to a valuable loss of output.* Large capital-intensive industries in particular incur very large fixed costs, and capacity must be used fully to spread these overhead costs over as large a level of output as possible. If there is a breakdown in one part of the factory and the fault cannot be by-passed, this can lead to a complete halt in production when products must flow continuously from one process to another. Heating, lighting and ventilation will also require attention, as a breach of the Factories Acts may lead to a stoppage until certain standards are re-established. Breakdowns and servicing will also have to be dealt with.

Much of the section's maintenance attention may be directed towards replacement schemes, which could involve the replacement of sound parts. Much of this is calculated upon the basis of probability and the expected life of the components comprising the plant, equipment and buildings.

(*i*) *The need for an efficient handling system from the initial receipt of raw materials and components, their processing and assembly, finishing and eventual packaging and final storage or warehousing, will be evident in most manufacturing organisations.* The success of a firm partly depends upon the development of a system for moving both components and products smoothly between operations, and perhaps also processing them while still moving. Handling costs can represent as much as 85 per cent of all production costs in some industries, and this means that efforts should be made to achieve a factory lay-out and handling system which helps to reduce such costs while still allowing other sections to function efficiently, not leaving labour idle waiting for materials.

(*j*) *An important factor in non-price competition between firms will be the maintenance of certain standards of quality in their output.* Production departments should be very concerned with aspects of quality control; a standard for quality should be established and a control system instituted to ensure that it is maintained. It can prove very expensive to rectify faults or defects once the product is in the hands of the consumer, particularly if a fault goes unnoticed in a large quantity of goods. Quality control may start with incoming raw materials and components, and still be in evidence at all the stages of production to correct faults as early as possible to avoid possible scrapping of large quantities of the final product.

Once standards of quality have been laid down, these will be administered by the **inspection** staff. The percentage of work which is actually subjected to inspection will depend upon the type of output and the seriousness of repercussions of departure from the standards of quality. Part of this inspection team will also be concerned with the periodic checking of tools and gauges to ensure that they still perform to their specification and allow the worker to operate within agreed tolerances. This will include dealing with such items as cutting tools for machines, drill bits, taps and dies, and testing equipment such as plug and screw gauges.

(*k*) *As production proceeds lessons may be learnt and faults corrected which will contribute to greater efficiency.* More positive action, however, can be taken by setting up a section actually to investigate possible areas for improvement. This involves **work study** to make a more efficient use of labour, materials and machine capacity by improving methods. Work study will also deal with producing the 'time allowed' for individual tasks involved in production, provide useful aids for costing, planning and for creating bonus schemes for operatives, especially where the work is of a repetitive nature.

Purchasing

The use of mass flow production techniques is only possible if there is an assurance that such important inputs as raw materials and components are always available at the correct time in the required quantities and qualities. If production comes to a standstill because of a lack of appropriate materials, this will prove very expensive for an organisation. To avoid the possibility of both men and machines standing idle, it is necessary to organise the purchasing side of a business as efficiently as possible. In many cases the costs of materials and other supplies can amount to more than 50 per cent of the total costs of production, so economic buying can have a very significant impact upon the competitive position of a firm. The purpose of a purchasing department is to obtain supplies of materials, equipment, tools and other items at the lowest possible price while also considering matters such as delivery dates and quality. (Fig. 2.3.)

(*a*) *The purchasing department will be in close contact with the production department so that any amendments to products can be met by corresponding adjustments in the purchase of supplies.* The purchasing department will need to be kept informed of

any contracts under consideration so that they can give an indication of what items may need to be bought from external suppliers. An early investigation will assist in determining possible sources and delivery dates for contracts which may depart from routine work.

The purchasing department must also keep in line with existing production schedules, so avoiding both shortages and also perhaps the overstocking of items for which the demand is falling. The purchasing department must liaise with the production department to inform them about the choice of supplier and the likely delivery of supplies, as this may have repercussions on the production programme and necessitate alterations that can be carefully planned rather than forced upon them at a late stage. The work of the buying staff will also keep them in close contact with the development of new materials and equipment, which may be of interest to various sections in the organisation. They can then arrange for the provision of samples and demonstrations for any interested parties. There must also be close co-ordination with the finance department to keep them informed of expenditure, as invoices must be settled and charged to the appropriate account or costed to the relevant contract. Similarly, keeping in close touch with the stores will provide details of items received, quantities issued for use and current balances to indicate the rate of usage and the timing and quantity of new supplies. The stores should also be kept up to date with orders placed and estimated delivery dates. In many cases the stores are controlled by the organisation's purchasing officer.

(*b*) *The purchasing department should play a part in helping to standardise items where possible, so that advantage can be taken of bulk buying, thus reducing the number of stock items.* When items depart from a standardised line, the production department will prepare its own specification. The purchasing department should be informed of this, so it can advise production staff on the actual possibility of supplies or likely substitutes which may meet their requirements.

A decision must also be taken concerning the extent to which buying is to be centralised or left with other parts of the organisation which may be located elsewhere. Centralised buying allows a greater degree of specialisation among purchasing staff, who become skilled in certain lines of work, and advantage can then be taken of bulk buying and the possibility of introducing greater stan-

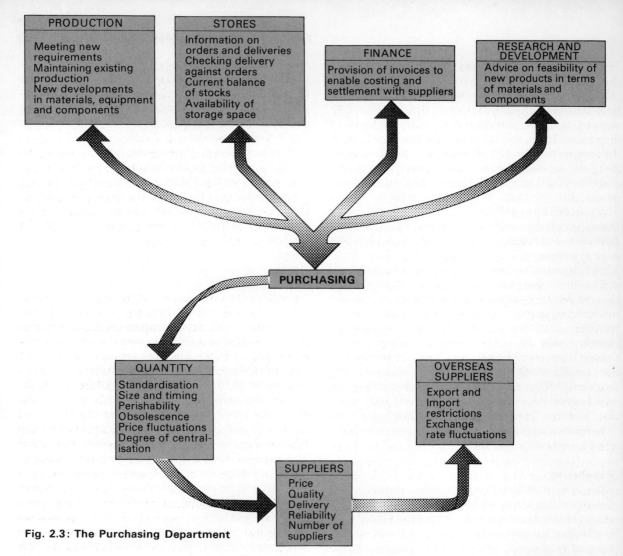

PRODUCTION
Meeting new
requirements
Maintaining existing
production
New developments
in materials, equipment
and components

STORES
Information on
orders and deliveries
Checking delivery
against orders
Current balance
of stocks
Availability of
storage space

FINANCE
Provision of invoices to
enable costing and
settlement with suppliers

**RESEARCH AND
DEVELOPMENT**
Advice on feasibility of
new products in terms
of materials and
components

PURCHASING

QUANTITY
Standardisation
Size and timing
Perishability
Obsolescence
Price fluctuations
Degree of central-
isation

SUPPLIERS
Price
Quality
Delivery
Reliability
Number of
suppliers

**OVERSEAS
SUPPLIERS**
Export and
Import
restrictions
Exchange
rate fluctuations

Fig. 2.3: The Purchasing Department

dardisation. Records will be centralised and give a more immediate indication of the present situation. If local purchasing is allowed it is essential that efficient communication exists between the various sections dealing with it.

(*c*) *The purchasing staff will build up their sources of supply over a period of time, and specialisation among them will allow a more detailed knowledge of various suppliers and what requirements they are capable of meeting.* Their experience can be supplemented by information available from trade directories and journals, suppliers' representatives, catalogues, advertisements and various trade exhibitions at either national or international level.

The purchasing department must decide whether it is beneficial to buy from a single source, or to spread the order to safeguard against a failure by a single supplier to meet the necessary quantity

and delivery dates. Similarly, the choice may be between dealing directly with the manufacturer or via a wholesaler, and between local or more distant suppliers, all of which will have their relative advantages and disadvantages.

Since material costs can be a very important part of total costs, prices quoted by suppliers will be of great importance. This may, however, have to be balanced against adherence to delivery dates and quality, as failures in these respects can be very disruptive to the production programme and also to the obligations of the marketing staff in fulfilling their sales. Every effort must be made to ensure that the supplier fully understands the specification attached to the order and conditions concerning discount, delivery, transport and packaging. This will permit the purchasing department to draw up a list of approved suppliers who have measured up to such standards particularly in providing items promptly and of a consistently acceptable standard.

If an overseas source of supply is selected, it will be necessary for staff to acquaint themselves with any regulations controlling the export of the product from the country of origin and its import into the country where the organisation is located, such as those relating to import duties, quotas or embargoes which may be placed upon certain products.

(*d*) *A difficult task facing the purchasing department is to decide upon an acceptable maximum and minimum level of stock for particular items, and consequently the most appropriate timing and size of new orders to replenish stocks.* The level of stock must always be sufficient to meet the demands and likely variations of production plans, while also paying attention to storage space, possible deterioration, obsolescence and delivery dates. Of prime importance in many cases where large sums of money are involved is the cost of tying up capital in stocks and the resultant effect upon the organisation's liquidity. This may mean sacrificing interest which may have been gained if the funds were used in some form of interest-yielding asset.

Attention will also have to be paid to market trends and how prices are likely to move as failure to purchase at the most opportune time may result in higher prices at a later date when stocks need replenishing. World commodity markets and exchange rates do tend to fluctuate widely over relatively short periods of time, and the buyer may be required to engage in a degree of speculative purchasing to avoid substantial increases in prices. However, as with all forms of speculation, market trends may be misinterpreted and the organisation may find itself at a competitive disadvantage, having mistimed its purchases.

Where price movements are small, the firm may buy on a contract basis. This reduces the need to hold large stocks, as agreement will have been made with manufacturers for the supply of items over a specified period of time and contact is then simply made to arrange delivery when required. Discounts can be obtained for large orders and the manufacturer in turn becomes very familiar with the firm's requirements.

Where non-standard items are concerned and storage space is limited, purchase may be limited to the minimum requirements consistent with efficient production; this will release capital for other purposes. Small quantities will, however, involve the loss of discounts and raise unit costs in terms of transport, handling and packaging.

(*e*) *A follow-up procedure will have to be instituted to check the goods received against the invoices and how they conform with the original order.* In some cases this may simply involve counting and measuring, but where more technical and sophisticated products are concerned, inspection may need to be carried out by an employee who has sufficient experience to check for the necessary quality and performance as indicated by the original specification. Results of inspection and any discrepancies must then be passed to the purchasing staff and finance department for action.

Personnel

No matter how sophisticated the technical means of production, the ultimate success of the organisation will depend upon securing a maximum contribution from its employees. The expenditure of human effort is a characteristic of even highly capital-intensive methods of production. Indeed, in such instances a failure to obtain certain standards from the relatively small work force can have repercussions upon the level and quality of output as severe as in places where the labour input exceeds that of capital. Personnel management will therefore be just as important, for example, in the capital-intensive power supply industries as it is in the more labour-intensive motor vehicle maintenance industry. Each department within the organisation will have its own requirements as far as certain skills and numbers of workers are concerned, and it will thus be the task of the personnel department to meet these needs and promote conditions which allow the potential of the work force to be used to the full. (Fig. 2.4, p. 34.)

(*a*) *The personnel department will keep in close contact with those areas which are likely to prove useful sources of new employees.* These include Job Centres, the Professional and Executive Register, the Youth Employment Service, Training and Retraining Centres, Private Employment Bureaux, as well as schools, colleges and universities. Some of these institutions may be used for advertising vacancies as well as space in newspapers, trade and professional journals. The actual content and style of the advertisement or communication to the media selected will have to be carefully devised in order that both the applicant, and the personnel department dealing with the replies, can act on accurate information.

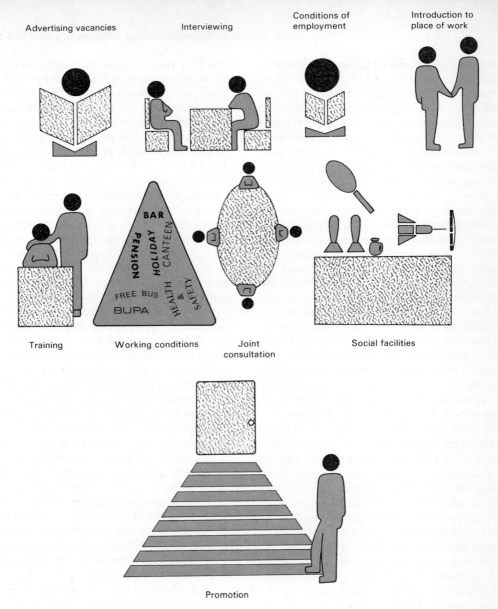

Advertising vacancies · Interviewing · Conditions of employment · Introduction to place of work

Training · Working conditions · Joint consultation · Social facilities

BAR
PENSION
HOLIDAY
CANTEEN
FREE BUS
BUPA
HEALTH & SAFETY

Promotion

Fig. 2.4: The Personnel Department

(b) Details received from applicants for vacancies must be studied, and this will be followed by a selection procedure. The suitability and personality of the candidates will involve an interview and the department will also need to be conversant with tests which can be employed to assist in determining basic intelligence, clarity and speed of thinking, special aptitudes and physical skills. Other tests may also be used to help give an indication of the applicant's general personality. Once these tests have been completed, it is important that they are interpreted correctly if they are to supplement a more immediate impression of the candidate's suitability.

As much information must be given as possible about the work involved, the terms of employment and any arrangements for medical examinations. A successful candidate will then need to be given more detailed terms and conditions of employment to supplement those dealing mainly with wages or salary, hours of work and holidays. In particular, the requirements of the Contracts of Employment Act 1963 stipulate that an employee must be given written particulars of the terms of employment and the period of notice, which may depend upon the length of service.

(*c*) *The new employee should be introduced into the work place and familiarised with the personnel with whom contact is likely to be made.* He will also need to know his position as regards other departments, and the safety regulations and break periods. This induction period is essential if the employee is to settle into the new post as quickly as possible.

(*d*) *Most employees will require some form of training ranging over various periods of time.* This can vary from the training for new recruits and apprentices to courses for more senior members of the organisation to keep them up to date with recent developments in their particular fields. An employee may undergo some form of training for a period of years, as often with apprenticeships, or may attend a course on a specific issue lasting only one or two days. Changes in technology and the resultant need to re-adapt or supplement existing skills will also necessitate training programmes.

If possible, the personnel department will aim at a training scheme which is geared specifically to its own requirements and it may seek to provide such programmes internally using its own facilities and staff. Specialist courses may also be provided by outside bodies that suit the firm's requirements such as further and higher education colleges, trade and professional associations. The firm may also operate within the context of the relevant Industrial Training Board established under the Industrial Training Act 1964, where both internal and external courses may be combined.

The Department of Employment and Productivity also provides staff to conduct courses for the benefit of supervisors in both large and small firms. In many cases this department's training staff will provide this facility on the firm's premises. The important role which the supervisory grade plays in organisations led to the provision of 'Training Within Industry for Supervisors'. This scheme deals with such points as the means of promoting harmonious working relations and developing the powers to give clear and effective instructions to others. The training staff suggest how to improve work methods to contribute towards a more efficient use of the capacity under the supervisor's control, while always being aware of the need for ensuring safe working conditions and the adherence to health and safety regulations by other workers.

A firm may also avail itself of the facilities provided by Government Skillcentres where a wide variety of skills are taught on a course generally of six months' duration. The firm's own instructors may also be taught educational techniques to supplement their own skills while at these same training centres.

(*e*) *Productivity and good industrial relations can be partly fostered by ensuring a healthy and safe working environment.* Certain working conditions are laid down in legislation such as the Factories Act and the Offices, Shops and Railway Premises Act, and the Health and Safety at Work Act. In other cases more specific steps may have to be taken to protect workers handling certain materials or performing particular operations. The workers' attitude will be influenced by conditions in terms of heating, ventilation, lighting and noise. A well-ordered plant or office lay-out will also help promote orderliness and cleanliness among the employees. Much of this work will be preventative in nature but there will doubtless be a need to provide medical and accident facilities which are capable of meeting the more immediate needs of the organisation, particularly accidents of an industrial and manufacturing nature.

(*f*) *The personnel department may also be delegated the responsibility for industrial relations as a whole and therefore given the task of establishing machinery for joint consultation.* This will act as a sounding board and channel of communication for keeping in close contact with the state of relations between employer and employee and the exchange of opinions on issues of mutual interest. The need for the personnel department to deal with the settlement of industrial disputes will be lessened if the joint consultative committees succeed in creating a forum for the explanation of policy, communicating the attitudes of employees to the firm's proposals and airing grievances. The bringing together of each side's collective experience and knowledge to deal with a matter in which both have an interest can avoid future contention.

(*g*) *Some organisations provide certain services which they regard as an additional means of promoting a contented work force and good working relations between different groups of employees.* Thus sports and social clubs and other facilities may be provided to extend the contact between employees in different areas, so helping to foster good working relations. The firm may also seek to assist the employee in such matters as accommodation, transport to the place of work, and the setting up of savings groups, pension funds and sick clubs.

(*h*) *As with other departments the personnel staff will need to keep themselves up to date with any changes that are likely to influence working conditions such as major advances in technology that have implications for certain workers and their skills.* Similarly they need to monitor any changes in the response of workers to various tasks and routines as these developments may inhibit the firm in its desire to achieve the greatest possible effort from its employees.

(*i*) *An additional function of the personnel department is to keep itself fully conversant with the firm's wages and salary structure.* They must have details concerning the grading system, other conditions of service and the current attitudes of trade unions, the TUC, the CBI and trade and employer associations to these issues. The details of the wage system should be readily understood and ensure that wages based upon time rates, or payments by results, are calculated at the agreed rates for the job. Clear indications must then be given regarding any additional earnings that the worker can expect. These earnings may arise from the nature of the job such as working shifts, working away from home, and any fringe benefits to which the employee is entitled. Of particular importance will be those other items with a monetary value such as travel allowances, luncheon vouchers, subsidised loans from the company, discount on company products and commission.

(*j*) *Workers are more likely to work to the best of their ability if they believe that a reward exists in the form of promotion for those employees judged on merit and ability.* Careful consideration must be given to the question of filling a higher post from existing workers or by recruiting an outsider. An applicant from outside the organisation may be well qualified for the position but such an appointment must be balanced against the effect upon incentives and general morale among employees. Existing workers must not form the opinion that promotions are not based upon sound and fair principles; repeated external appointments will lead to a frustration of their career aspirations.

(*k*) *Not only should the line of promotion be clearly evident to employees but they should be given further indication of work undertaken by the personnel department in the fields of job evaluation and merit rating.* Analysis of jobs within the organisation will be undertaken to produce a job specification which contains details of the manual and mental activities involved in a particular job, its purpose, scope, duties, responsibilities and the requirements necessary to fulfil such activities. Job evaluation involves a process whereby these different jobs are compared in terms of their relative value in achieving the organisation's objectives, and are given rankings according to their relative value. This investigation and appraisal will then allow them to be grouped into wage and salary scales.

One of the purposes of job evaluation is to compare the analysis which it provides with the standards of attainments which must be reached by an individual if a vacant or new position is to be filled on the basis of a promotion. The suitability of an employee for promotion involves merit rating where the past record of the individual can be looked at from the point of view of those areas which are important to the new job. These activities of the personnel department will make a valuable contribution to the organisation in that they will assist in the preparation of job specifications for recruitment, selection, promotion and training. In more general terms, it will perhaps highlight certain shortcomings in some performances that can be looked into and appropriate action taken to improve the situation. Similarly, it will help identify particular talents, abilities and attitudes that may qualify for more responsible and valuable positions. Supervisors will then be more aware of the need to observe the performance of employees. Workers will also be more staisfied if they are aware that their efforts do not go unnoticed and that ability rather than favouritism is the real basis for promotion.

(*l*) *The personnel department will also have to deal with matters which involve the dismissal or redundancy of staff.* Such action must be seen to be fair and within the terms of any legislation such as the Redundancy and Protection of Employment Acts. Where redundancies are concerned, consultation must exist with the employees' representatives to discuss the numbers involved, the basis for redundancy and the agreed formula for financial compensation for those made redundant.

(*m*) *Detailed records should be maintained concerning employees, and in particular an analysis conducted to provide information on labour turn-over and the reasons for dismissals or employees leaving on their own accord.* Recruiting and training labour to fill vacant positions can prove a very expensive business and it will be the aim of the firm to keep labour turnover as low as possible and to take appropriate action to deal with what may be developing into a significant factor in causing workers to leave the organisation.

Research and Development (R and D)
The distinguishing mark of R and D activities is the presence or absence of an element of novelty

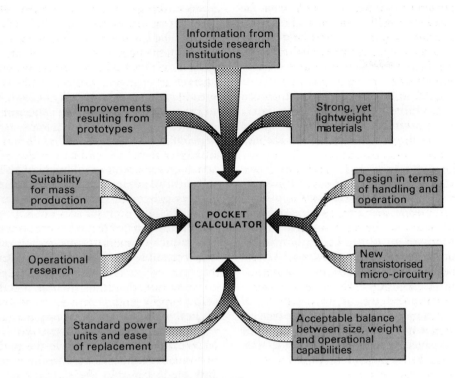

Fig. 2.5: The Research and Development Department

or innovation. If activities involve departure from routine and break new ground then they can generally be classified under the heading of R and D, and this is one of the aspects of the organisation's work which plays a vital role in securing its future prosperity. R and D is generally associated with the use of science and technology in projects involving new products, techniques and processes. It should be remembered that other departments within the organisation may perhaps have sections which seek to raise their productivity through analysing existing methods and improving upon them, such as work study undertaken by the production department. Similarly, the personnel department may be involved in discovering and developing abilities among the labour force. The following section will, however, concentrate primarily upon R and D which is characterised by a very high scientific content. (Fig. 2.5.)

Basic or fundamental research is undertaken primarily for the advancements of scientific knowledge without a specific practical application, and is only likely to be financed by private firms which regard the expenditure as worth while in that it could yield some future advantage to the company. A large company may be engaged upon a wide range of activities and the opportunities for making use of any advancement in scientific knowledge are greater. **Applied research**, on the other hand, is work undertaken with either a general or a particular application in mind. It is the investigation into practical problems by utilising the knowledge which has been produced by basic research. The **development** aspect is then regarded as the use of the results from such applied research, and is aimed at the introduction of useful materials, processes, products, equipment and systems, or the improvement of existing ones.

The total expenditure on scientific research and development by British industry in 1975 was £1,345 million and 55 per cent of this expenditure was accounted for by salaries and wages. The total employment of 180,000 was made up of scientists and engineers (33 per cent); technicians, laboratory assistants and draughtsmen (36 per cent); and administrative, clerical, industrial and other staff (31 per cent). Industries with very strong scientific and technological characteristics, such as electronics, telecommunications, chemicals and aerospace, account for a very large part of scientific research and development.

(a) *Some work may be put out by industry to outside bodies, or reference made to consultants or research institutions on particular aspects of their work.* For example, the government established the Scientific and Industrial Research Department to promote scientific research, particularly in subjects likely to effect trade and industry. It has fourteen main stations for different branches of its work, such as buildings, chemical and fuel research, and is administered by the Department of Trade and Industry.

(b) *Membership of a Trade Association may enable an organisation to benefit from the results of joint research, since member firms will have made a financial contribution to such work.* The organisation itself, or its trade association, may sponsor work in the research departments of institutions of higher education, such as universities and polytechnics. Useful information may also stem from the activities of the National Research Development Corporation, which is financed by the Department of Trade and Industry and seeks to give British industry the opportunity of benefiting from the work of British inventors which would otherwise be neglected through a lack of support from industry itself in its early stages.

(c) *The research and development department can be expected to work in very close contact with the market research, design and production workers.* The market research results may indicate areas for successful scientific research and development. The design teams, involved at a later stage, will consider results from many areas of research to produce a product that strikes an acceptable balance between meeting the needs of both consumers and the production department. The latter department will ultimately have responsibility for harnessing the organisation's resources to its production.

(d) *A project can expect to pass through several clear stages, after ideas have been discussed, to form an initial concept of what may prove a worth-while venture.* A feasibility study will be undertaken to identify likely problem areas and to estimate the potential sales, thus allowing the commercial viability of the project to be considered. Close liaison will continue with other departments and sections while a prototype is developed. If the project is still considered viable then a full-scale working model will be constructed to allow additional but more detailed information to be gained by interested parties. Even at this stage the project may be shelved or scrapped, as the pace of technological change and the fluctuations of consumers' tastes and preferences are such that it may become obsolete before it is actually put into production.

(e) *R and D can be expected to embrace many projects aimed at maintaining or improving the organisation's competitive position. A project may concentrate upon examining the firm's essential raw materials with a view to improving their quality through new processing techniques or a process which may even allow the use of what was previously regarded as a low-grade material.* If the raw material is cultivated, then productivity may be raised by developing a new seed strain or soil additives. This may also make possible cultivation in geographical areas that had previously proved unsuitable as commercial propositions. Totally new sources of supply may be investigated and developed in different areas as fresh techniques of exploration and development are made possible by technological and scientific advances.

Some raw materials such as metal ores are in finite supply and R and D may promote techniques to utilise waste and scrap materials or to develop substitutes from alternative raw materials. Man-made metal alloys, plastics and fibres have not only revolutionised consumer products, but also made possible the development of capital goods which no longer have to operate within the limits imposed by the traditional materials from which they were previously made. The creation of materials which can combine attributes such as strength, lightness, flexibility, longevity and a lack of bulk, has opened up whole new areas for industry and ensures that the pace of technological change continues.

(f) *The R and D department may also be delegated some responsibility in production development for the avoidance of waste and the elimination of inefficiency.* In particular, recent years have seen the growth of **operational research** which tackles business problems by considering and evaluating all the possible alternatives in order to find the best solution by balancing and reconciling conflicting aims. The purpose of operational research is to make a more effective use of the organisation's resources in terms of productive capacity and assets, methods, materials and labour.

(g) *The R and D staff may also be given a very wide brief in terms of ergonomics.* This can be defined as the study of the relationship between the capabilities of a worker and the extent to which the actual physical design and lay-out of equipment is suitable to these capabilities. The aim may be to minimise physical effort in performing certain operations by ensuring that such things as controls are designed and located in such a way that fatigue and accidents, for example, are minimised.

(h) *Periodic reviews will also be conducted in some organisations to ensure that where possible nationally and internationally agreed standards are adhered to.* This should comply with those promoted by the British Standards Institute and design staff must be given the relevant guidelines in such matters as dimensions, sizes, quality, performance and other characteristics. In particular, such features may need to be embodied into the product if the customer requires it to be used in conjunction with complementary activities and products, or if it needs to undergo repair or servicing later.

Attention must be paid to minimising what may be wasteful and uneconomic variety. The research and development work on innovations or existing practices in the organisation can contribute to a greater standardisation in such matters as components, processes and materials. Unit costs of production will be much higher if alterations in the productive processes are continually having to be made to provide products which are widely differentiated. However, a balance will have to be struck between the need of the marketing department to satisfy its customers' requirements and the advantages to the production department of longer production runs giving lower unit costs.

Finance

Most business organisations have a finance department. This has the responsibility for running the financial affairs of the organisation and for providing financial information to other parts of the organisation or to members of society. They may require this information for varying reasons and so purpose, content and communications are important in this connection. As no one set of accounts are unique, in the modern business world a medium-to-large size organisation would have a variety of accountants. The three most common are the financial accountant, the cost accountant and the management accountant.

(a) *The financial accountant would be the person to provide the board of directors with the overall profit achievement.* The most important document from the point of view of the shareholders and any creditors would be the year's results. They will be the main basis on which future objectives and plans will be set. The shareholders will be interested in growth and profitability, whereas creditors are more likely to be interested in stability and liquidity. It is a legal requirement that the organisation's results and a report are filed with the Registrar of Companies, and also they have to be audited by a professional team of auditors to make sure everything complies with the Companies Acts 1948–81.

So it would not be uncommon for a finance division in a large organisation to have a separate department for taxation and another department called Internal Audit. This department exists for verification and performance purposes and might report direct to the financial director. Nowadays, in the rapidly changing economic and business environment, one document representing a year's results does not provide sufficient information to gauge an organisation's performance. It must be remembered that a financial accountant is always dealing with historic costs and these costs are worth no more than a legal or information document for comparative purposes. Therefore, it would not be uncommon for the directors to have monthly accounting information and issue a half-yearly statement. The monthly statement could be elaborated to show the up-to-date position and also include forecasts. Some organisations employ financial analysts to incorporate changes on the previous month and previous year comparisons, so allowing a more detailed picture of the company's performance. All this information is supplied as an aid for senior management to make better 'calculated' decisions.

Obviously with detailed and complex information being supplied, it is most important that certain aspects be adhered to.

(i) It must be accurate, since if information contains errors it might never be trusted again.

(ii) It must be clear and easy to understand, otherwise when the information is passed to senior management it may be virtually ignored because of a lack of time to digest it.

(iii) It must be consistent. If a problem has arisen, then management must make a corrective decision and it can only do so by analysing trends. If the information is inconsistent then those trends might not be readily identified. Trends help management to diagnose potential problems, highlight new opportunities and allow a more accurate projection.

The financial accountant's main role, then, is to prepare accounts by basic book-keeping methods and to provide that information to other members of the company, to the shareholders and to the creditors.

(b) *Whereas the financial accountant deals with actual historic values, the cost accountant deals with the costing of selected products or services.* This is done by putting estimates to a 'unit' (a unit being a process of production) and therefore building a standard. This is invaluable to the organisation when attempts are being made to deal with actual costs. Most manufacturing organisations to-day employ the principles of standard costing. The principle hinges on the identification and classification of costs. Input costs can either be **direct** or **indirect**. An example of direct costs would be labour and materials. They are called direct because their costs can be easily identified. What cannot easily be identified are the indirect costs. For example, the overall costs of heating, lighting and rent cannot be attached directly and solely to a job or process. By a process of apportionment and allocation a standard overhead rate can be applied to each job or cost centre. There is not one unique apportionment basis. Heating might be apportioned according to floor space, whereas insurance would be apportioned according to the capital value of equipment used. Depending on whether the manufacturing process is labour or machine orientated, the total collection of these costs and the total machine hours or labour hours would form a standard labour overhead rate or a standard machine overhead rate.

Obviously during the course of a period, say a month or a year, not all costs are going to be standard. Costs can vary for many reasons, one of them being inflation. Variances will then arise when actuals are measured against standards. For these reasons, **variance analysis** is an important tool for control purposes.

These detailed records of expense help management in their decision-making process. It aids product selection, imposes tight organisation and defines responsibilities. Examples of the more common type of variance are in materials and in labour. Variances in materials might lead to questions on buying techniques, and a counteractive decision might then call for substitutes. Or if inflation was causing the problem, the standards themselves might need to be changed. Variance analysis therefore helps to highlight inefficiencies, aids cost production and can suggest performance techniques and productivity agreements that help to smooth out these inefficiencies.

The cost accountant has a close relationship with all departments concerned with manufacturing. The costs are incurred from the time the materials are bought to the time they are issued to production and to the time they are made into complete units. These departments provide the cost accountant with the necessary facts and figures. The cost accountant must digest these figures and present them to the management of those departments so that the information can be used as an aid to better decision-making.

(c) The **management accountant** *is not unlike the cost accountant in that he is dealing with actual costs, but he also provides management, at all levels, with financial information on a variety of projects.* These projects can range from detailed budgeting to investment appraisal on capital projects.

Basic management accounting originates from a plan. Planning is a difficult process in itself and there are basic rules and guidelines to be adhered to. For instance, one of the problems is that planning is insufficiently responsive to latest events and therefore it is most important to state the basis for the plan and the date when it was issued. It is the management accountant's responsibility to keep management informed of variances from the budget. If a critical decision on accepted criteria is made, then a forecast or target should replace the budget as the means of achievement.

In times of inflation and environmental uncertainty, a budget should not be treated with rigidity but should be flexible in its approach. For instance, a management accountant in a sales division should be able to provide product sales figures in an easily understandable form so that management can make the right decision. Threats and risks must be reduced and opportunities seized. If one product is more profitable than the others, obviously that is the product which the resources of the company can best be invested in.

Some large organisations use a system called **divisional responsibility** whereby each division is treated as a profit centre. Services provided between divisions are charged for under this system.

Most organisations today have a finance department with a finance director. It is not uncommon, however, to have a finance director with responsibilities other than finance. His responsibilities could include the Data Processing Division and the Corporate and Business Planning Section. There is no single financial structure for an organisation. For example, a company using a divisional responsibility system might appoint a controller for each division, who would then report to the divisional director, who in turn would be responsible to the finance director.

3. The Nature and Role of Law for the Organisation

The nature of law

This chapter will examine the different types of law and its effect on the organisation and the community. We are particularly concerned with those laws specifically establishing a rule of conduct which is imposed and enforced. This means that if this particular rule of conduct is disobeyed, then the state may intervene to punish the offender or provide facilities by which any victim of this disobedience can seek redress. (The British 'state' is the United Kingdom of Great Britain and Northern Ireland, but English law only applies to England and Wales.)

The emphasis that must be placed on a rule of law is that it is *binding* on the community. However, in a democratic country the laws should be a reflection of the wishes and feelings of the members of that community. The democratic process will ensure that laws will be changed and amended as attitudes change and different pressures are brought to bear on the government in power. The general aim of law is the attainment of **justice**. This is a difficult concept, but basically it means that everyone is treated fairly and equally. Justice should be both formal and substantial.

A particular law may not always achieve justice, but it will nonetheless be binding. The aims of the modern state have often conflicted with what is the traditional view of justice. There has been an attempt to achieve a measure of justice based on broader social and economic principles, which sometimes deprive individuals of their rights. For instance, the idea of compulsory purchase of land may be ideal for the community at large, but to take away an individual's property is hardly just. The reduction of public spending by the government may not be thought just by those affected by the cuts, but nonetheless it is regarded as an essential ingredient of an overall economic package intended to benefit everyone in the long run.

Therefore to achieve justice for the whole community is highly problematical because of the many conflicting interests. At best a successful government will achieve a uniform, objective system of laws which are at least *certain* in their application, and are free from ambiguity. The community will want to see that these laws are applied systematically and without bias and prejudice. The measure of fairness of a particular law will perhaps reflect its acceptability by the people.

The classification of law

Law can be divided into a number of distinct classes (see Table 3.1).

Public Law

Within this classification are all the rules which require direct state involvements namely:

(i) *Constitutional Law*

Unlike many foreign countries, there is no written British Constitution but it is based on the ordinary laws of the land, e.g. legislation, case law and partly on convention. Constitutional law is the collection of rules which govern and regulate the government itself, the powers of the Houses of Parliament, the powers and privileges of MPs, the rules relating to the Civil Service, the police, and armed forces, the courts, the voting rights of the population, their freedom of speech and movement, the interaction between central government and local authorities. Within the constitutional legal framework is the means by which all of the laws affecting the community are made and enforced.

(ii) *Administrative Law*

This is the body of rules which is concerned with the regulation of the government's influence in those areas which affect individual freedoms and rights. The legislature has intervened much more freely in recent years in areas which were once the concern of the individual, i.e. social welfare, social security, industrial relations, town and country planning. The great bulk of detailed rules which relate to the role of the state and its institutions as they affect its citizens is administrative law. The more abstract principles upon which these institutions are run is constitutional law, i.e. the rules of natural justice.

Table 3.1: Classification of law

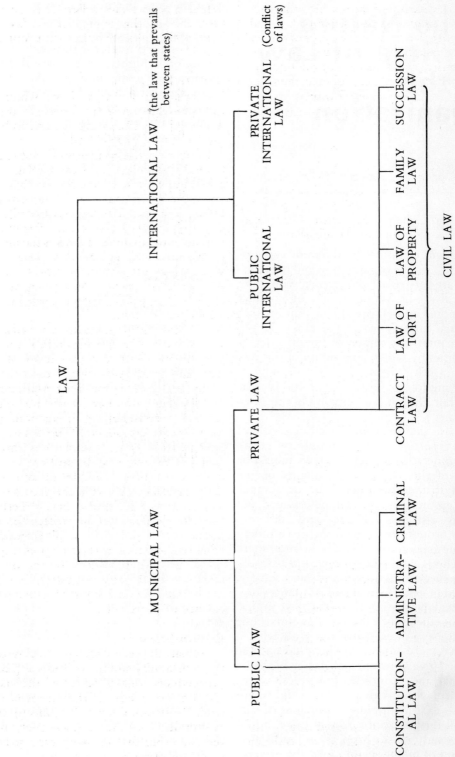

LAW
- MUNICIPAL LAW
  - PUBLIC LAW
    - CONSTITUTION-AL LAW
    - ADMINISTRA-TIVE LAW
    - CRIMINAL LAW
  - PRIVATE LAW
    - CONTRACT LAW
    - LAW OF TORT
    - LAW OF PROPERTY
    - FAMILY LAW
    - SUCCESSION LAW

    (CONTRACT LAW, LAW OF TORT, LAW OF PROPERTY, FAMILY LAW, SUCCESSION LAW = CIVIL LAW)
- INTERNATIONAL LAW (the law that prevails between states)
  - PUBLIC INTERNATIONAL LAW
  - PRIVATE INTERNATIONAL LAW (Conflict of laws)

(iii) *Criminal Law*

Criminal Law deals with offences which the state recognises as contrary to continuance of law and order. The importance of different types of crimes depends on the valuation by the state. They can be further classified by the nature of the offence, e.g. offences against the person, property, the state, public morality. Crimes are now usually prohibited by statute law. Offenders against such law are **punished** by the state.

Private Law

The state is not primarily concerned with private law, but provides the laws, court facilities and powers with which private individuals can pursue claims against each other if they wish. There are many subdivisions within this classification:

(i) *The Law of Contract*

This allows the individual to pursue a grievance resulting from a pomise made between two parties which is intended to be legally enforceable. An action in contract is based on a wrong which is complained of as a breach of contract. (The more detailed rules of contract will be considered in volume 2). Also largely based on the law of contract are a number of specialised areas of legal agreement, mostly governed by statute, i.e. sale of goods, agency, partnership, insurance, hire purchase, collectively known as commercial law.

(ii) *The Law of Tort*

Examples of torts are nuisance, trespass, defamation, negligence. A tort is a wrong independent of contract which imposes a duty that must be observed towards others generally. A breach of this duty can lead to an award of damages.

(iii) *The Law of Property*

The rather complex law relating to property involves the rights and duties people have over land, e.g. absolute ownership, the interests they may create in land, wills, marriage settlements, and associated encumbrances (leases, mortgages, rights of way, light, etc.). All other forms of property are considered to be personal property which includes goods, patent privileges, copyright, stocks and shares, etc.

(iv) *Family Law*

This deals with the rights, duties and obligations concerning the status of husbands, wives, children and other members of the family.

(v) *Succession Law*

When a person dies others may succeed to his property and this branch of the law deals with how, when and to whom such property is distributed.

Civil Law

The branches of Private Law, which define the rights and duties of individuals in their relationship with each other, can also be placed under the heading 'civil law' (Table 3.1).

Civil law concerns the rights, duties and obligations of individuals and their relationships with other individuals in society (individuals can of course be a company, or a firm of partners, or a public utility such as the Gas Board). Actions of litigation in civil law reflect the individual involvement in that the case takes the heading of the parties involved, e.g. *Smith* v. *Jones*. The person who brings the action is represented first and the defendant second. However, if there is an appeal, the appellant's name is listed first, with the respondent second.

The basic distinction between civil and criminal law is that in the former there is no element of punishment (with the exception of exemplary damages). In the majority of cases the plaintiff is suing the defendant for compensation in the form of damages (although there are additional or alternative remedies, e.g. injunction, specific performance, rescission, etc). There is no obligation, unlike criminal law, to see the case through to the end, and an action can be withdrawn at any time in the proceedings—usually because a settlement has been reached between the parties out of court. The court system is, of course, different for civil cases. In criminal cases the prosecution must prove the accused's guilt beyond all reasonable doubt, whereas there is no such strict presumption in the civil courts. There is no favouring one party (i.e. innocent until proven guilty), but the courts decide the issue in favour of either party on the balance of probability.

Criminal Law

Criminal offences are recognised as wrongs against the community and the offender is punished with proceedings usually taken in the name of the Crown. The report of the case is headed with a letter 'R' standing for *regina* (queen) or *rex* (king) as the head of state. (However, it is worth remembering that in many cases private individuals can bring a prosecution.)

There are two sources of criminal law—the common law and legislation, the latter now being the most important as Parliament (i) attempts to codify the criminal law, (ii) has to pass more laws as society develops and becomes more complex. Consider, for example, the plethora of Acts relating to consumer protection, e.g. the Trade Descriptions Acts 1968, 1972, Food and Drugs Act 1955, Weights and Measures Acts 1963, 1976 and 1979, Prices Act 1974, Unsolicited Goods and Services Acts 1971, 1975, etc. These all relate to one specific aspect of our society, all have criminal sanctions, and were all recently introduced.

Some behaviour offends against what we all recognise (perhaps through our culture and background) as being against our moral principles or the correct standard of conduct. This feeling may be expressed through the media, pressure groups or individuals, until the legislature recognises a justifiable complaint and, if it is politically acceptable, acts upon it—sometimes immediately but usually as a result of an enquiry by a committee or commission, plus further political and public debate following the publication of government papers. For example, the Health and Safety at Work Act 1974 was based on the Robens Report, and the Consumer Credit Act 1974 stemmed from the Crowther Committee's investigation into consumer credit.

There are also categories of statutory offences which are not centred on moral principles but have been passed mainly out of legal necessity to ensure the ordered working of society and the economy, for example, the Acts relating to the law of the road, the collection of revenue and government legislation to regulate the economy.

Punishment

If convicted of an offence, the accused will be **punished** by the courts. Basically the idea of the punishment is to emphasise that the criminal laws of the land cannot be broken without penalty. Also behind sentencing is the idea of deterrence, so that not only is the defendant aware of the consequences of his offence but so too are the public who may read an account of the trial in local or, for serious cases, national newspapers.

Unless the crime carries a fixed penalty, the judge can exercise his **discretion**. In common law crimes, the judge has unlimited discretion to punish, but where a punishment is stated in a statute there is normally a maximum punishment and the judge can exercise his discretion up to that maxi-

mum. As an example, the maximum fine for failing to observe a speed limit is £50, but the usual fine is £5–£20, depending on the actual excess of speed, and the previous record of the driver.

The use of discretion allows the judge to take into account mitigating factors in each case—whether the commission of the crime was deliberate, reckless or through ignorance, and whether or not it was a first offence. It is interesting to note the recommendations of the advisory council on the penal system (1978) who have suggested that the majority of indictable crimes have their maximum sentences reduced.

Types of Offences

The crimes in this country are classified into **summary** and **indictable** offences; that is, either triable before a magistrate or before a judge and jury. The swing is towards increasing use of the magistrate as recommended by the James Committee Inquiry in 1975 and therefore the division is somewhat hazy as many indictable crimes, e.g. theft, can at the choice of the accused be tried at a summary level. Furthermore, those summary crimes carrying a penalty of three months or more can be transferred for trial at the Crown Court, again at the wish of the accused.

There is an increasing number of more recent statutes, e.g. the Health and Safety at Work Act 1974 and the Trade Descriptions Act 1968, which have alternative actions, either summary or indictable. The latter is usually reserved for those instances where a serious or persistent breach of the Act has occurred and a stronger deterrent is required.

An alternative classification of crimes is into **arrestable** and **non-arrestable** offences, a distinction introduced in the Criminal Law Act 1967. An arrestable offence is one where the sentence is fixed by law or the arrested person could be sentenced for five years imprisonment for a first offence. With a few statutory exceptions all other offences are non-arrestable.

With regard to the business community, the distinction between arrestable and non-arrestable offences is not usually significant. For serious offences such as theft, false pretences, burglary, arrest is technically possible, but care has to be taken and a proper arresting procedure established. The use of excessive violence to restrain someone may result in the victim suing for assault and battery. Also the arrest will only be legally correct if an arrestable offence is, or has been committed. Unlike the police, the ordinary citizen cannot arrest on grounds of suspicion. A wrongful arrest may lead to a claim for damages for false imprisonment.

Before a conviction can be obtained, the rules of criminal procedure require the prosecution to prove the guilt of the accused 'beyond all reasonable doubt', either to the magistrate in a summary trial or to the judge and jury in a Crown Court indictable trial.

Confirmation of guilt usually requires two basic elements (i) there has been a guilty act or conduct (*actus reus*) (ii) there was also a guilty intent (*mens rea*). The latter element can vary from deliberate intent to negligent or reckless behaviour. However, Parliament has passed some Acts which do not require any proof of *mens rea*. Thus a purely innocent act can be penalised if it contravenes a statute, e.g. if a trader attatches a false description to goods by mistake. He can still be prosecuted under the Trade Descriptions Act 1968. It is therefore no defence to claim to be unaware that an offence has been committed. Liability is absolute.

Sources of English law

As we have already seen, there is a distinction between 'laws' or codes of conduct which the people themselves enforce, and the laws of the state. These latter laws are *made*; therefore, they have a source. There are several sources in fact, and we shall examine those which play a major role in the making and developing of law today.

Case Law
Case Law is where judges lay down legal principles concerning the cases before them. The reason why case law is so important is because judges apply the legal principles after following the examples of earlier cases. This is known as the **doctrine of precedent.** A particular case then becomes an authority even if it is based on the interpretation of a statute. Despite statutes being a supreme source of law, it is the case which is examined and not merely the words of the statute. The English courts have adopted the doctrine of precedent, whereby they follow the previous decisions of other judges, since the introduction of the system of common law in Norman times. Not all that a judge says in reaching his decision is important in the development of a precedent. The basis of a binding precedent is the legal reasoning (*ratio decidendi*) a judge uses in reaching his decision. The legal reasoning is a complete amalgam of known principles of law, experience, references to literary sources, all applied to the case under consideration. The precedent is developed by subsequent judges applying these abstract principles to a similar case. This case law then stands as a binding precedent and by convention must be followed by judges in a court in the same hierarchy when a similar case arises. Precedents created in the lower courts can, of course, be overruled in the Appellate Courts. Furthermore, these senior courts have now granted themselves increased power to deviate from the custom of following precedents. In 1966 the House of Lords announced that it would uphold the convention of precedent, but would deviate in those circumstances where it felt that justice would be best served by doing so.

The Court of Appeal (Criminal Division) also occasionally declines to follow its own precedent when it feels that the liberty of the accused is more important than the convention. Even the Court of Appeal (Civil Division) under the strong influence of Lord Denning has recently deviated from normal practice. By doing this the appellate courts are introducing an element of uncertainty into the role of precedents. But if the decision-making is improved and justice is done, the whole structure of the law is improved. Moreover, the very nature of legal reasoning makes for some uncertainty anyway. As an abstract principle, there will of course be difficulties in applying it to subsequent cases, and the judge may decide to '**distinguish**' the earlier decision from the case before him on the basis of the material facts. The approach judges adopt in developing precedents is generally extremely cautious. What must be emphasised is that the precedents will not conflict with fundamental principles of law already laid down, and the judge will follow them within fairly closely defined guidelines. His discretion occurs when the facts of a current situation apparently do not seem to fit the previous rules. There is then a gap in the law which the judge must attempt to fill. In most cases the gap is small and often trivial, but sometimes a major development in the law ensues.

Because the courts abide by previous decisions, the individual is in a better position to know the outcome of a dispute he may have with another individual. This therefore prevents the need to seek recourse to the courts every time a legal problem arises. It means, for instance, that businessmen should realise the consequences of a breach of contract, of being negligent in not providing a safe system of work for an employee, of unfairly terminating a contract of employment, or of polluting the atmosphere. With regard to the criminal law, precedent assists the maxim that *punishment should only be inflicted for a breach of the criminal law clearly formulated beforehand*. The process of laying down legal rules gives notice of the consequences of disobeying them.

Legislation

Legislation is a written source of law. It is enacted by the British Parliament (which will be dealt with in detail in Vol. 2). Much of the contemporary law of this country is now embodied in statute form. These statutes (Acts of Parliament), must begin their life as Bills, receiving the approval of both Houses of Parliament and the assent of the monarch.

The intention to introduce legislation is usually expressed in a party's election manifesto. In order to stay loyal to supporters the programme is usually introduced during the government's term of office (although it may be modified as extra information is obtained, circumstances change, or serious objections are raised). During any term of office unexpected issues may arise that have to be dealt with promptly, e.g. the Counter-Inflation (Temporary Provisions) Act 1972–3. Also there will be a flow of reports from the Royal Commissions, Committees and the Law Commission, which recommend reform or new legislation. There are also the annual Finance Acts, Consolidation Fund and Appropriation Acts authorising the collection of revenue and its expenditure.

Although many of the statutes passed each parliamentary session reflect the government's continued intervention into the economy and society (e.g. the establishment of the National Enterprise Board, nationalising a company, introducing extended trade union laws or restructuring local government), much of the legislation involves revising and updating laws which have become outmoded or are presenting administrative difficulties.

An important element of the legislative process is that Parliament is regarded as **sovereign**. In theory there is nothing about which Parliament cannot legislate. Obviously Parliament would not enact any laws which were immoral or unnecessarily unjust (except in true emergencies), because the democratic process would see that the term of office of such a government was a short one. Usually the government takes advice from as many sources as possible before introducing legislation. Prospective controversial legislation is discussed either by Parliament after a White Paper has been issued, or through a Green Paper which encourages public discussion.

The government is aware of the great difficulty in enforcing legislation which does not have the backing or acquiescence of the public. However, once passed, an Act must be obeyed even if it is 'good' or 'bad' law. Only Parliament can amend or repeal legislation. The courts must obey the intention of Parliament and interpret accordingly.

Interpretation of Statutes

Although the parliamentary draftsmen attempt to write statutes in a clear, precise, unambiguous form, there will always be difficulties in interpretation as was indicated in the Law Commission's report of 1969:

> There are practical limits to the improvements which can be effected in drafting. Account must be taken of the inherent frailty of language, the difficulty of foreseeing and providing for all contingencies, the imperfections which must result in some degree from the pressures under which modern legislation has so often to be produced, and the difficulties of expressing finely balanced compromises of competing interests which the draftsman is sometimes called upon to formulate. Difficulties may also arise when words are inserted into a Bill in the course of discussion in Parliament without sufficient regard to its overall structure as originally planned.

It is essential that judges have a consistent approach to interpretation and over the years they have developed a number of rules and principles to aid them in their interpretation. The **Literal Rule** suggests that judges should interpret the words of a statute as they stand. Only if there is an obvious absurdity will the judges resort to the **Golden Rule** when the judge can apply a commonsense interpretation. A third major rule of interpretation is the **Mischief Rule** which refers the courts in cases of doubt to the pre-Act situation: what defect was there in the Common Law and what has Parliament done to remedy this defect? Interpretation should be based on furthering this remedy.

Although the judiciary cannot ignore or disobey

a statute, a number of presumptions they have evolved ensure that there is no misuse of power. For instance:

1. Any law which attempts to remove or reduce the rights of individuals must be clearly stated. Compensation is assumed unless an Act specifically mentions that there is to be no compensation.

2. Legislation is assumed not to act retrospectively.

3. The existing law is presumed to remain unchanged unless there is a specific contrary reference in the Act.

4. No criminal liability is presumed unless there is fault (see page 50).

5. There is a presumption against any abuse of power or arbitrary conduct.

However, it must be emphasised again that no court can challenge a statute on its merits, no matter how harsh or unfair the legislative decree appears to be. The only challenge exists through the normal democratic process of choosing a government, plus the opposition and debate within the Houses themselves.

Codification and Consolidation

The establishment of the Law Commission in 1965 under the chairmanship of a High Court Judge was a recognition by the legislative authorities that the law is at the best of times difficult to follow and understand. With successive governments passing 60–70 statutes a year, and with over 2000 statutory instruments, it is obvious that the businessman as well as members of the public will find the law confusing. The Law Commission attempts to make the law more intelligible by recommending to Parliament that various aspects of the law should be updated, amended or repealed. One way of making the law more compact is by codification. Very little of this has been accomplished in this country. It involves the gathering of all the existing law on a particular subject and incorporating it into one Act, e.g. Sale of Goods Act 1979, Theft Act 1968 (amended by the Theft Act 1978).

On a more modest scale are the attempts made at consolidation. This is where several pieces of legislation on some aspect of law are brought together and re-enacted. Consolidated legislation does not usually have to subject itself to the rigours of passing through the normal stages of enactment. A joint committee will examine any proposal by the Lord Chancellor for consolidation and if satisfied the Bill will pass through the various stages with the minimum of delay.

There are also other bodies, e.g. the Criminal Law Revision Committee and the Law Reform Committee, which are involved in improving the legal system, not to mention the host of other committees, commissions and other unofficial bodies which may examine or comment on some aspect of British law, perhaps with a view to legislative reform.

Delegated Legislation

Much attention is given by the media to statutes but delegated or subordinate legislation is rarely given much publicity. This is because the rules, orders, regulations, and bye-laws which make up delegated legislation are usually enacted in a procedural fashion. Under a 'Parent' Act, Parliament delegates the power to make law to various bodies, e.g. ministers and local authorities. Much is gained from this process for it enables laws to be made and altered quickly and usually without reference to Parliament. It frees Parliament from much of the detailed specialist work and allows it to concentrate on broader issues.

Delegated legislation has the force of law, but it is not supreme. Those passing laws through delegated legislation can only do so within the legal powers granted to them. If there is an abuse of this power, the courts have the right to declare the legislation void (*ultra vires*).

English Law and Europe

Now that Britain is a signatory to the EEC Treaty by virtue of the European Communities Act 1972, it is arguable that the accession to Europe creates a further source of law—**Community Law**. At the moment the amount of legislation issued by the Community is quite small. What has been passed is in pursuance of the major objective of creating a single market within the Community which allows for the free movement of goods, businesses, capital and labour.

The 1972 Act immediately introduces Community Law by providing:

1. for the removal of customs duties;

2. for the introduction of a Common Agricultural Policy;

3. for the amendment of Company Law so that greater harmonisation with European law is achieved;

4. for the maintenance of competition by the outlawing of restrictive practices.

The executive powers of the European Community are exercised by the **Commission** and the **Council** (which, with the European Court of Justice, will be discussed in more detail in Vol. 2). These two institutions can issue a variety of orders, namely:

1. *Regulations* These are the main source of legislation and have a binding and direct effect on the Member States.

2. *Decisions* These are directed at the Member States and are usually issued where uniformity with Community Law is not a high priority. Usually each Member State is left to introduce decisions in the form of subordinate legislation.

3. *Directives* These are issued direct, e.g. to a company. They have immediate binding effect.

4. *Recommendations* } As these imply, they are
5. *Opinions* } both a source of advice only. They are without legal effect, but it is hoped of course that the advice will be accepted.

The interpretation of Community Law is by the **European Court of Justice**. It is expected that before passing judgement on a case which involves a European Treaty, the national courts will refer any point of law to the Court of Justice.

Section 2 of the European Communities Act 1972 supports this view when it says that the European Treaties 'are without further enactment to be given legal effect' and to 'be enforced, allowed and followed accordingly'. In the event of a conflict between Community law and national law, then Community law must prevail.

The only possible confusion that may arise is where a subsequent statute is unintentionally passed by Parliament which contravenes Community Law. As parliamentary law is regarded as supreme, the courts have no power to declare such a statute invalid. The courts would have no choice but to follow the law of Parliament. Perhaps Parliament will issue guidelines under a new Interpretation Act stating that unless it is clearly stated to the contrary, Community Law must be regarded as the most authoritative source of law.

The European Communities Act 1972 does not bind successive Parliaments—this would be fundamentally unconstitutional. But to create a harmonious working relationship with the Community, obedience to Community Law is self-imposed by Parliament. However, if it was regarded as necessary, the European Communities Act 1972 could be repealed.

The European Court of Justice can also be used by Member States, companies or individuals to appeal against measures or fines imposed by the Commission or Council.

Common law and equity

All English law consists either of common law or equity, which complement each other. **Common law** comprises the judicial precedents developed in the courts, all legislative enactments and, to a minor degree, ancient customs. The title 'common law' has its historical origins in the days following the Norman Conquest, when the process of developing a legal system common to all the people in England and Wales began.

Equity is a term which introduces the concept of fairness and natural justice. The law relating to equity is based on the rules developed by the Chancery Court prior to the rationalisation of the courts by the Judicature Acts 1873–5. Equity complements the common law allowing discretionary remedies where the common law is regarded as somewhat rigid and harsh. In particular the remedies of specific performance, injunction and rescission were developed by equity.

The position of judges in the English legal system

As we have seen, judges play a role in making and interpreting law. It is necessary to examine their position in the English constitution.

Constitutionally judges are **independent** of the executive. They are appointed on the recommendation of the executive, but can only be removed by the Queen on the address of both Houses of Parliament. Their salaries are paid from the Consolidated Fund. Judges tend not to be criticised by Parliament unless a vital legal dispute has arisen, and certainly no discussion is allowed on cases which are pending or ongoing.

Judges are appointed and not elected and the fact that on the whole they have attracted little publicity suggests that they are very aware of their role and power. It is fair to say that only the judges in appellate courts are the true lawmakers and their approach is usually conservative, those in the lower courts being deciders of fact and assessors of damages and sentences.

As a general rule the judge tends not to play an active role, but is responsible for seeing that the case is properly conducted in the right atmosphere and in compliance with the rules of procedure and evidence.

Some fundamental principles of English law

We will now examine some of the basic principles or concepts of English law, some of which are referred to in Chapter 6 (page 106).

Vicarious Liability

If a civil wrong has been committed, the court has the power to award compensation in an action in the form of damages, or it can order someone to do something. But this does not necessarily mean that the victim of some wrong will necessarily receive the compensation given out by the court, as the defendant may have insufficient assets to meet an award. In order to protect innocent victims against these 'men of straw', the doctrine of vicarious liability has been developed. Perhaps this type of liability occurs most in the field of employer-employee relationships, and it makes an employer liable for any tort committed by his employee in the 'course of his employment', even if the act or omission had not been authorised (*Century Insurance Co. Ltd. v. Northern Ireland Road Transport Board (1942)*). It must be stressed that the employer is liable only for wrongful acts which are connected with the employee's actual and apparent duties. Some criticism may be levelled at this doctrine because it means that the employer is held responsible even though he is not personally at fault, which is contrary to basic legal principles. But there are many reasonable arguments in support of the principle of vicarious liability:

1. It is the employer who is generally the wealthier and the more likely to be able to afford any compensation. Moreover, the efficient employer is likely to have widespread insurance to cover such eventualities. Some insurance is compulsory, e.g. third-party cover for motor vehicle use, and as a result of the Employers' Liability (Compulsory Insurance) Act 1969, protection must be given for an employee's injuries to his colleagues.

2. The employer has the responsibility of recruiting his employees, and therefore if his judgement is at fault, why should he not take the consequences?

3. The employer also has the power to instruct, train, supervise, control and discipline his employees, which if correctly carried out should remove most of his employees' untoward activities.

4. It must also be noted that the wrongful act would probably never have occurred if it had not been for employees' job requirements.

5. Finally, it is generally recognised as a matter of course, that the employee represents the employer, and his acts are also the acts of his employer.

Both fraud and theft have involved employers in liability, even though there has been no personal gain on their part. Professional advisers and employees who are in a position dominated by a special relationship must be careful of the information they give, as if it is unsound, misleading or erroneous they are liable—and so are their employers vicariously. The principle of vicarious liability can be extended to contractual situations where agreements are made with third parties by employees on behalf of their firms, or where agents arrange contacts for their principals. These contracts will be binding even if unauthorised and in breach of the employee's contract or agency agreement, if the contract is made with the authority that the employee has or seems to have.

Strict Liability

The concept of strict liability is an attempt by Parliament and the courts to recognise that some wrongs are so serious that responsibility must be borne, irrespective of fault. Strict liability is not always synonymous with absolute liability. There may be circumstances where a defence is permissible, for example, if an artificial lake overflowed its banks and damaged property, there would be no liability if it was the result of an unusual freak storm—an 'act of God'. It can be argued that a further example of strict liability occurs with the tort of nuisance; the courts will simply be concerned with deciding whether there is a nuisance and whether it should be prevented.

Business organisations are subjected to a variety of statutes and statutory regulations which impose obligations on the employer and sometimes on their employees. Much of this legislation is involved with improving safety standards, working conditions and the general safety of employees, visitors and others who come on to business premises (see Chapter 6, pages 105–6). For example, the Factories Act 1961 lays down that flywheels, moving parts and every dangerous part of machinery should be securely fixed. If, therefore, an employee is injured after coming into contact with part of a machine, the employer is strictly liable, the issue of fault being immaterial.

Making the employer liable is perhaps the only way of enforcing some statutory legislation, such as the Trade Descriptions Act 1968 and the Food and Drugs Act 1955, and no defence is effectual if the employer has not executed reasonable care.

Fault

With criminal cases the courts adopt the presumption that a person is not guilty of a crime unless the accused is at **fault**. This is an essential element of liability in the criminal law, although many of the modern statutes do expressly lay down that a conviction can be obtained regardless of fault.

Conflict Resolution by the Courts

There are many courts established under the Constitution of England. The powers, jurisdiction and location of these courts have been established by relevant statutes, e.g. the Courts Act 1971 which set up the Crown Court. The English legal system is divided into civil and criminal courts in a hierarchical structure. The less serious criminal and civil cases are taken to the magistrates and to the county courts respectively. Indictable offences are taken to the Crown Court (although after consultation between the police, magistrate and defendant, some indictable offences can be tried summarily at the magistrates court (see p. 44). Cases involving demands for large sums of damages, or equitable remedies, such as injunctions, specific performance or rescission and defended divorces, are taken to the High Court.

Each party in an action or prosecution normally has the right to appeal, or at least if permission is granted by the appellate courts. The English legal system is perhaps unusual in that there are two senior appellate courts, the Court of Appeal and, as an ultimate court, the House of Lords.

Business organisations will probably only use the courts when litigation is really necessary. For instance, an action to recover damages in the Queen's Bench Division of the High Court is both costly and time-consuming. Much of this is caused by the technical procedure in presenting a case. The issue of the writ is only the first stage in a lengthy business. If the defendant intends to enter a defence, his entry of appeal will be for the purpose of asking for an adjournment in order that his defence may be prepared. If the defendant successfully survives the preliminaries and a judgement is not entered in default, then the two parties enter into further preliminaries by way of

pleadings. The plaintiff's main pleading is the **statement of claim** which sets out his case. If a defence is entered after receipt of the statement of claim then this can be on the basis of alternative defences, or it can admit the plaintiff's claim is without substance. The plaintiff, like the defendant, has the right to ask for further particulars on points which are not clearly defined.

Further complications arise when the defendant is involving third parties to indemnify all or part of the claim. The plaintiff must also give this third party an opportunity to defend and resist the action. Furthermore, each party must supply each other with a list of all relevant documents.

This outline is purely an indication of the work done before a contested dispute reaches the court. It is time-consuming and exacting because each side is attempting to prepare its case in secret, thus giving away as little as possible to its opponent. The costs of this preparation for trial can be enormous, and the bill rapidly escalates during the trial because of the insistence that evidence is given orally which incurs expense claims from witnesses. Subsequent appeals can push the total bill for expenses and fees in excess of £10,000. Thus it can be seen why so many businessmen prefer to use arbitration as a means of settling disputes.

Not all cases are so expensive. Companies make great use of the County Court for collecting debts. Costs are fixed by the court and in many cases the actions are not defended and a judgement can quickly be obtained.

Remedies in civil actions

Damages
The successful litigant will usually be seeking redress in the form of compensation. Damages awarded can be in several forms.

Ordinary
These are damages assessed as having arisen naturally from the breach of the law, or if in a tort action, what the court feels is the damage done to the plaintiff.

Special
These are damages which the court will not presume to have arisen unless the plaintiff makes a special substantial claim, e.g. loss of profits.

Aggravated
Where the court takes into account the defendant's actions in the dispute and feels a greater sum is necessary to show true compensation.

Exemplary
These are rarely given, but are used as a punishment or deterrent.

Liquidated
These damages have been expressly stated in a contractual agreement and will be automatically awarded if the case is proved unless, in the court's opinion, the damages are a penalty and not a true assessment of expected loss.

If the plaintiff is successful in his action, yet the court is unable to discover any real loss, then an award of **nominal** damages is made (about £2) merely to show the plaintiff's justification in bringing a case. If the plaintiff succeeds in a case but the court is unhappy about his conduct in bringing such an action, then **contemptuous** damages (e.g. ½p) will be awarded (often without costs) as an indication of the court's displeasure.

Damages are the traditional remedy available to those successful in civil litigation, and in many cases the assessment of damages is relatively easy with the courts applying the principle of putting the plaintiff back in the position he would have been if the wrong had not been committed.

If a debt is owed, the calculation of the award of damages is straightforward. If there is a breach of contract where goods have not been delivered, damages are based on the difference between the contract and the market price, and the loss incurred in buying goods elsewhere.

However, if there is difficulty in assessing damages, the courts must not shirk their responsibility but must do the best they can. For instance, it is often difficult to calculate a satisfactory award of compensation for physical injury, loss of future earnings or loss of future profits, particularly as the courts usually abide by the principle of settling a claim once and for all and award a lump sum. A good illustration is the High Court case where Dr Lim Poh Choo was awarded £243,000, at the time a record award, after she had suffered irreversible brain damage after a minor operation. Mr Justice Bristow, recognising the arbitrary nature of court awards, recommended that the award should be contested in the Court of Appeal, particularly as a factor for inflation had been built into the award. This departure from the traditional approach suggests that perhaps judges are becoming more sensitive to the ravages of inflation over a period of years, which prudent investment would not necessarily alleviate.

There is, however, some criticism over the 'rule of thumb' method used. Although judges have many guidelines and a wealth of experience to draw on, some decisions tend to be made in an amateurish way. A further complication in the assessment of damages is where the 'cause and effect' of loss is not easily definable and the courts may then feel that the claim for damages is 'remote'. If a plaintiff is successful, an award of damages is always possible, even if it is only nominal. However, there is very little protection from the 'man of straw' who has inadequate assets. Some protection is offered by compulsory motor insurance, and by the doctrine of vicarious liability.

Injunction
This is a court order requiring (a mandatory order) or prohibiting (a prohibitory order) some act, e.g. prohibiting the publication of libellous material or prohibiting a trade union official from blocking the movement of a firm's supplies. It can be part of a trial or can be interlocutory—a temporary restriction to stop further damage pending a trial. An injunction is a discretionary award and will only be granted if an award of damages is unsuitable, e.g. to prevent an ex-employee from divulging company secrets.

Specific Performance
The Chancery Division of the High Court has the sole power to grant a decree of specific performance which compels a person to carry out a promise that has been made. It is mainly confined to sales of land or leases, or occasionally for breaches of contract where the goods are of a unique type. Again it is a discretionary award, granted only when damages are insufficient. To ignore the granting of an injunction or specific performance is contempt of court and can be punished by a fine, committal or sequestration.

There are other means by which the courts remedy a dispute. Breaches of contract have the additional remedy of rescission and rectification. Also the plaintiff may claim remuneration for work done on a *quantum meruit* basis instead of claiming damages.

Contempt of Court
Contempt may be either civil or criminal and is based on the rules of common law supported by statute. Civil contempt is the refusal to obey court orders, for instance an injunction. Criminal contempt could be in the form of insulting behaviour

during a court hearing, intimidating witnesses and jurymen, or perhaps publishing some comment about a pending trial or one in progress.

The penalties for contempt are perhaps severe but are designed to prevent disobedience or conduct which, if allowed, would challenge the fair and efficient administration of justice. Both civil and criminal contempt is punishable with imprisonment, but this tends not to be a method of punishment until other alternatives have been examined. The power to punish for contempt is by judge alone without a jury.

Prerogative Orders
All tribunals, inquiries, arbitration and lesser courts, government ministers, civil servants and local authorities, are subject to the control of the prerogative orders *Mandamus*, Prohibition or *Certiorari* which are issued from the Queen's Bench Division of the High Court. These ancient orders are discretionary and are usually sought where there are procedural errors, rather than problems of substantive law, which would be settled in the courts and on appeal.

(i) *Mandamus*
This commands a person or body to carry out a public duty or exercise its power. For instance, it has been used to order a local authority to produce its accounts for inspection by a ratepayer. Or it can be used to compel magistrates to hear a case, or a tribunal to hear an appeal.

(ii) *Prohibition*
This is only used where proceedings have not been concluded and in circumstances where there is an abuse of jurisdiction or the demands of natural justice. Under this order proceedings can be halted.

The above two orders are rarely used as they provide no compensation to the victim of any abuse of procedural law and most wronged individuals can find a satisfactory remedy through the normal routes of appeal.

(iii) *Certiorari*
This is used slightly more frequently and has many of the features of the prohibition order but is used to quash the decision of some lower court or body after its proceedings have been concluded. *Certiorari* is granted where it is apparent that the principles of natural justice have been ignored, e.g. where there is obvious bias towards one of the parties, or one of the parties has been denied a proper hearing. Also if the inferior court has acted beyond its powers (*ultra vires*) then this want of jurisdiction will be corrected. Finally, where a tribunal has made some error of law on the face of the record, then *certiorari* will have the decision of the tribunal quashed.

(iv) *Habeus corpus*
This ancient writ was perhaps more important in the past, but basically through it anyone can challenge his unlawful imprisonment.

Tribunals
It has already been shown that the use of the court system can be slow and costly. Recognising the problems of litigation, particularly for the ordinary citizen, Parliament has set up a large number of tribunals, especially in those areas of jurisdiction relating to benefits or rights, e.g. industrial tribunals, social security tribunals, National Insurance tribunals, etc.

Tribunals perform quasi-judicial functions. They are not part of the regular court system but the statute setting up a tribunal will insist on procedural guidelines and the application of law to ensure fair decisions. The Tribunal and Inquiries Act 1971 keeps under review the constitution and workings of many tribunals. For instance, it requires that the Lord Chancellor appoints the chairman of the tribunals. Further protection of the parties is ensured by insisting that reasons accompany the tribunal decision and also a route of appeal to the High Court is allowed.

The composition of tribunals varies but basically the format is that a legally qualified chairman is appointed, assisted by two lay specialists representing each side of the dispute. This is the constitution of the industrial tribunal established by the Industrial Training Act 1964—the procedure tends to be formal, and the normal rules of evidence are applied. Appeal lies to the Employment Appeals Tribunal with a further appeal to the Court of Appeal (Civil Division).

Tribunals are a short cut to a legal decision. They do not employ the same exacting standards and practice of the court system, which suggests that the decision-making may not always be as satisfactory, but they are here to stay. They remove from the court system a large number of cases which could cause further backlog and delays. For the parties involved it means a faster, less expensive hearing, presided over by specialists.

The emphasis is on a broad approach to the problem—hence the addition of laymen, and the parties are encouraged to be voluble and at ease by removing some of the formalities encountered in the courts.

Arbitration

An alternative method of settling a conflict or dispute is to resort to arbitration. This is favoured in many cases, particularly by businessmen, as a means of resolving contractual problems, and it is not uncommon for contracts between business organisations to insist on arbitration first as a means of resolving disputes, with parties free to use the courts if dissatisfied with the arbitration decision.

Despite being outside the normal court system and the arbitrator being an independent third person who is not necessarily a court official, the arbitration procedure is governed by the Arbitration Act 1950. Thus the hearing must be conducted judicially according to the normal rules of English court procedure (unless the parties agree to the contrary).

Although there is no basic right of appeal to the courts, there is a limited control by the High Court. Arbitration is often referred to the High Court for an opinion on a point of law or any award. Any serious breach of the normal rules of justice may be quashed or prohibited by use of prerogative orders.

The attractions of arbitration to the businessman often outweighs the disadvantage that complex issues of law are probably best solved by the High Court. Obviously the privacy of the hearing and decision are appealing. Lengthy, open litigation in the High Court could damage the goodwill of the company, whatever the merits of the claim. A final advantage is the cheapness of this type of hearing. It can be expensive in terms of fees paid to a professional man to act as arbitrator, but overall the cost is usually only a fraction of an average High Court case.

The effectiveness and demand for arbitration has been recognised by the granting of the right to settle small civil claims in the County Courts. Also, the Administration of Justice Act 1970 allows judges of the Commercial Court to be appointed as arbitrators.

4. The Organisation and Demographic Factors

Every organisation, whether in the public or private sector, is affected either directly or indirectly by demographic changes, that is, alterations in the size and structure of the population. If such organisations are to fulfil their objectives they should be constantly adjusting their level and type of activity to reflect the changing needs of this changing population.

The needs of the population

The changing needs of the population arise out of the dual role of members of society as both consumers and producers, which in many cases they perform simultaneously. As consumers they have certain material and collective needs, and as producers certain economic, social and employment needs. These basic needs may be classified under three main headings.

Material Needs
These refer to those items of consumption necessary to sustain the expected and accepted standard of living of the community. Obviously these will vary according to a country's relative stage of development. In a developing country they may be as basic as the provision of shelter, warmth, food and clothing, whereas in a highly developed economy such as the UK they are likely to include such things as washing machines and split-level cookers.

Collective Needs
These concern the general collective wants of society, and consequently confer economic and social benefits on both the individual and community at large. They encompass such areas as law and order, defence, public and general health facilities, transport and communications, and educational services.

There is a strong relationship between these collective and material needs. Basically, the improvement of a nation's material standards is generally accompanied by the creation of more collective wants. For example, as the number of cars on the roads increase, then it is necessary to provide more motorways, car parks, traffic signs, traffic wardens and to spend a larger amount on dealing with the pollution associated with the internal combustion engine.

Employment Needs
Every member of the population needs to live in an economic and social environment which enables him to command sufficient resources in order to satisfy his material and collective needs. This means that opportunities must exist for members of the community to find employment for themselves so that they can produce sufficient to meet their own needs and also support those who are dependent upon them, for instance their families, the elderly and infirm.

As the size and structure of the population alters it will be necessary for all organisations concerned with the satisfaction of these three basic needs to adjust the scale and nature of their activities accordingly. For example, central and local government departments have to adjust the provision of educational facilities to keep pace with the number of children of school age. They base their expenditure decision on the type of population figures shown in Table 4.1. These have been taken from the Conservative Government's

Table 4.1: The relationship between educational expenditure and the size of the school population

| | 1980–1 | | 1983–4 | |
	Numbers	Current expenditure	Numbers	Current expenditure
Under 5's	424,000	176m	394,000	160m
Primary	3,808,000	1,633m	3,332,000	1,440m
Secondary	3,830,000	2,349m	3,623,000	2,270m

Current expenditure is expressed at 1980 survey prices.
Source: The Government's Expenditure Plans 1981–2 to 1983–4.

ublic expenditure plans 1981–2 to 1983–4, and
learly indicate how expenditure reflects the pro-
cted alterations in the size of different educa-
ional age groups in the schools.

As a result of the general reduction in the size
f the school population current expenditure was
rojected to fall for each category by 1983–4. In
similar way the private sector would have to
lan its productive and service activities to reflect
he changing nature of its population of con-
imers. For instance, if the birth rate increased,
hen initially the producers of nappies, cots, prams
nd so on would have to respond by increasing
heir output to meet the increase in demand.
hen, as this group became older it would be
ecessary to produce more dolls, action men,
vendy houses, and train sets. As they reached
heir teens there would be an increased demand
or records, motor-cycles and fashionable cloth-
ng. The onset of marriage would be accom-
anied by a larger demand for housing, washing
nachines, and cars. Finally with the approach of
ld age more retirement homes, painting sets,
vheel chairs and false teeth would be required.

he size of the total population

Table 4.2: The United Kingdom popu-
lation, 1931–2001

Year	Home population (000s)
1931	46,038
1941	n.a.
1951	50,225
1961	52,709
1971	55,515
1981	53,870
1991*	57,192
2001*	58,373

* Projections
Source: *Annual Abstract of Statistics*, 1982.

The figures in Table 4.2 show how the popula-
ion of the United Kingdom has increased since
931. The growth rate in both absolute and per-
entage terms is analysed in Table 4.3. As the
gure for 1941 is not available the period from
931–51 has been taken for comparison. The
verage rate of growth per decade during this
eriod is 4·55 per cent.

Table 4.3: The growth rate of the United Kingdom population

Period	Absolute (000s)	Percentage
1931–51	4187	9·1
1951–61	2484	4·9
1961–71	2806	5·3
1971–81	355	0·6
1981–91	1322	2·4
1991–2001	1181	2·1

The analysis reveals that there has been a fairly
steady increase in the population of approximately
5 per cent for each decade up to 1971. There was
a considerable fall in the 1970s to around 0·6 per
cent but it is predicted that during the 1980s and
1990s there will be a rise of about 2–2·5 per cent
each decade.

Factors influencing the size of the population
The alterations in the total size of the UK population have been caused by changes in the **birth
rate**, **death rate** and the **rate of migration**.

The birth and death rates are expressed as the
number of births or deaths per year per 1000 of
the population. Table 4.4 shows how these have
altered during the period 1946–81, and also how
they have contributed to the rate of population increase. The table shows that the variations in the
rate of increase have been largely due to fluctuations in the birth rate rather than in the death rate,
which has remained relatively constant.

The birth rate peaked in both 1946–51 and
1961–66. In the first case this was due to the very

Table 4.4: The United Kingdom birth rate and death rate, 1946–81

Period	Birth rate (average annual figure)	Death rate (average annual figure)	Rate of increase (%)
1946–51	18·28	12·01	6·27
1951–56	15·68	11·78	3·9
1956–61	16·74	11·63	5·11
1961–66	18·34	11·81	6·53
1966–71	17·16	11·7	5·46
1971–76	14·14	11·9	2·24
1976–81	12·56	11·78	·78

Source: adapted from Office of Population Censuses and
Surveys; General Register Office (Scotland); General
Register Office (N. Ireland).

high marriage rates immediately after the war. In the second it was caused partly by the substantial increase in the number of immigrants coming from countries with high fertility rates and partly by the relative economic calm which encouraged people to marry younger and have children earlier.

Since 1966 there has been a steady decline in the birth rate and all of the signs seem to suggest that this is likely to continue. This has been due to a variety of factors. First, the average age of marriage has stopped falling and those who have recently married are having fewer children in the first years of their married life than in the past. Secondly, the changes in the law concerning abortion and the spread of free provision of contraceptives has tended to reduce the number of unwanted children. Thirdly, due to the changing role of women in society the activity rates of women in the working population have increased. This has meant that the immediate economic burden involved in having a child is greater than it used to be as the mother's earnings have to be sacrificed at least during the final months of pregnancy, and in the majority of cases until the child

is of school age or even older. The long-term costs associated with bringing up children have also risen, as due to the raising of the school leaving age and the increased provision of further and higher education places children remain a burden to their families for a longer period of time.

The magazine *Which?*, in an article entitled 'What Children Cost' (December 1977) attempted to quantify the effects on a family budget of having children. Fig. 4.1 shows the average proportion of a parent's income that needed to be spent in order to support either a family containing one child or two children. *Which?* based this diagram on a study carried out by the Department of Health and Social Security. It clearly showed that on average about 18p of each £1 spent by a family with one child went on supporting the child up to the age of 18. For a family with two children the figure went up to 28p of each £1. This meant that, on average, a family earning £5000 a year and spending the whole of its take-home pay of £330 or so, would spend £600 a year on supporting one child, £900 on two. Obviously these amounts varied with the child's age and the parents' income. Inevitably costs like

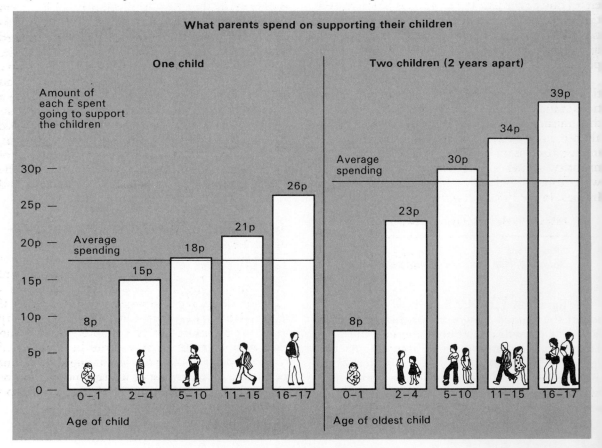

Fig. 4.1   Source: *Which?*, December 1977

these, plus the initial sacrifice of the wife's income, made potential parents think twice before embarking on a family, and as a result acted as a contributory factor to the decline in the birth rate.

The death rate has been relatively stable since the war because mortality rates had already reached fairly low levels by 1945, and so there was very little chance of them improving.

Mortality in childhood and early adult life is very low. Of those who live until their first birthday, 95·1 per cent of the males and 96·8 per cent of the females survive until they are 45. Consequently, the loss of life in the child-bearing years up to 45 is so low that it is almost impossible for there to be any fundamental improvement in the death rate, which could significantly influence the size of the total population.

The main cause of death amongst the elderly has tended to be the degenerative diseases such as cancer and diseases of the circulatory system. Unless a significant breakthrough occurs in the treatment of these diseases, the pattern of death rate established since the war for this age group is likely to continue indefinitely. It may be concluded therefore that the stable death rate experienced during the past thirty years is likely to continue into the foreseeable future, and that the death rate is likely to continue to play a fairly minor role in determining changes in the total size of the population.

The total size of the United Kingdom population has been considerably influenced by alterations in the level of net migration. Table 4.5 shows that during the period 1951–61 there was an almost equal balance between emigration and immigration with a net balance of 57,000. The majority of the immigrants during this period were from the old commonwealth countries and Ireland. In the 1960s outward migration exceeded

Table 4.5: Net migration, 1941–2001

Period	Net Migration (000s)
1941–51	n.a.
1951–61	+57
1961–71	−428
1971–81	−346
1981–91 *	−500
1991–2001 *	−500

* Projections.

Source: *Annual Abstract of Statistics*, 1975 and 1982.

inward by 428,000. This change was brought about initially by the 1962 Commonwealth Immigrants Act and then perpetuated by subsequent restrictive measures imposed on immigration. This situation continued in the 1970s and the projected net migration figures indicate that it is likely to continue in the future, running at about 500,000 each decade.

It is not only the numbers involved in net migration that is important but also the demographic characteristics of the populations involved. During the past thirty years the majority of the immigrants entering the United Kingdom have been relatively young. This is because most immigration has been of people coming to work in the UK, and their families. Consequently, they have increased the size of the population of child-bearing age, and hence account for a fairly high number of births. The immigrant population has also tended to produce families which have been larger than the national average. Due to their relative youth, the death rate amongst immigrants has been relatively low.

In general the emigrants leaving the United Kingdom have been older than their immigrant counterparts entering the country. The term 'brain drain' has often been applied to these emigrants as many of them have been highly qualified people who have been attracted by high salaries and better opportunities abroad. Many people have gone to the United States of America and Canada, although more recently there has been a flood of people to the Arab States where it is possible to earn three times the equivalent United Kingdom salary as a doctor, scientist, technician, engineer or football coach. Obviously, the loss of such talented people must reduce the ability of the United Kingdom to satisfy all its collective and material needs.

The Significance of Changes in the Total Size of the Population

The significance of the increase in the size of the United Kingdom population since the war, and the projected increase for the next two decades can only be appreciated when viewed in terms of the availability of resources to support it. A study of this relationship between population size and the available resources may either be approached from the point of view of considering the amount of food necessary to sustain a larger population or alternatively by looking at the effect of population growth on the level of national output.

The **Malthusian approach**, so called because it was originally described by the Reverend Thomas Robert Malthus in his *Essay on Population* in 1798, is that the size of the population grows geometrically whilst the food supply, which is the means of sustaining that population, only grows arithmetically. This suggests that an ever-increasing population will eventually outrun its means of subsistence. On the evidence he had available to him, Malthus was justified in his fears. However, he had not foreseen that the country would experience an industrial revolution which would enable it to improve production to such an extent that an ever-increasing population could be supported by exporting surplus production of manufactured goods in exchange for imported foodstuffs. It has to be remembered that although the United Kingdom and other developed countries have been able to operate under this system, there is still a large proportion of the world that has not been so fortunate and suffers from serious malnutrition and famine. Perhaps the developed world has only been able to survive because of the uneven distribution of world resources, which have enabled them to satisfy their needs while others have not. The question that needs to be answered is whether this uneven distribution will continue to be tolerated if, as is predicted, the world's population doubles during the next thirty years. If it is not, then countries like the United Kingdom could be in an extremely vulnerable and potentially dangerous position. This has already been shown in the early 1970s in the case of the United Kingdom's dependence upon imported oil. If a similar situation arose in the case of food, then the Malthusian fear of the eighteenth century might become the reality of the twentieth or twenty-first. Obviously, to ensure that such a situation does not arise, and that such a basic material need as food is available for the United Kingdom citizen, the government will either have to move the United Kingdom towards greater individual self-sufficiency in food or encourage collective self-sufficiency within Europe.

The concept of an **optimum population** relates the size of the population to its output. Basically, an optimum population is that which, given the amounts of human and physical resources available to a community, is such as to maximise output per head in that community. This means that if the population were smaller, production would be smaller per head, and if it were larger, production would also be less per

head and therefore there would be a problem of overpopulation. This is a more satisfactory approach than that taken by Malthus because it acknowledges that both population size and output are dynamic factors and so a country's optimum is constantly changing. Changes in the total size of the population may be caused by alterations in any of the three factors already considered, whereas changes in the level of output might be caused by developments in technology, productivity or trade. By attempting to control and influence these factors, it is possible for the government to move the population towards its optimum size.

It is generally considered that the United Kingdom's population is already near to its optimum size. However, for reasons already indicated, this does not mean that the United Kingdom will be incapable of supporting the projected population for 2001 of 68,373,000. The experience of the United Kingdom in the past has been that output and resources have expanded in line with the population increase. For example, people living a century ago would never have thought it possible that the United Kingdom would ever have been able to support a population of 55,515,000 in 1971.

However, it would be naïve to consider that countries like the United Kingdom will be able to go on maintaining output per head indefinitely by merely improving production as the population increases, or that such adjustments in output will not have implications on other aspects of the life of the community. In fact, there are three fundamental problems associated with the continual increase in the population and resultant adjustment in the level of output.

1. Any adjustment will inevitably affect the distribution of the fruits of production amongst the population. Continual change would provide the opportunity for either the creation of greater equality or greater inequality.

2. There are certain goods which rely on scarce resources which are very difficult or expensive to increase. This is because the resources necessary for this output are in relatively fixed supply. For instance, the quantity of land is fixed so that there is a limit to the area which can be used for agriculture, especially when you consider that land is also needed for housing and recreational uses.

3. Social problems such as excessive noise, pollution and urban congestion are often associated with an expanding population unless adequate plans are made to deal with these a long time in

advance. Even then, plans may prove inadequate: an example recently is the motorway network which was built in the 1950s and 1960s to standards which seemed adequate given the forecasts made then of traffic growth. As it turned out, traffic has grown much more quickly than forecast, so that the motorways are now inadequate for present needs.

Finally, consideration should be given to the significance of a **declining population**. Although it is unlikely that such a situation would arise in the United Kingdom in the foreseeable future, it is important to appreciate the implications of a declining population in order to secure a complete picture of the significance of changes in the total population. There are four main implications to consider.

1. From the point of view of the optimum concept, output per head will expand if the country was originally overpopulated and contract if it was underpopulated, or at the optimum.

2. A declining population is usually accompanied by an older population since the birth rate will be lower. This older population is likely to be less receptive to new ideas. Obviously such attitudes may tend to hold back the development of the economy. The older population, especially the relatively high number of pensioners, will make greater demands on the welfare services, which in turn will impose a larger burden in terms of taxation on the already declining numbers making up the working population.

3. Patterns of consumer demand and investment would need to be fundamentally altered to meet the smaller requirements of the declining population.

4. The major advantage associated with a smaller population is that it would be likely to lead to a reduction in congestion and pressure on the fixed supplies of certain resources such as land.

The sex structure of the population

The sex structure of the population refers to the relationship between the number of males to the number of females in the total population. Table 4.6 indicates that since the war, the United Kingdom population has always contained a larger number of females than males. This is revealed by both the total figures for all ages and

also the sex ratio which shows the number of males per 1000 females. Since 1941 this gap between the sexes has become increasingly smaller, though the projections suggest that it will continue. It is interesting to note that this female dominance has persisted in spite of the larger number of male births. The larger number of male births is revealed by the fact that for each decade the 'under 15' classification of males has been greater than that for females. Consideration of the sex ratio for the 'under 45' group suggests that this male dominance continues up until middle age. Then the situation is completely reversed as is shown by the category designated as '45 years and over', which indicates a considerably larger number of females than males in the total population. The reason for this reversal is the longer life expectancy of women over men, and the loss of predominantly male lives in the two world wars.

Table 4.6: The sex and age structure of the United Kingdom population, 1941–2001

	Mid-year estimates				Projections		
	1941	1951	1961	1971	1981	1991	2001
Total population							
(millions)	48·2	50·6	53·0	55·7	56·3	58·2	59·9
Males							
Under 15	5·1	5·8	6·3	6·9	6·1	6·6	6·9
15–29	5·8	5·3	5·3	6·0	6·5	6·6	6·0
30–44	5·5	5·5	5·3	4·9	5·5	6·0	6·6
45–64	5·0	5·6	6·4	6·5	6·1	6·1	6·7
65–74	1·4	1·6	1·6	2·0	2·2	2·2	2·0
75 and over	0·5	0·7	0·7	0·8	1·0	1·2	1·2
Males—all ages	23·3	24·4	25·7	27·1	27·4	28·5	29·6
Females							
Under 15	5·0	5·6	6·0	6·5	5·8	6·2	6·6
15–29	5·8	5·2	5·1	5·8	6·3	6·3	5·8
30–44	5·8	5·7	5·3	4·8	5·4	5·9	6·4
45–59	4·6	5·1	5·5	5·2	4·8	4·7	5·4
60–74	3·0	3·5	3·9	4·5	4·5	4·2	3·0
75 and over	0·8	1·1	1·5	1·8	2·1	2·4	2·4
Females—all ages	24·9	26·1	27·3	28·6	28·8	29·7	30·4
Sex ratio (males per 1000 females)							
All ages	933	934	941	947	953	961	969
Under 45 years	990	1008	1027	1038	1042	1039	1040
45 years and over	819	808	810	811	817	833	854

Sources: *Census of Population Reports; Population Projections*, No. 5 (1974); *Social Trends*, 1975.

The long-term projections of the sex ratio may have to be revised if the activity rates of women in the working population continue to increase. In 1951 the activity rates stood at 34·7 per cent; by 1976 they had grown to 47 per cent and by 1986 it is projected that they will have increased to 50·6 per cent. This will mean that an increasing number of women will be exposed during their lives to both the rigours of child-rearing, plus the additional stresses associated with employment which have traditionally shortened male life expectancy. It is quite possible that the life expectancy of women may be reduced by the shouldering of these additional pressures.

The age structure of the population

The significance of the changes that have taken place in the age structure of the United Kingdom population since 1941 become more apparent if they are classified in the three age-group categories: '0–15', '15–64', and 60+ in the case of women, and 65+ in the case of men.

Table 4.7: Age composition of the United Kingdom population

| Year | Males (%) | | | Females (%) | | |
	Under 15	15–64	65+	Under 15	15–59	60+
1941	21·88	69·95	8·17	20·08	65·06	14·86
1951	23·77	67·21	9·02	21·45	61·30	17·25
1961	24·51	66·14	9·35	21·97	58·24	19·79
1971	25·46	64·2	10·34	22·72	55·24	22·04
1981	22·26	66·05	11·69	20·13	57·29	22·58
1991	23·15	65·61	11·24	20·87	56·90	22·23
2001	23·38	65·42	11·2	21·71	57·89	20·40

Table 4.7 clearly indicates that the proportion of both males and females under the age of 15 increased for the three decades from 1941. Due to the fall in the birth rate the figures for the 1970s show that for both sexes this youngest category has declined in proportionate terms. However, in the 1980s and 1990s the increase is likely to be restored. Since 1941 there has been a gradual expansion in the proportion of both males and females in the older categories. This trend contin-

ued until 1981 after which it was felt that the numbers in these categories would begin to decline. The changes in these youngest and oldest age groups have meant that up to 1971 *the middle group became progressively smaller*. This was caused by two factors. First, the low interwar birth rate, which resulted in a relative decline in the number of middle-aged people. Secondly, the slightly higher birth rate of the 1950s and 1960s. Thus, since the war, the population tended to become top and bottom heavy, which meant that the proportion of the population of approximately working age (the middle group) became increasingly smaller, and was required to support an ever-increasing number of dependents in terms of children and the elderly.

This situation had very serious economic and social effects. The larger number of dependents required an ever-expanding education, health and social service system. To finance such an expansion, taxes had to be increased on those who worked, which had an adverse effect on 'work effort' and encouraged demands for inflationary wage increases to compensate for the higher proportion of income being taken in taxes. Social factors, such as the decline of the extended family, aggravated the situation still further, in that the state had to accept a larger responsibility towards the elderly. In the past this might have been partly shouldered by the immediate family. It became the acknowledged responsibility of the state to provide adequate properly heated and supervised accommodation for senior citizens, and to ensure that old people were properly fed and received appropriate medical treatment. Even though the size of the middle group grew in the 1970s the projections suggest that the burden of the dependents will exist for many years to come.

The working population and its occupational distribution

The **total working population** is made up of all those people who are willing and able to work. It consists of people in employment, those in HM Forces and women's services, those who are self-employed and those who are registered as unemployed.

Table 4.8 reveals that between 1961 and 1971 *the working population declined as a proportion of the total population*, but in the 1970s this trend was reversed. Three main factors contributed to these changes.

Table 4.8: The working population and activity rates in the United Kingdom, 1951–80

Year	Population (000s)		All ages	15+	Activity Rates (%) Males and females					Females		
	Total	Working			15–19	20–24	25–44	45–64	65+	20–24	25–44	45–64
1951	50,225	23,809	47·4	59·6	81·3	79·7	66·7	59·5	15·9	65·4	36·1	28·7
1961	52,709	25,345	48·1	60·5	72·9	76·8	69·4	66·0	12·7	62·0	40·8	37·1
1966	54,806	26,174	47·7	62·1	68·6	77·2	72·6	60·6	13·1	61·6	47·1	46·1
1971	55,515	25,421	45·8	61·1	58·4	75·1	74·4	71·5	11·3	60·1	50·6	50·2
1980	55,945	26,380	47·1	59·8	53·8	78·0	79·7	71·0	5·2	68·5	61·0	53·0

Source: Adapted from Department of Employment, *British Labour Statistics: Historical Abstract 1886–1968*; Department of Employment, *Gazette*, November 1973 and April 1981; *Annual Abstract of Statistics*, 1982, Central Statistical Office.

1. Adjustments in the birth and death rates caused changes in the number of people of working age, that is the 16–65 age group.

2. Due to greater provision of pension and welfare facilities for the elderly, there was a widespread acceptance of a retirement age of 65 for men and 60 for women. This meant, for example, that the activity rates of the 65 + group fell from 15·9 per cent in 1951 to 5·2 per cent in 1980.

3. The activity rates of the 15–19 group fell from 81·3 per cent in 1951 to 53·8 per cent in 1980. This was caused by the progressive raising of the school leaving age to 16 and an increase in the number of young people continuing their education after this minimum school leaving age.

Table 4.8 also reveals that *female employment has played an increasingly important role in the size of the total working population.* In particular there has been a large and continuous increase in the number of women aged between 25–64 in the work force. Obviously the majority of the women in this age group are married, and they have been able to increase their activity rate for a number of reasons.

1. The recent decline in the birth rate and the wider availability of creche facilities has reduced the number of women who either want or have to fulfil the 'traditional fulltime' role of wife and mother.

2. The greater application of technology to housework has allowed women to devote far more time to activities outside the home.

3. There are more jobs available that are suitable for women, such as those with flexible hours, or those in the service sector, or those of a light industrial nature.

4. There has been a general change in attitude towards the role of women in society, and their right to be treated equally in the jobs market. This has been supported by such legislation as the *Equal Pay Act* of 1970. This was later amended when the *Sex Discrimination Act* of 1975 was introduced, and in the same year the *Employment Protection Act* came into force, further extending a woman's right to return to work after having a child.

If the government is to meet the employment needs of the population it must try to stimulate the economy to a level of activity which will satisfy the requirements of the working population, and also acknowledge and make provision for the larger number of women in the total working population.

The **occupational distribution** of the population may be categorised under four main headings. First, those working in the **primary** industries which refers to the activities of agriculture, forestry, fishing, mining and quarrying. Secondly, those employed in **manufacturing and construction**. Thirdly, those people who operate all the various **services** in the country, such as the public utilities, distribution, commerce, transport and communications, professional and scientific services, catering and hotels, and national and local government. Fourthly, those people who are members of the **armed forces**.

Table 4.9 (p. 62) shows that since 1951 there has been a large proportionate movement of people out of the primary sector, and gradual movement out of manufacturing and construction and the armed forces into the service industries. This has been caused by a number of factors. Increased mechanisation has tended to reduce the numbers

Table 4.9: Distribution of employees in employment in the United Kingdom, 1951 and 1980

| | Estimated proportion (%) | |
	1951	1980
Primary	8·5	3·1
Manufacturing and Construction	44·4	35·4
Services	44·8	60·1
Armed Forces	2·3	1·4

Source: adapted from Department of Employment, *British Labour Statistics: Historical Abstract 1886–1968; Social Trends*, 1982.

working on the land and in the extractive industries. Similarly, the numbers employed in the manufacturing and construction sector have been reduced by the introduction of new technology which has resulted in higher productivity and the loss of jobs in this sector. The increased number of people employed in the services reflects the growing expertise and reputation of the United Kingdom in such fields as insurance, banking, finance, business services and the professional and scientific services. These activities have become very large contributors to the invisible earnings side of the balance of payments. The growth in the service sector also reflects the increasing number of people who are now employed by central and local government, which has been forced to expand its services to keep pace with the growing collective needs of society.

What the figures fail to reveal is the growing **occupational mobility** of the nation. It is now considered likely that the average person will have to change his occupation at least three times during his working life. This will be necessary because of the ever-changing collective and material needs of society in its demand for goods and services, and the tremendous technological changes that have brought these about. For example, the electronics industry, producing a wide range of goods from televisions to computers, has grown up since the war, mainly because technological advances have made possible new products, and hence have created new jobs. This essentially dynamic situation in the needs of the labour market has encouraged the government to introduce a number of measures to increase occupational mobility. Through the Manpower Services Commission they have provided advice for firms on

training programmes and tried to promote the development of certain required skills and crafts. They have also set up retraining programmes in their own Skill Centres and in local colleges, where, for example, the Training Services Agency has run its 'Training Opportunities' (TOPS) courses.

Geographical distribution of the population

Table 4.10 shows that since 1951 there has been a drift of population away from Scotland, Northern Ireland, Wales and the whole of the north of England. This has been largely due to the relative economic decline in these less prosperous areas. People have moved into those regions where there have been better employment opportunities, housing and general amenities, such as the whole of the South of England and the Midlands. Governments have tried to stem this migration of people away from the depressed areas of high unemployment. They have attempted to increase employment in these areas by a variety of regional policy measures such as the offer of grants, tax incentives and other inducements to firms to move to areas of high unemployment.

These shifts in the geographical distribution of the population have also made it necessary for organisations concerned with satisfying collective and material needs to alter their scale of operations to take account of the changes in the demand for

Table 4.10: Geographical distribution of the United Kingdom population, 1951 and 1980

Area	1951 (%)	1980 (%)
North	6·2	5·5
Yorkshire and Humberside	9·0	8·7
East Midlands	5·7	6·8
East Anglia	2·8	3·4
South East	30·0	30·2
South West	6·4	7·8
West Midlands	8·8	9·2
North West	12·8	11·5
Wales	5·2	5·0
Scotland	10·1	9·2
N. Ireland	3·0	2·7

Source: Office of Population Censuses and Surveys; General Register Office (Scotland); General Register Office (Northern Ireland); *Regional Trends*, 1982, Central Statistical Office.

housing, education, entertainment, and transport.

Another important feature has been the general movement of the population away from the rural areas into the urban conurbations. This now means that over 80 per cent of the population live in urban areas and over one-third of the population in vast conurbations like Greater London, West Yorkshire, South-East Lancashire, Merseyside, Tyneside, Central Clydeside and the West Midlands. The government have tried to control this situation by the use of town and country planning controls, the designation of 'green belt' areas, the controlled development of new towns and the expansion of existing ones.

The creation of this essentially urbanised population has in itself caused the development of collective social needs that have acted as an additional drain on the government's resources. It has resulted in the break-up of the extended family and of basic social ties.

This has meant that central and local government departments and organisations like the church have had to try to forge new social links by running clubs, societies and classes in further education. The concentration of wealth in a confined urban area has caused more problems of vandalism and petty crimes to occur. Physical problems have developed over the provision of adequate housing and traffic facilities, and over the means of dealing with air and water pollution and waste disposal. For transport agencies, the emphasis has been on providing adequate facilities for people and goods to move about *within* towns, as well as *between* towns. In the 1960s and 1970s, British Rail, for example, closed down a number of lines serving rural areas while improving services such as 'Inter-City' passenger trains. In education, retailing and local government, there have been changes towards larger units (schools, supermarkets, local government reform) to take advantage of the economies of scale possible with a highly concentrated, large urban population.

5. The Economic Aspects of the Acquisition and Use of Resources

The economic problems arising from scarcity of resources in relation to demand

The basic economic problem is that, in any society, resources are limited but human wants are infinite. All economies, no matter what their stage of development, are faced with the **problem of scarcity**. This arises because there are not enough resources to produce all the goods and services that people would like to consume. Economies are thus faced with having to make a choice between what will be produced and what will not be produced. An economy will therefore require a system through which its members can jointly decide to what extent its scarce resources should be utilised towards satisfying certain wants while other wants remain unsatisfied. Professor Lord Robbins described economics as the 'science which studies human behaviour as a relationship between ends and scarce means which have alternative uses'. A feature of the following sections is that it is human behaviour which produces a system that contributes towards the allocation of scarce resources between alternative uses. The organisation plays a major role in the system which is to be described, as the activities of organisations are themselves guided by human behaviour, and have an important role in deciding what should be produced.

Resources as Scarce Means with Alternative Uses

Resources are the facilities available to a community which can be utilised to produce goods and services to satisfy certain wants. They are generally classified into three or four main groups:

1. Natural resources in the form of land, mineral deposits and natural vegetation which grows on the land are grouped together and known as **land**.

2. Human resources in the form of manual and mental skills are known as **labour** whether such skills are natural aptitudes or acquired and developed over a period of time.

3. The term **capital** is used to describe all those man-made aids which assist in production, such as machinery, tools, factory buildings, offices and communications and transport systems. These are items of real capital and money is not included, as money *per se* does not assist directly in production. Filling a factory space with pound notes will not further the output of goods and services!

4. Some classifications of resources identify a particular human skill and remove it from the general heading of labour to form a separate classification known as the **entrepreneurial skill**. This skill displays the ability to bring together quantities and combinations of the other resources to obtain an output, and measures such decisions against the risks involved. The entrepreneur is the organising factor in production and bears the risks arising from the uncertainty that surrounds market conditions. In a sole proprietorship the entrepreneurial function is readily identified, as the individual both manages the organisation and accepts the entire risks associated with the business. Similarly, in a partnership the members share the role of entrepreneur. In a public limited company, however, management and risk are separated in that the board of directors accepts the responsibility for the organisation's policy, while the shareholders accept the risks. This same division will exist in other organisations, such as nationalised industries, where control is again separated from ownership.

These resources are known as **factors of production** and a common feature is that they have alternative uses. It is possible to use land for agricultural purposes or for the siting of industrial and commercial premises, and even within these broad uses scope exists for alternatives in terms of different types of agricultural products, and a wide range of industrial products and commercial services. Land may even be left untouched and allowed to contribute to the satisfaction of wants associated with environmental pleasures.

Labour is also flexible in that the skills of a carpenter can be employed in a wide range of industries, such as furniture making, the construction industry or the fitting out of ships. Similarly the skills of an accountant can readily be employed in a wide range of industries.

Items of real capital have a surprising degree of flexibility in that a drilling machine, for example, can perform its operations on a wide range of components that make up totally different end products. Commercial vehicles are able to carry a great variety of freight, and as items of capital they therefore have alternative uses. The talents of the entrepreneur can be applied to many industrial and commercial activities and so again have alternative uses.

Another common feature of these factors of production is that at any one moment their total availability—from what are, in some cases, finite sources—is limited. This is in direct contrast to human wants which are infinite. Thus arises the problem of choice regarding what is actually to be produced and in what quantities. A further element of choice is involved in terms of how wants are to be satisfied. It is possible to combine factors of production in different ways to achieve the same end product. For example, cotton shirts can be made through the employment of a large quantity of labour assisted by a relatively small utilisation of tools and machinery. In this case the production technique is said to be labour-intensive, and this would be in contrast to a capital-intensive technique where most of the work is performed by machines with relatively little assistance from labour.

A further element of choice arises in deciding for whom goods and services are to be produced; meeting more of the wants of certain members of the community implies that less of the wants of others are to be satisfied. Thus the economic problems arising out of scarcity are those based upon choice, and can be summarised as *what* to produce, *how* and *for whom*.

The Role of an Economic System

Since some wants of some groups of the community are satisfied, and certain factor combinations are used, then some form of decision-making process must exist in an economy. The economist is concerned with such systems and their respective mechanisms, which operate to make decisions on the issues arising out of choice. They are also concerned with the efficiency with which the systems operate. Efficiency is looked at from the point of view of determining the extent to which the sys-

tems maximise the total welfare of the community. Welfare or satisfaction is derived from consuming the output of organisations which employ factors of production. The optimum allocation of resources, which these factors represent, is said to have been reached when it is not possible to raise total welfare any further. If the movement of resources from one line to another adds more to welfare than is sacrificed by such a movement, then resources were not previously allocated in an optimum way. An optimum allocation of resources will have been reached if any further re-allocation will result in a sacrifice of welfare which is not outweighed by the welfare gained elsewhere as a result of the re-allocation.

The efficiency of an economic system involves a concept of efficiency which differs from that of the scientist or engineer. The economist is concerned with achieving output at the lowest possible cost and the cost is defined as what is sacrificed elsewhere. The welfare derived from the output of a product should thus be achieved at the lowest possible cost in terms of welfare sacrificed elsewhere. This involves the concept of **opportunity cost** and arises from the fact that resources have alternative uses. If, for example, resources are to be devoted increasingly to the production of iron and steel, this will involve an opportunity cost in terms of the alternative outputs which the resources shifted to iron and steel production could have produced if employed in their alternative uses.

The contrast between the economist's concept of efficiency and that of other interpreters can be seen in the following example. It is possible to derive heat from burning a tonne of coal and a tonne of oil, and it may well be that the technology available means that the heat derived from the oil exceeds that gained from the coal, i.e. more calories per tonne of oil compared with a tonne of coal. The economist, however, is concerned with the opportunity cost of the respective operations in terms of the resources involved in all the relevant processes. It may well be that the desired amount of heat can be obtained at a lower opportunity cost from coal, as this involves the smaller sacrifice in terms of a loss of welfare elsewhere.

A great deal therefore is being asked of a system which is not only expected to deal with the problems arising out of scarcity and hence choice, but is also expected at the same time to achieve this optimum allocation of resources whereby the total welfare of the community is at a maximum. The pattern of output, the factor combinations and the distribution of output, must all be working towards this objective. These are some of the areas which the economist studies and investigates. There may perhaps be scope for improving the system and its mechanisms to take advantage of 'killing two birds with one stone'. The ultimate, of course, would be to kill as many birds as possible with the smallest possible stone and try and get the stone back!

It is possible for an economic system to be imposed upon an economy by some form of economic overlord who takes it upon himself to decide upon the range and quantities of goods to be produced, the production techniques to be employed, and how the output should be distributed among the community. If he is seeking to conduct his plans with a view to maximising welfare, the problems would be insurmountable. Information would be required on each individual's scale of tastes and preferences, the total available supply of factors of production and their productive potential in various uses, different factor ratios and potential outputs. The output would then have to be distributed according to the criteria decided upon for meeting consumer wants. The problems confronting such an economic overlord in an advanced complex economy can hardly be exaggerated. The remainder of this section will, therefore, concentrate on the workings of an alternative system based upon the role of a price system which is allowed to operate freely in a market economy.

The price system in a market economy as an influence upon the decisions of an organisation in terms of *what*, *how* and *for whom* to produce

Under a price system the economic decisions and the eventual allocation of resources are based upon the relative strengths of the forces of demand and supply interacting with each other in markets. The organisation plays a vital role in a price system and contributes to the eventual results of what, how and for whom output is to be produced (Fig. 5.1).

A market is formed by the existence of the forces of demand and supply and is the means by which buyers and sellers are brought into contact with each other. The market is a mechanism which determines prices, and a market economy permits the allocation of resources to be determined by a price mechanism.

The Price System and *what* to Produce

Prices perform the task of registering the relative strengths of consumers' tastes and preferences. The organisation functions between the markets for final products and the markets for factors of production, and is instrumental in bringing about an allocation of resources in response to changes in consumer demand. This is because the decisions of an organisation regarding what to produce will depend upon the signals it receives from product markets and the relative strength of those signals. The signals are the prices in these markets and the organisation reacts to them, as relative prices will affect relative profitability. The organisation is motivated by the simple fact that it pays to produce what people want.

The product market can be compared to an election box which registers consumers' votes for the possible candidates, which are the alternative products available. Unlike a political election, however, each consumer will have a number of votes depending upon the amount of money which he is prepared to spend. When voting money for particular products, the consumer will have distributed spending power according to a scale of preferences. When the millions of such decisions are collected in markets, they will reflect the relative strength of different consumer demands. Let us assume that, for reasons of changes in tastes and preferences, the votes are recast, and this means that consumers are now dissatisfied with the existing pattern of resources and their current allocation. These signals will be communicated to the firm by a change in relative prices, and will thus have an impact upon the relative profitability of producing the products involved. The higher prices of the goods in greater demand will open up profitable opportunities for the firms involved (which we will call Group A), while firms associated with the goods now in less demand (Group B) will experience a fall in profitability (Fig. 5.2, p. 68).

Group A will now be in a much more powerful position when they in turn cast their votes in the markets for factors of production. They are now keen to attract more resources whose additional employment, in the absence of the higher product prices, would not have proved profitable. Group B will now be obliged to release some resources whose employment now proves unprofitable. Both Group A and Group B are transmitting the initial change in tastes and preferences to the markets for factors of production, and bringing

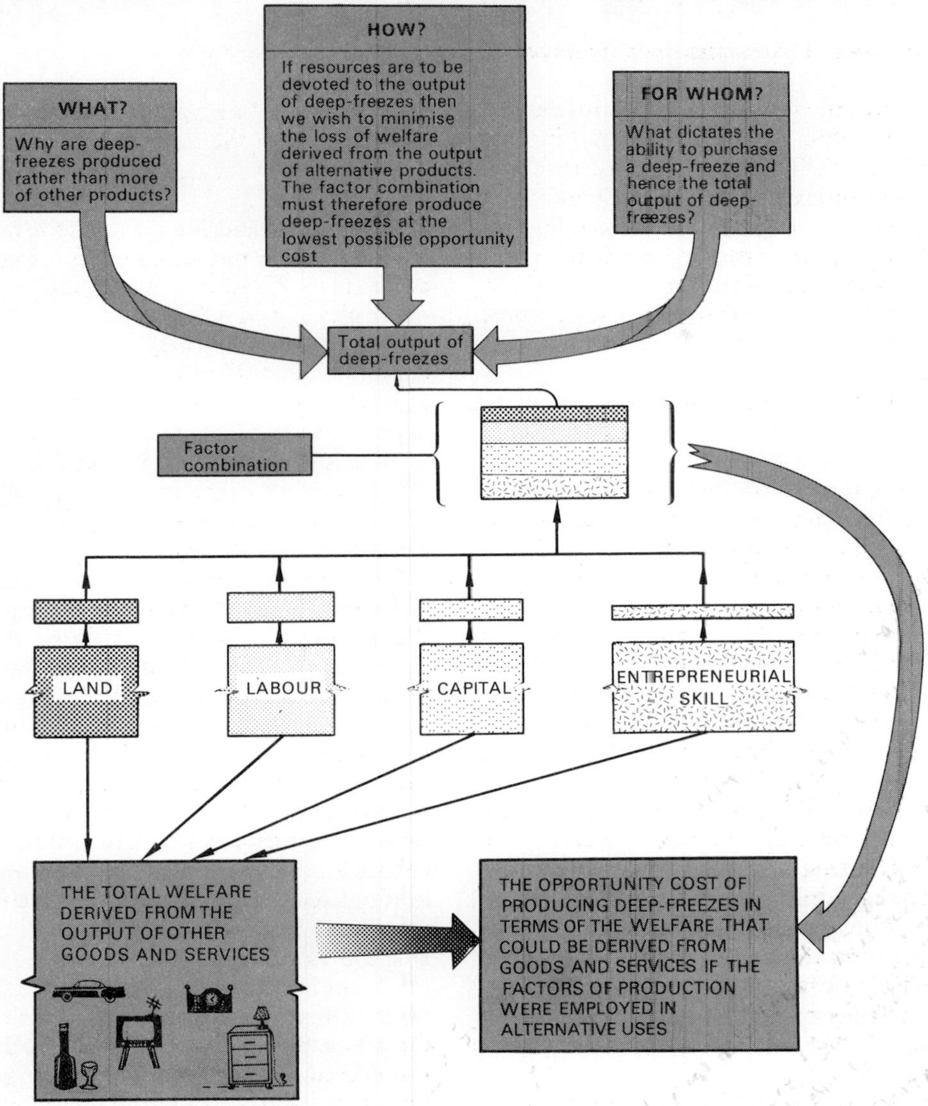
HOW?
If resources are to be devoted to the output of deep-freezes then we wish to minimise the loss of welfare derived from the output of alternative products. The factor combination must therefore produce deep-freezes at the lowest possible opportunity cost
WHAT?
Why are deep-freezes produced rather than more of other products?
FOR WHOM?
What dictates the ability to purchase a deep-freeze and hence the total output of deep-freezes?
Total output of deep-freezes
Factor combination
LAND
LABOUR
CAPITAL
ENTREPRENEURIAL SKILL
THE TOTAL WELFARE DERIVED FROM THE OUTPUT OF OTHER GOODS AND SERVICES
THE OPPORTUNITY COST OF PRODUCING DEEP-FREEZES IN TERMS OF THE WELFARE THAT COULD BE DERIVED FROM GOODS AND SERVICES IF THE FACTORS OF PRODUCTION WERE EMPLOYED IN ALTERNATIVE USES

Fig. 5.1

about a re-allocation of resources. This will continue until the relative prices for the products involved, and their effect upon relative profitability, prevent either any further expansion of Group A or any further decline of Group B. As Group A expands it will be obliged to pay attention to the effect which increased supplies of its products on to the market will have on prices, as they will start to fall from their previous peaks produced by the original increase in demand.

At the same time, Group A will incur higher costs in its efforts to attract more resources and thus its revenue and cost situations will eventually place a limit on what is a profitable level of increased output. The decline of Group B will be arrested by the revival in price which occurs for its products. This is because when supplies to the market are reduced, the prices will pick up and eventually allow a profit to be made. The net result is that Group A have expanded the scale of their operations; total output is now higher and their market price will also have settled at a higher level. Group B on the other hand, has contracted the scale of its operations which is reflected in a lower output and lower market prices.

This re-allocation of resources comes to an end when relative prices no longer make a further shift of resources worth while and both groups, taking account of the risks involved in their respective activities, are making an acceptable or 'normal profit'. The firms therefore play an important role by reacting to relative prices in product markets and giving further expression to the changed pattern of consumer demand in the markets for factors of production. This leads them to take decisions about *what* to produce.

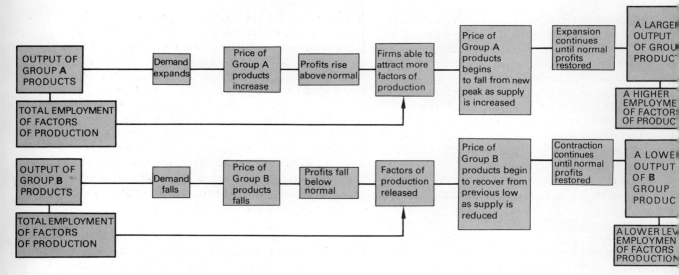

Fig. 5.2

The Price System and *how* to Produce

The prices of factors of production should be a reflection of the value which consumers attach to their contribution to output. If, for example, a particular type of labour commands a very high price, this will imply that consumers value its contribution to output very highly, and the prices they are prepared to pay for the resulting output allows the firm to employ that particular type of labour. In this case the relative prices of factors of production will in fact reflect their respective opportunity costs. A firm can only attract additional units of factors of production from other uses by offering a price that overcomes its value in an alternative use, and this it can only do if consumers are willing to pay a higher price for the end products. In our example, Group A found this venture worth while as the higher prices in product markets meant that consumers had given their 'permission' for such factors to be attracted, whereas the lower prices for Group B's product indicated that they wished them to be released from such uses. Thus the relative prices of factors of production not only reflect their respective opportunity costs, but they also cause firms to adopt a combination of factors of production that minimises the opportunity cost of achieving output. The firm will seek to economise on the use of high price factors of production to keep costs down, and this contributes to the working of an

efficient economic system which operates to ensure that output is achieved at the lowest possible opportunity cost in terms of output and hence welfare sacrificed elsewhere. Thus the firm makes decisions concerning *how* output is to be produced by taking account of relative factor prices and this contributes to the maximisation of total welfare.

The Price System and *for whom* to Produce

The question remains, however, *for whom* output should be produced. The pattern of output will be a reflection of the relative strengths of consumer demands and in the earlier analogy with an electoral system it was said that it depends upon the number of votes cast. The number of votes cast will depend upon the purchasing power of consumers, and this will be dictated by income. People are both consumers and suppliers of factors of production, and the share of the total income going to a particular provider of a factor of production will depend upon the price received for its factor service. Those factor services therefore which command a large share of the total income of an economy do so because of the decisions of firms in factor markets which influence factor prices and levels of employment. It is again a price system which dictates the distribution of output and hence *for whom* goods and services should be produced.

The decision of an organisation in terms of *where* to produce

The geographical location of industry is the end result of a combination of factors—economic, social and political. The very complexity of location decisions has made it difficult to outline general laws and theories regarding industrial location. The main models formulated in connection with the topic show that an industry may be located so as to provide a profit maximum, or it may be located at a least-cost site. The 'least-cost' model was set out by Weber, who devised a technique of mapping the spatial variations in transport costs in order to find the location where costs of production are minimised. This involved the use of **isodapanes** (lines joining places of equal transport costs). The best location is the place where transport costs per unit of production are least, or where the benefits of agglomeration (that is, concentration of industrial activity) and/or labour availability offset the disadvantages caused by not locating where the transport costs are least.

In contrast, the 'profit maximising' theory analyses demand. In the theory by Lösch, the best location is that which commands the largest market area, and the main transport costs considered are those from factory to consumer.

All models necessarily overgeneralise the complex situations of reality. In siting an industry, all factors of production should be considered and a location chosen where favourable factors outweigh any disadvantageous ones. The assembly of raw materials, the processing itself with inputs of labour and power, and the transport of the finished product to the market, are all important factors, and their influence on location varies from industry to industry.

Major Locational Factors (Fig. 5.3)

Raw Materials
Some industries are tied to a location near the source of raw materials, especially where there is considerable weight loss during processing. The raw materials are often from forests, mines and farms; the industries include saw-mills, pulp-mills, ore concentration plants, sugar- and flour-mills. Perishable products are also processed near the source, such as the canning of fruit, the making of butter and cheese and the freezing of fish. However, raw materials exert a decreasing location pull and this is mainly because of improvements in the transport of bulky materials, especially by water and because of specialised transport facilities, such as the refrigerated milk tanker.

Markets
These exert an increasing influence. Industries making goods which are more expensive to transport than the raw materials are usually located at the major markets. Transport costs for the finished product may be higher because of an increase in bulk during processing (as, for example, in brewing, making furniture and vehicles) or because products are fragile, perishable or highly packaged. Also, certain industries may benefit from personal contact between producer and consumer.

Power
Early industries were all power orientated, even before the Industrial Revolution took place. For instance, early iron works could be set up only where plentiful charcoal supplies were found near the iron bands, e.g. the Forest of Dean, the Weald of Kent. Mills using water-wheel power were located along swiftly flowing streams, e.g. con-

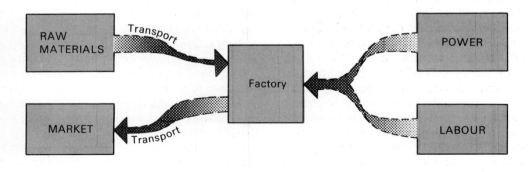

Fig. 5.3: Major locational factors

centrations of textile mills along the valleys flanking the Pennines, and along the 'Fall Line' of the eastern USA where the Appalachian Mountains reach the coastal plain. With the coming of steam power, industry was rapidly attracted to the coalfield areas, a pattern which frequently remains because of the immobility of plant and equipment. Energy itself has now become very mobile, as electricity can be transported great distances with very little loss of power, thus eliminating regional variations in power costs. There is a group of industries, however, whose power requirements are very great, and these are the electro-chemical and electro-metallurgical industries. They are often located close to plentiful supplies of relatively cheap hydro-electric power, for example, Invergordon, northern Scotland; Tema, Ghana, using Volta power; and Kitimat, British Columbia.

Labour
Labour supplies must be considered in terms of quantity, cost, skills and efficiency. Some large factories may require a work force in excess of 20,000 people (many vehicle-producing factories, for example) and labour supplies may therefore dominate the location decisions. Such large plants are generally located close to large cities (e.g. British Leyland, Longbridge, near Birmingham; Mercedes Benz, Stuttgart.)

Some industries may be attracted by relatively low wage levels. This was important in the initial development of industries in the southern USA where wage rates were below the national average. It was also an important factor in the recent expansion of labour-intensive industries in countries like Japan, Hong Kong and Taiwan.

Finally, there are some industries requiring such specialized skills that they locate close to a reservoir of skilled workers, e.g. potters around Stoke, gunsmiths in Birmingham, watchmakers in parts of Switzerland.

Transport
Assembly of raw materials and distribution of the finished product incurs costs which may influence the location decision. Mode of transport is also important. In Great Britain, early industries often showed a linear pattern along the canals and, later, along the railway lines. Waterside locations are still of importance when bulky raw materials are being handled as these can be transported more cheaply and conveniently by water. For example steel works, oil refineries and flour-mills are very frequently located along the coast or along inland waterway systems. Modern road transport networks have caused greater flexibility in the choice of location and have helped to cause a more dispersed pattern of industrial development.

Other Location Factors
Industries will tend to concentrate in an area, and advantages may be gained from such clustering. The product of one industry, for example, may be used as a raw material by another. Also, money made in one industry may lead to the setting up of further industries in the same area, for **money capital** is obviously important in the development of industry. This is a relatively mobile factor, although some countries may exert official controls restricting transfers of money. **Physical capital** (existing plant and capital) may also be distinguished. This is very immobile, and may lead to the continued development of an industry at an existing site. The presence of existing physical capital may also attract new industries. For example, closed textile mills in Lancashire were promptly re-occupied by a variety of industries.

Personal and government factors may also influence the location decision. The founder of a firm may choose an area of special natural beauty, or an area with a favourable climate in which to establish a factory, or very often his home town as, for example, Ford cars at Detroit, Players tobacco at Nottingham. Government influences may be at the national or regional level. Financial incentives in Great Britain which may influence location are provided by the Department of Trade and Industry, but a feature of regional policy is that it is two-edged in that the expansion of industry in areas of high activity and concentration is controlled through the use of Industrial Development Certificates (IDCs). Since 1947, a firm wishing to establish a new factory of over 3,000 sq. ft. in certain parts of Great Britain has had to apply for an IDC from the Department of Trade and Industry. IDCs are not required in the parts of Great Britain eligible for government aid.
varies from one industry to another and also through time. Finally, there are still some industries which are not greatly influenced by the location factors discussed, and these are known as 'foot-loose' industries.

The organisation and the influence of the law of diminishing returns upon output

The reaction of a firm to more favourable market conditions that leads to the decision to increase output will be influenced by the time period considered. In the short run it is possible to identify certain restraints under which the firm operates in its efforts to increase output.

The Short Run

This is defined as a period of time during which the input of some factors of production are regarded as fixed and output can only be raised by increasing the employment of those factors which the firm regards as being variable. This involves the firm in an increase in output, which is achieved by using the existing capacity, as dictated by the fixed factors, more intensively through the addition of more units of variable factors. Because of this inability to vary the input of all factors in the short run, the firm will be susceptible to the law of diminishing returns. This law predicts that if increasing quantities of variable factors are added to a fixed quantity of other factors, then eventually the resulting increases in output will get progressively smaller.

If, for example, capital equipment is fixed and the firm increases output by employing more units of labour, the marginal product of labour will eventually start to diminish. The marginal product of labour is the addition to total product (output) which results from the employment of an additional unit of labour. The implications which this law holds for the firm in the short run is shown in Table 5.1. This firm cannot increase its inputs of capital and employs additional units of labour to raise output in the short run.

When one unit of labour is employed total product is 20 units, and the employment of a second unit of labour raises total output to 120 units. The marginal product (MP) of the second unit of labour is thus 100 units, as this is the increase in total product which results from the employment of this second unit of labour. Similarly, total product increases from 120 to 290 units when the third unit of labour is employed and thus the MP of this unit of labour is 170. The initial employment of labour results in an increase in its MP and this implies that there are some economies of scale associated with increases in output, such as being able to take advantage of the division of labour. The MP of the fifth unit is 280 units, but this is

Table 5.1

Units of labour	Total product	Marginal product	Average product
1	20	20	20
2	120	100	60
3	290	170	96·7
4	520	230	130·0
5	800	280	160·0
6	1120	320	186·7
7	1450	330	207·1
8	1770	320	221·2
9	2060	290	228·9
10	2300	240	230·0
11	2480	180	225·4
12	2560	80	213·3
13	2560	0	196·9
14	2460	-100	175·7

not to say therefore that this fifth unit personally contributes 280 units to the total product. There is a direct contribution from this additional unit of labour but its presence also allows certain economies that make other units more productive. The MP of labour increases at first but eventually the point of diminishing marginal returns is reached when 7 units of labour are employed, as beyond this point the MP of labour declines.

The data in Table 5.1 is transferred to Fig. 5.4

Fig. 5.4

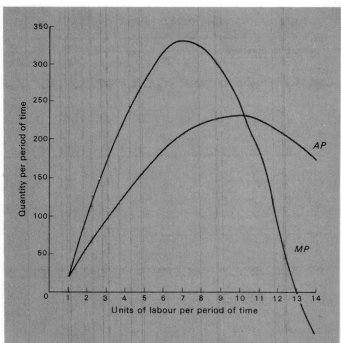

and the point of diminishing marginal returns is indicated at the peak of the curve showing the MP of labour. The employment of the thirteenth unit of labour leaves total product unchanged and thus the MP of this worker is zero. The employment of the fourteenth actually leads to a decline in total product and so the MP of this unit of labour is actually negative.

The average product (AP) per unit of labour is shown in Table 5.1 and this has also been transferred to Fig. 5.4. An interesting feature is that the *MP* and *AP* curves intersect at the latter's highest point and it is useful to understand this relationship as it contributes to the understanding of cost curves dealt with in subsequent sections of this chapter. Both the data and the curves show that after the employment of the seventh unit of labour the AP of labour continues to rise, despite the fact that the MP of labour is failing. This occurs because although the MP of labour (the addition to output) is declining, it is still greater than the existing AP of labour and thus the latter must be pulled up. For example, the MP of the ninth unit of labour is 290 units, and this is greater than the AP of 221·2 units relating to the previous 8 units of labour. Thus the AP of 9 units of labour must be higher than the AP of 8 units of labour. In fact, as long as the MP of labour is greater than the existing AP of labour, the latter will continue to rise. Once, however, the MP of labour falls below the existing AP of labour, then the AP of labour will also start to fall. Thus it is no coincidence that the *AP* curve falls once it is cut by the *MP* curve, and this point of intersection is the point of diminishing average returns.

The Long Run

Firms will eventually experience diminishing returns during their efforts to increase output in the short run to meet a change in market demand. In the long run however, the firm is freed from the restraints imposed by some factors of production being fixed. This long run is defined as a period of time which enables the firm to vary the input of all factors of production and adjust more fully to a larger level of output. There will be scope to introduce more units of capital, train more labour and generally have an opportunity to exploit greater economies of scale. The actual duration of the short run will vary between industries according to the nature of their products and the technical conditions surrounding their production. If, for example, there is an increase in the demand for ceramic floor tiles, firms may at first expand production by using their existing capital items, such as kilns, more intensively through employing more labour. It may, however, be only a question of weeks or months before producers can obtain and install more or larger kilns and train the necessary operatives. Similarly, the oil-refining industry may be able to expand output in the short run by increasing the employment of variable factors such as labour. It may be a question of years, however, before a long-term adjustment can be made as oil refineries are large complex plants and this will be reflected in the time taken to construct them. The actual decision to expand the scale of operations to accommodate a larger demand will be taken only if the firm believes that the more favourable conditions are of a fairly permanent nature and so make investment expenditure worth while. Business expectations are therefore an important factor in determining the extent of the long-term adjustment.

The influence of the law of diminishing returns upon the costs of production

The identification of time periods is important since it highlights the expected relationships between inputs and outputs and these relationships will have repercussions upon a firm's costs of production according to the time period considered. Changes in costs will affect profits and it is important therefore to distinguish between the main categories of costs and how they are likely to vary with output.

Fixed Costs

These are costs which do not vary no matter what changes occur in output. In many cases they can expect to include such items as the interest that must be paid on borrowed capital and the repayments on such loans, the depreciation on items of capital equipment, rent and rates levied by local authorities. Fixed costs are also known as overhead or indirect costs, and the latter description implies that, since fixed costs are incurred regardless of the level of output, they cannot be directly related to any particular unit of output. Fixed costs must also be paid even if the firm ceases production.

Variable Costs

These costs vary directly with the level of output and are only incurred when output actually takes place. If output increases so will the variable costs associated with such items as labour, raw material and power. These costs can be more readily attributed to certain units of production and therefore are also known as direct costs.

This division into fixed and variable costs does become a little blurred on occasions as the category into which some costs are placed depends upon the time period considered. Some costs may remain constant over a particular range of output but then suddenly jump once output reaches a certain level. For example, plant and machinery are to varying degrees indivisible and their capacity cannot be increased by marginal amounts to cope precisely with an increase in output. In the long run this involves the installation of more items of capital and thus costs can be of a variable nature when the firm expands output. These costs become fixed over the next range of output before further capacity is installed. It also becomes possible to reduce some fixed costs in the long run if the firm believes that it should reduce the scale of operations because of business expectations of a more permanent fall in the market demand for its output. In these circumstances, the firm will not replace machines as they wear out, it will reduce the size of its plant and also produce an administrative structure more in keeping with its reduced output. Some variable costs may, in turn, display a certain degree of indivisibility. For example, a firm may require more man-hours to increase output, but the nature of the conditions surrounding the employment of labour may oblige the firm to hire an additional worker on a full-time basis, although this additional labour may not be fully utilised by the desired increase in output. Similarly, raw materials may only be available in standard amounts that may be surplus to immediate requirements, while services such as heating and lighting cannot always be controlled in line with changes in output. Within a firm it will be the task of the cost accountant to identify the firm's total costs and provide management with the unit costs of their finished products for purposes of establishing the relative profitability of its activities.

This greater variability of all costs in the long run does not prevent a useful division of costs into our two categories, as the firm will decide in its own interest whether they should be regarded as fixed or variable. Subsequent sections will thus concentrate upon using the two broad headings under which costs are generally placed by a firm.

Marginal Costs (MC)

This is the addition to total costs as a result of producing and selling one more unit of output. As output is expanded the increase in costs will be those attributable to an increase in variable costs which rise with output, since by definition fixed costs remain unchanged. Marginal costs are therefore comprised entirely of marginal variable costs.

Table 5.2 (p. 74) can be used to show the likely characteristics of a firm's marginal costs as output changes. The MC of the first unit is £280 as this is the addition to total costs as output is raised from zero. The MC of the second unit is £100 as total costs increase from £480 to £580 as a result of this extra unit of output. Column 5 shows that this firm's MC falls quite rapidly at first, but then the fall becomes less pronounced, and eventually reaches a minimum level when the eighth unit is produced. Beyond this point MC rise at an increasing rate. This is reflected in the *MC* curve in Fig. 5.5. which relates to the data contained in column 5 of Table 5.2.

Fig. 5.5

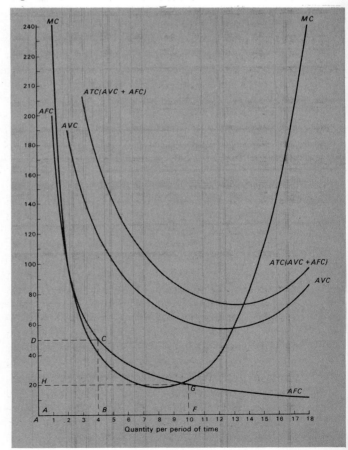

Table 5.2: Costs (in £)

1. Units of output	2. Fixed costs	3. Total variable costs	4. Total costs	5. Marginal costs	6. Average fixed costs	7. Average variable costs	8. Average total cost (6 + 7)
0	200	0	200	0	0	0	0
1	200	280	480	280	200.0	280 0	480
2	200	380	580	100	100.0	190.0	290
3	200	440	640	60	66.6	146.7	213.3
4	200	480	680	40	50.0	120.0	170.0
5	200	510	710	30	40.0	102.0	142.0
6	200	534	734	24	33.3	89.0	122.3
7	200	554	754	20	28.5	79.1	107.6
8	200	572	772	18	25.0	71.5	96.5
9	200	592	792	20	22.2	65.8	88.0
10	200	614	814	22	20.0	61.4	81.4
11	200	644	844	30	18.2	58.5	76.7
12	200	682	882	38	16.7	56.8	73.5
13	200	742	942	60	15.4	57.1	72.5
14	200	822	1022	80	14.3	58.7	73.0
15	200	932	1132	110	13.3	62.1	75.4
16	200	1082	1282	150	12.5	67.6	80.1
17	200	1282	1482	200	11.8	75.4	87.2
18	200	1542	1742	260	11.1	85.7	96.8

The shape and direction of this *MC* curve will be influenced by the marginal product of the variable factors which are associated with its marginal costs. Since labour is generally a variable factor then Table 5.1 can be used to illustrate the impact of the marginal product of labour upon marginal costs. This table shows that in the initial stages a proportionate or percentage increase in the employment of labour brings about a larger proportionate or percentage increase in output. For example, an increase in the employment of labour from 4 to 5 units resulted in an increase in output from 520 to 800 units. This amounts to changes of 25 per cent and 53·8 per cent respectively. Thus initial increases in output would require a much smaller proportionate increase in the employment of labour, and total variable costs would therefore increase by a smaller proportion than the desired increase in output. This prospect of certain economies as output is expanded is also reflected in Table 5.2 where the increase in output from 3 to 4 units causes total variable costs to increase from £440 to £480. These are changes of 33·3 per cent and 9·1 per cent respectively. Thus, because the firm's marginal product associated with variable factors, such as labour, can be expected to increase quite sharply at first, then the marginal costs will fall.

This influence of the marginal product can be identified at other stages of the cost data since, as the marginal product slows down, so also will the decline in marginal costs. Eventually of course the point of diminishing marginal returns will be reached and this will exert an upward pressure on marginal costs at higher levels of output. For example, the increase in the level of employment from 10 to 11 units in Table 5.1 raises output from 2300 to 2480 units, and these are changes of 10 per cent and 5·1 per cent. Thus a proportionate increase in the employment of a variable factor is now met by a much smaller proportionate increase in output. This relationship can again be seen in Table 5.2 where the increase in output from 14 to 15 units causes total variable costs to rise from £822 to £932. An increase in output of 7·1 per cent has required an increase in variable costs of 13·4 per cent and marginal costs are now increasing.

This upward pressure on the firm's marginal cost can also be added to by what may soon become another important factor. Not only is the firm being forced to employ proportionately more units of variable factors to achieve the desired increase in output, but at the same time may eventually be obliged to pay a higher price to obtain them. Increased demand for labour may involve firms in paying a higher wage or salary for labour in order to secure its services. Thus marginal costs may start to rise even before the point of diminishing marginal returns is reached.

Average Variable Costs (AVC)

These are the total variable costs of producing any given level of output divided by that level of output. The data in column 7 of Table 5.2 shows that the average variable cost per unit produced falls as output is at first expanded. Again this is partly explained by the expected increase in the average product associated with the employment of additional units of variable factors. In the case of the firm in Table 5.2 the average product per unit of labour increases at first as total output rises at a faster rate than the employment of labour. The firm in Table 5.2 is experiencing a similar rise in the average product of its variable factors as it employs more of them. When, for example, output is increased from 5 to 6 units, the total variable costs (which reflect the employment of variable factors) increase from £510 to £534. Thus output has increased by 20 per cent with an increase in total variable costs of only 4·7 per cent, and so the average variable cost associated with each unit of output must fall, and column 7 of Table 5.2 shows this to be the case.

Eventually, however, the firm will experience a fall in the average product of its variable factors, as total output will increase at a slower rate than the employment of variable factors. For example, the increase in output from 17 to 18 units requires an increase in total variable costs from £1282 to £1542 and these are changes of 5·8 per cent and 20·2 per cent respectively. The average variable costs associated with each unit of output must therefore increase, as is shown by column 7 of Table 5.2. Not only will the fall in average product be exerting an upward pressure on the average variable costs but they will also be pushed up by the increased price that the firm may be forced to pay in order to obtain additional units of variable factors. The average variable costs may therefore start to rise even before the point of diminishing average returns is reached and the general shape and direction of such a curve is illustrated in Fig. 5.5.

Average Fixed Costs (AFC)

These costs will fall continuously as output is expanded, as a fixed amount is being divided by a progressively larger level of output. Average fixed costs fall quite steeply at first but the fall becomes less significant as higher levels of output are reached, as shown by column 6 of Table 5.2. The average fixed cost curve is depicted in Fig. 5.5 and its shape is that of a rectangular hyperbola. The feature of such a curve is that if a level of output is selected and then multiplied by the average fixed costs associated with that output, the result must always be the same, i.e. total fixed costs. The curve in Fig. 5.5 shows average fixed costs are £50 when output is 4 units and this produces the total fixed costs of £200. The same result is achieved when 10 units is multiplied by their average fixed costs of £20. These amounts are represented by the areas ABCD and AFGH. They must be the same and equal to any other areas shown by a combination of output and corresponding average fixed costs. A rectangular hyperbola will have this particular property.

Average Total Costs (ATC)

These are determined by adding together the total fixed cost and total variable costs and dividing them by the level of output in question. The same result would be achieved by adding together the average fixed costs and average variable costs associated with a particular level of output. Column 8 of Table 5.2 shows that average total costs fall at first and then eventually rise. The initial fall is due to the fact that both the average variable costs and the average fixed costs fall as output is expanded. Eventually, however, the average variable costs start to rise, and although the average fixed costs fall continuously, the progressively larger increases in average variable costs will more than outweigh the progressively smaller fall in average fixed costs. The average total cost therefore starts to rise, as shown by the curve in Fig. 5.5. Note that the gap between the average variable cost curve and the average total cost curve in the diagram is equivalent to the average fixed costs at a particular level of output. The average total cost curve is after all the result of adding the average fixed cost curve to the average variable cost curve.

It may have been noticed in columns 5 and 7 of Table 5.2 and in Fig. 5.5 that in a range of output beyond 8 units the marginal costs are rising, while the average variable costs are still falling. The explanation is that as long as the addition to total costs (i.e. marginal costs) is still less than the existing average variable costs, then production of one more unit will still cause the average variable costs to fall. Once, however, the marginal costs exceed the existing average variable costs, the latter must start to rise. This occurs between the production of the twelfth and thirteenth units, and therefore it is no coincidence that the marginal cost curve cuts the average variable cost at the latter's lowest point. Similarly, the average total cost curve is cut by the marginal cost curve at its lowest point.

If cost curves are to be used to illustrate a particular point, it is important that they are drawn in a manner which does demonstrate their basic shape and direction. Points of intersection should occur at the correct places rather than being drawn in a haphazard fashion. Cost curves can prove useful aids when discussing and illustrating the output decisions of firms that seek to maximise their profits.

Long-run Costs

The analysis of the firm's costs has so far been conducted from the point of view of the likely impact on costs of increases in output in the short run (see Fig. 5.6). When diminishing returns were an important influence on these costs, the firm had to make the best of the situation by employing more units of those factors of production which were more immediately variable, and was not able to expand the scale of its operations by varying the inputs of all factors of production and combine them in the most productive way. The firm has fixed factors, such as plant and equipment, geared to its current level of output and these will not be the most economic means of producing a higher level of output.

In the long run, however, all factors of production are variable and the firm can be expected to adjust the quantity and combination of its inputs of any factors of production in order to achieve the higher output at the lowest possible unit cost. The firm will be able to take advantage of potential economies of scale, with the result that a proportionate change in output will be met by a smaller proportionate increase in costs. Some likely opportunities for economies of scale were outlined in Chapter 2. The long-run cost curves show the cost associated with producing a higher level of output when a period of time has elapsed which allows all factors of production to be varied, and Fig. 5.7 can be used to illustrate the likely shape and direction of such curves.

It is assumed that the firm is currently producing OQ_1 units of output and this output is produced with a combination of inputs specifically geared to this level of output. This position represents a production technique that is the result of a previous long-run and planned adjustment to this level of output OQ_1, and this is produced at an average total cost of OC_1. If market conditions now change and this firm wishes to increase output, then in the short run it will have to operate with some factors such as plant and equipment being fixed. The average total costs associated with the higher level of output OQ_2 is shown by a movement along the curve ATC_1 and produces OC_2. In the long run the method of production

Fig. 5.6

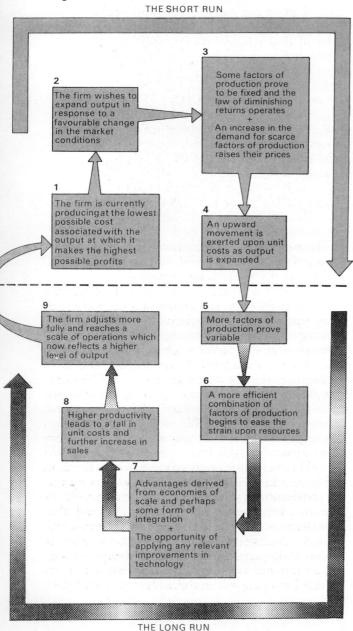

THE SHORT RUN

2 The firm wishes to expand output in response to a favourable change in the market conditions

3 Some factors of production prove to be fixed and the law of diminishing returns operates + An increase in the demand for scarce factors of production raises their prices

1 The firm is currently producing at the lowest possible cost associated with the output at which it makes the highest possible profits

4 An upward movement is exerted upon unit costs as output is expanded

9 The firm adjusts more fully and reaches a scale of operations which now reflects a higher level of output

5 More factors of production prove variable

6 A more efficient combination of factors of production begins to ease the strain upon resources

8 Higher productivity leads to a fall in unit costs and further increase in sales

7 Advantages derived from economies of scale and perhaps some form of integration + The opportunity of applying any relevant improvements in technology

THE LONG RUN

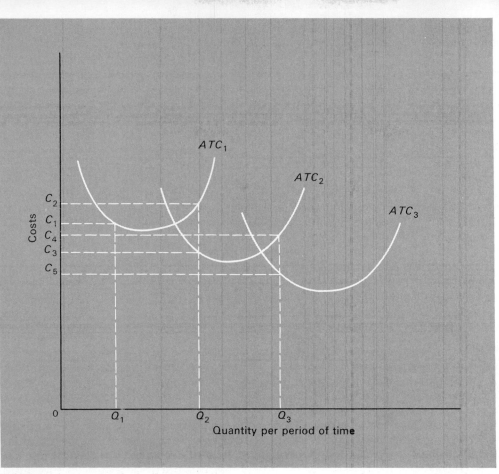

Fig. 5.7

can be adjusted more fully to cope with the increase in output by, for example, expanding the capacity of plant and equipment. Because of the economies of scale associated with such a move, it then becomes possible to produce OQ_2 units at an average total cost of OC_3. The curve ATC_2 now represents the likely experience of the firm as far as unit costs are concerned if it again varied output in the short run with its new set-up of plant and equipment being regarded as fixed. Thus a further increase in output, in response to market changes, to OQ_3 will see an expansion along ATC_2 to produce an average total cost of OC_4. A long-run adjustment will permit output OQ_3 to be produced at an average total cost of OC_5, as ATC_3 is the new relevant cost curve. This exercise can be repeated and gives rise to costs which reflect a complete adjustment to increases in output and traces the shape and direction of the long-run average total cost curve ($LRATC$). Such a curve is illustrated in Fig. 5.8 (p. 78) and shows that at any one moment a firm can only produce on a single short-run average total cost curve ($SRATC$) because some factors are fixed. In the

long run it will select the most suitable combination of input and this will have its own $SRATC$ curve at any given level of output.

The decline in the $LRATC$ curve shows that the firm benefits from economies of scale, and in our example in Fig. 5.8 the eventual rise in the $LRATC$ curve indicates that this particular firm does experience diseconomies once output is increased beyond a certain level. Some possible sources of diseconomies of scale are suggested in Chapter 2. It should be noted that the $LRATC$ curve envelopes the $SRATC$ curve, and is always at a tangent to a point on a $SRATC$ curve. No point of a $SRATC$ curve could lie below the long-run curve as this would imply that a certain level of output could be produced at a lower unit cost in the short run than in the long run. It is very unlikely that opportunities for reducing unit costs would be taken advantage of in the short run and then neglected in the long run. The flatter nature of the $LRATC$ curve suggests less dramatic changes in costs as output is expanded when compared with the short-run situation. This situation is thus reflected in a long-run marginal cost curve ($LRMC$)

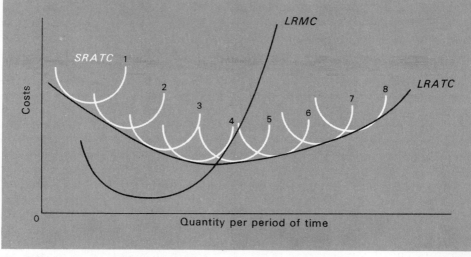

Fig. 5.8

which is also flatter and indicates that additions to costs are less significant when compared with the experience in the short run.

The previous analysis has shown that unit costs will be lower in the long run than in the short run when output is expanded. This will also be the case, however, when the firm is obliged to contract output because of unfavourable developments in its market. The firm in Fig. 5.9 is currently producing OQ_1 at the lowest possible unit cost of OC_1. If the firm is forced to reduce output to OQ_2, the new unit costs are shown by a movement along the relevant curve ATC_1 and produce

Fig. 5.9

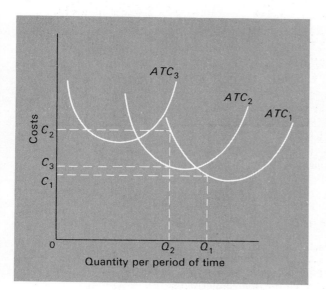

an average total cost of OC_2. The capacity set by the fixed plant and equipment is now too large for the lower level of output for which it was not specifically designed. In the long run the firm will adopt a combination of factors of production more closely geared to the lower level of output. Plant and equipment may be fixed in the short run, but in the long run they can be reduced by not replacing items as they wear out and installing units that provide a capacity that is more suitable to the lower level of output. The long-run adjustment results in OQ_2 being finally produced at a unit cost of OC_3 on ATC_2 which is also a point on the $LRATC$ curve. This $LRATC$ curve is thus relevant for both increases and reductions in output that the firm believes are to be sufficiently permanent to warrant an alteration of its scale of operations.

In conclusion, it should be pointed out that for most of the analysis of costs is has been assumed that the fixed factors were items of real capital such as plant and equipment. However, there may be circumstances where the skills of labour are such that additional employees are not readily available and certain types of equipment may prove more variable. In this case, a short-run situation would involve the addition of extra units of capital in order to use the existing labour force more intensively. Again the concept of diminishing returns would apply and influence short-run costs as the marginal and average returns from additional units of capital would eventually decline. A long-run adjustment may then involve the firm in concentrating upon training extra labour to meet its specific requirements.

The acquisition of human resources by an organisation and the labour market

The Recruitment of Labour

If a firm is large enough, the size of its labour force may justify the establishment of a specialist personnel department and, as described in Chapter 2, this section will have a special responsibility for recruiting labour. They will use their own advertisements in appropriate newspapers and journals and keep in close contact both with educational institutions and the Youth Employment Service when dealing with school and college leavers. Recommendations from existing employees may also prove a valuable source of recruitment.

Otherwise the services of an independent selection or appointment counsellor may be employed. The Department of Employment is a useful source of manual and clerical workers via Job Centres, and it also maintains a Professional and Executive Register and a Graduate Recruitment Register.

Fig. 5.10 shows the various ways in which people first heard of their jobs, as reported by the *General Household Survey* of 1974. Information on vacancies from friends or relatives was the most common way of finding a job, both among men and women. Between one-fifth and one-quarter of all jobs were found through advertisements and a similar proportion through a direct approach to the employer. Women favoured the advertisement more than men, while more men went for the direct approach. Over 11 per cent of male workers found their jobs through what used to be known as employment exchanges, but only 2 per cent went to private agencies. Agencies were used mainly by women, perhaps because of their dealings in secretarial skills, as women found about 7 per cent of their jobs through private agencies, while only 6 per cent were obtained through employment exchanges. This survey would seem to reduce the relative importance of consultants and private agencies, but they themselves will be using advertisements as part of their activities and therefore they play a more significant role than this survey would seem to suggest.

The labour market as a means of allocating resources

If the labour market is to perform the function of allocating human resources into areas of production which reflect the relative strengths of consumer demands, then this will depend both on the mobility of labour and on the labour market producing wage and salary differentials that will attract labour into the appropriate lines of production. The following sections will therefore examine both the mobility of labour and the extent to which the price (i.e. wage/salary) of labour will contribute to an efficient occupational distribution of the work force.

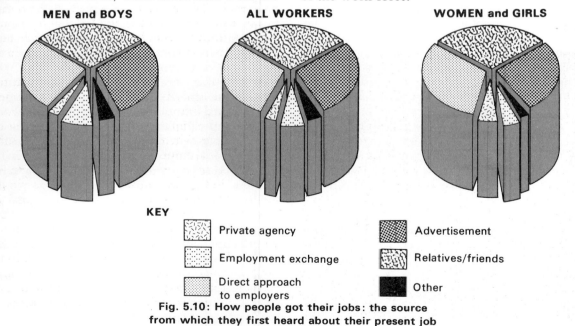

MEN and BOYS   **ALL WORKERS**   **WOMEN and GIRLS**

KEY

Private agency   Advertisement

Employment exchange   Relatives/friends

Direct approach to employers   Other

Fig. 5.10: How people got their jobs: the source from which they first heard about their present job

Mobility of Labour

This term refers to the extent to which labour can move geographically to different areas or regions and also between occupations. A firm may at first be able to increase its input of labour, in response to an increase in the demand for its final product, by encouraging its existing work force to work longer hours by offering overtime rates. The labour force may be further enlarged by offering attractive rates of pay to recruit the necessary skills from the working population in its immediate vicinity. However, once these sources are exhausted it may suffer from labour shortages, as higher wages may not succeed in attracting labour from other geographical areas for in this sense labour tends to be relatively immobile. People tend to become attached to their immediate environment and develop strong family and social ties which they may not be prepared to break. In addition, such people may face the problem of securing satisfactory accommodation in a new area of the country.

These factors may be of less concern to younger workers than to older and more established people to whom family and social ties may be of greater importance. The government seeks to increase the geographical mobility of labour by offering financial contributions towards expenses incurred in travelling to interviews. Financial support may also be available for any temporary accommodation the worker requires and for eventual removal expenses.

Even if geographical mobility could be increased, there is the additional problem that if the scarcity of a certain skill in a particular sector is to be alleviated, some workers may have to change occupations. The government does provide some facilities to encourage workers to retrain or adapt their existing skills but the success of such a policy depends upon the scale of such provisions and the willingness of people to take advantage of them. For reasons of simple inertia and lack of ability, workers tend to be occupationally immobile but this condition can be further aggravated by the ex-istence of man-made barriers to entry. Trade unions, for example, may demand years of apprenticeship, and professional bodies may also have regulations that inhibit mobility. Thus despite increases in relative incomes making the acquisition of certain skills more attractive, it may be a number of years before a noticeable increase in workers possessing the necessary skills actually occurs. New entrants on to the labour market can contribute to a change in the composition of the working population's skills. This will only happen if young people are guided into occupations for which demand is growing, but again time may elapse before they have developed practical skills in their jobs.

Despite the existence of relatively high unemployment in the economy as a whole, labour shortages can still exist and have been a recurring feature in the UK since the decline of the staple industries, such as textiles, shipbuilding, coal mining and iron and steel, which tended to be heavily concentrated in certain parts of the country. The newer, faster-growing light industries, such as consumer durables, are located in the main in the Midlands and the South-East, where the rapidly growing service industries have also concentrated many of their activities. Table 5.3 shows how unemployment was regionally distributed in the UK at the end of 1973 when there was a relatively rapid period of industrial expansion. This demonstrates the geographical immobility of labour which can frustrate the growth of those firms which are facing an increase in the demand for their end-products. At the end of 1973, unemployment excluding school-leavers stood at 524,700, yet vacancies notified to employment offices totalled 360,7000, indicating that vacancies could not be alleviated any further due to both the geographical and occupational immobility of the work force. Even in September 1980 when unemployment varied from 4·8 per cent to 13·7 per cent between the main regions of the country and totalled over 1·4 million, there were still 128,000 vacancies in terms of those notified to employment offices.

Table 5.3: UK Regional Unemployment Rates (1973)

North	Yorkshire and Humberside	East Midlands	East Anglia	South East	South West	West Midlands	North West	Wales	Scotland	Northern Ireland	United Kingdom
3·9	2·3	1·8	1·6	1·3	2·1	1·7	2·9	3·0	3·8	5·3	2·3

Factors Influencing Wage Rates

There are several factors that can exert a significant influence upon wage rates and produce differentials that are not necessarily a close reflection of the relative strengths of consumer demand for final output, as was assumed in our previous analysis of the price system operating in a market economy.

(a) *The collective bargaining power of a trade union will be an important factor in determining certain wage rates in an economy.* In the UK more than 10 million people belong to unions and a large proportion of the remaining part of the working population work in industries where wage rates are influenced by the activities of unions to which they do not belong. Another section of the working population may have wages negotiated via Wages Councils where there are no adequate arrangements for collective bargaining between employers and employees. The extent to which relative bargaining power diverges from the relative strengths of consumer demand will result in wage differentials that fail to act as a mechanism for bringing about any necessary re-allocation of labour. Wage differentials between firms and industries as a whole that would perhaps arise if market forces were allowed to operate may also be limited by the tendency for unions to negotiate on behalf of their members on a national scale irrespective of the firm or industry in which they are employed. Thus the Amalgamated Engineering Union and the Transport and General Workers Union will negotiate wage increases and working conditions for its members irrespective of the end product to which these workers contribute.

(b) *Changes in relative wage rates according to the forces of demand and supply may also be prevented by the existence of what are regarded as traditional and acceptable differentials by workers and their union leaders.* These may have been produced by an entirely different market situation which existed for a considerable period in the past and which resists market forces operating to bring about a change. Broad differentials may not only exist between industries themselves but also between skills within the same industry. If an increased wage rate is secured by a particular group of workers because of an increase in the demand for their skills, this may produce claims by other groups. This initial increase in wages will have eroded the gap between that particular group and those that traditionally earned more, while also widening the differential over lower-paid workers. These other groups can then be expected to seek wage increases to restore the traditional differentials and may prevent a change in relative incomes that might otherwise eventually have produced a reallocation of labour between firms and industries in accordance with the changing patterns of tastes and preferences expressed by consumers.

(c) *The creation of differentials to reflect the changing pattern of demand may also be inhibited by wage claims on the basis of comparability.* For example, increased wages for one group of workers may provoke similar claims by workers performing comparable tasks in other firms and industries where the same skills are employed. If, for example, motor vehicle assembly workers in one company obtain a wage increase, those in another company may demand equal treatment from their employers. This may then spread to other sectors of the economy as the question of differentials will help to increase the number of wage claims.

(d) *Government intervention in the determination of wages can be a major influence in the economy as a whole when seeking to control the level of wage claims in order to help reduce the rate of inflation via an incomes policy.* Such policies may have statutory backing or be of a voluntary nature to keep wage increases within an agreed 'norm'. A wage freeze will replace both market forces and other influences, such as collective bargaining, where wage increases are concerned. It can be assumed in this situation that overcoming inflation is the major concern of the government which is therefore willing to accept that a reallocation of labour will be prevented in such circumstances. Such wage freezes have been relatively short-term policies and are generally followed by an incomes policy that seeks to keep further increases within an agreed monetary limit, such as £6 per week, or a percentage of income, such as 10 per cent. The government may also attempt to secure agreement that a minimum period of time elapses between wage increases and this can slow down the creation of new wage and salary differentials.

(e) *The government is also a major employer in the UK and therefore has direct control over the wage rates of approximately 12 per cent of the total work force.* Social services, such as health and education, are not sold on a free market since central and local government authorities do not compete among themselves for doctors, teachers, etc. by offering different pay scales; therefore market forces are largely removed from these sectors of the economy. Instead the government must gauge the relative importance of such services as far as total welfare is concerned, and it will determine total employment and rates of pay according to the need for such services. There would not, however, seem to be a means by which governments can establish the position of social services in a list of consumer's priorities.

(f) *Employment in the nationalised industries and wage rates will be more open to market forces as the end products are sold on open market.* Collective bargaining power, however, also tends to be strong because of the importance of such items as energy, transport and iron and steel. Non-economic factors have often guided decisions relating to the prices of end products and the levels of employment in nationalised industries, as was seen in Chapter 2. Thus market forces in both product and labour markets may be distorted by a combination of social, political and overall economic considerations.

(g) *The government's demand management policies can also contribute to an allocation of labour that would not otherwise arise if market forces were allowed to operate.* A government faced with growing unemployment may increase employment in central and local government services, as was the case in the UK from 1962 onwards; by 1972 total employment in local government alone had increased by 53 per cent. This increase may be in excess of the growth in the demand for social services and in the later years could be seen primarily as a means of creating employment. In times of an upturn in the level of productive activity, however, the possibility exists that labour will not be released from the public sector and firms in the private sector may experience labour shortages.

In particular, the growth of the private sector may be frustrated if employment in the social services has become relatively more attractive through movements in wage differentials. Public sector earnings tended to lag behind the private sector in the 1950s and 1960s, but in the 1970s they moved ahead in an unprecedented fashion. Traditional differentials were therefore upset. This may have been an instance where market forces did play a major role in moderating wage increases in the private sector, as the depressed state of total demand in the economy for much of this period will have had a greater impact upon the private than upon the public sector, as the latter tends to be isolated from market forces. The government was in a stronger position to raise revenue to meet wage claims and so pay the full amount permissible by any incomes policy currently in operation.

The subsequent decline in the relative size of the manufacturing sector in particular, may see governments allowing greater flexibility in the determination of wages via an approach to incomes that seeks to restore differentials that produce a redistribution of labour in favour of the wealth-creating sector of the economy.

(h) *On occasions the government may seek to bring about a reallocation of labour which it believes market forces are failing to produce.* The scarce nature of certain skills and their major role in production results in some firms 'hoarding' certain types of labour during a downturn in the economy, as they anticipate difficulty in regaining them during a more buoyant period when they wish to expand. The possibility exists therefore that firms experiencing the strongest demand from consumers will not necessarily be able to secure key workers from those currently unemployed. The introduction of the Selective Employment Tax in 1966 was partly aimed at encouraging the tertiary sector to employ fewer workers. This tax was designed to raise the cost of employing labour in *services* relative to manufacturing, in an effort to release workers into manufacturing itself, which had tended to suffer labour shortages. This tax was abolished in 1973 but it does illustrate that by deliberately raising the cost of employing labour in certain sectors of the economy, the government can directly intervene in the labour market if it wishes to encourage a different allocation of labour.

Market Forces versus Government Intervention in the Labour Market

The previous section analysed some of the factors which operate to determine wage rates and which may produce an allocation of labour which does not closely reflect the relative strengths of consumer demand. It should not necessarily be assumed, however, that such imperfections in the labour market unfairly disrupt market forces, as one cannot treat labour in the same way as non-human factors. The question arises as to the extent to which an individual's income, and hence standard of living, should be left solely to market forces. Perhaps a faster rate of economic growth could be achieved if the forces of demand and supply were allowed to create wage differentials, so leading to a re-allocation of labour in favour of the rapidly growing industries. However, would the costs in terms of unemployment, due to the problems of immobility and wage differentials produced, be considered as acceptable when the question of fairness is considered? Is it fair, for example, that a worker who has spent a large part of his working life making a valuable contribution to the economy suffer a setback in his living standards because market forces no longer create a need for his skills? Similarly, should relative living standards be determined by the collective bargaining power which unions use on behalf of some members of the work force, when other workers may possess little in the way of bargaining power? It is for these reasons that governments may adopt economic measures that cushion unemployment by stimulating total demand in the economy, and replace collective bargaining power with some form of control over incomes. The government must accept, however, that in doing so it will slow down the mechanism for re-allocating labour.

In the long run, however, market forces may influence the situation as firms must eventually release labour because of higher labour costs and if the declining demand for their output proves to be of a permanent nature. Similarly, the more profitable and expanding firms may create income differentials in excess of those set by union-negotiated wage rates, through the process of **wage drift**. This is a term used to describe the tendency in some sectors for actual earnings to be above what they should be according to the wage rate. This wage drift results from bonus payments, overtime rates and shorter working hours, and so allows expanding firms to attract more labour. The government must attempt to strike a balance between recognising the need for market forces to operate and what is considered to be a socially acceptable result produced by such forces in terms of employment and wage differentials.

The acquisition of capital and the capital market

Capital as a Factor of Production
The acquisition of new fixed capital assets by organisations will help raise their future productive capacity, and so the extent to which a community is willing to devote some of its limited resources to this purpose will play a major role in determining future living standards as measured by the level of consumption. A failure to invest in capital goods and an over-emphasis upon devoting limited resources to increasing immediate consumption, will have repercussions in a later period when production is inhibited by a capital stock which is worn out and out of date. If final consumption from limited resources is to be maintained or increased, some resources must be directed to the production of capital goods so that future productive capacity and living standards can be safeguarded.

The acquisition of capital goods involves not only the allocation of funds by firms in the private sector to the purchase of such items as plant and equipment, but also the protection by the government of future welfare—in the form of health and education—by the construction of hospitals, clinics, schools and colleges. The government is concerned both with raising the quality of labour (to which improved health and educational facilities can make a valuable contribution) and with influencing future productivity in the economy in a more direct way. Investment expenditure by the government in transport, communications and energy sectors is vital for user industries.

Since every country possesses a limited supply of factors of production, the production of capital goods requires the reduced employment of resources for output to meet consumption, in order that these resources can be released for more productive use in the future. This will raise output per head of population and allow an increase in future consumption. A more productive use of resources will also permit the government to increase the provision of social services which, in the absence of higher productivity, would only be possible by demanding an actual cut in consumption to release resources for such a purpose.

The Importance of Savings
If living standards are not only to be maintained but also to improve at an acceptable rate, it is necessary for some potential consumption to be sacrificed. Incomes which households receive allow them to make a claim upon resources according to the level of these incomes, and the extent to which resources can be devoted to the creation of capital assets will depend largely upon their willingness to save. Households, however, will only be willing to postpone their claim upon resources if the sacrifice is tolerable in that their present incomes permit such a sacrifice. This highlights the difficulties facing countries with incomes which are very low, as the sacrifice which saving entails will not be possible if incomes are not far removed from subsistence levels. In fact a vicious circle operates, because the reason why incomes are low is that output per head is low, which in

turn may be largely attributed to a lack of fixed capital assets which help to raise productivity and thus the income per head of the population.

However, once this vicious circle is broken, it then becomes progressively easier to increase the stock of capital assets as higher incomes will make savings less of a sacrifice. This process will then be further assisted by the improved return which households can expect to receive on their savings.

Savings may be placed with a financial institution of some kind to earn a rate of interest, or perhaps take the form of contributions to pension funds or insurance companies, as a means of safeguarding the future standard of living of the saver or that of a beneficiary. Institutions which receive savings in various forms are the means by which the claims upon resources are channelled to organisations wishing to purchase fixed capital items.

The Price System and the Allocation of Capital Assets

Capital as a factor of production has so far been referred to in terms of real assets, but it is now necessary to relax this definition as a value must be given to such assets, and thus the value of resources allocated to their production. Capital will now therefore be used in the context of the money that must be raised to purchase items of real capital.

In the previous analysis of the price mechanism (pages 66–8), the claim which an organisation could place upon resources in factor markets was dependent upon the power which it derived from the market for its final output. The expanding firms in Group A became more profitable and this provided them with an incentive to expand output; to achieve this they required more factors of production and among them would be capital assets. Higher profits would allow them to increase their fixed assets from internal resources, as some profits could be saved for this purpose, and in the case of limited companies it would be possible to 'save' on behalf of shareholders by maintaining a certain level of undistributed profits. Not only will higher profits produce funds permitting capital expenditure on fixed assets, but will also make it easier for the company to raise capital from external sources. This is possible as the company is able to offer an attractive future return (i.e. price) for such funds in the form of a dividend or rate of interest, and the most profitable companies will thus be provided with a greater influence in

determining the allocation of capital assets. Producers of capital goods will in turn be susceptible to these pressures, and resources will move in favour of those items of capital required by the expanding companies. After all, it pays to produce not only what people wish to consume but also the plant and equipment to help meet changes in the pattern of consumer demand.

Subsequent sections will deal with how organisations acquire capital, as this is the means by which various parts of the UK economy expand and others may be obliged to reduce their claim upon those resources currently being allocated to the output of capital goods.

Internal Sources of Capital via Retained Profits

Retained funds within a company are the prime sources of finance for investment by firms in the UK. On the basis of the information in Table 5.4, these internal funds have accounted on average for about 70 per cent of companies' total sources of funds. The extent to which internal finance is available will depend on current and past levels of profits and on the levels of taxation and the dividend/retention policy of the firm. As far as company taxation is concerned, the company will seek to take advantage of tax allowances for investment in fixed capital and stock appreciation to reduce their tax liability. Where the payment of dividends and the retention of profits are concerned, a company has discretion (subject to the upper limits of government controls) over what dividends, if any, it pays to shareholders. The price of shares, however, is closely related to the expected flow of future dividends, and a failure to pay adequate regular dividends discourages the purchase of shares, thus creating problems when the company decides to raise fresh share capital. Share prices may then undervalue the company and render it liable to a take-over bid.

Retained profits form the major part of the company's internal source of funds and the information in Table 5.4 shows that they play an important part in financing the gross domestic fixed capital formation of companies. Share issues, however, fall a long way short of investment in fixed assets, to which a large part of total funds are allocated.

Profitability in companies is thus an important condition if investment is to take place in new plant and equipment. A high level of private investment occurs where there is confidence that it will be profitable and the massive investment in

Table 5.4: Sources and uses of funds of industrial and commercial companies, 1964–75 (£m)

	1970	1971	1972	1973	1974	1975
Sources of funds						
Gross income	8,779	9,975	11,468	15,496	19,274	18,122
Tax payments	−2,927	−3,179	−3,345	−3,533	−5,620	−4,320
Dividend payments	−810	−930	−933	−1,396	−1,517	−1,483
Interest payments	−1,238	−1,253	−1,448	−2,326	−3,299	−3,242
Total internal funds	3,804	4,613	5,742	8,241	8,838	9,077
Bank borrowing	1,126	732	2,988	4,504	4,411	700
Share issues	636	765	988	1,216	274	1,576
Total external funds	1,762	1,497	3,976	5,720	4,685	2,276
Total source of funds	5,566	6,110	9,718	13,961	13,523	11,353
Uses of funds						
Gross domestic fixed capital formation	3,354	3,470	3,796	4,718	5,848	7,028
Stocks	1,331	759	943	3,526	6,089	2,382
Acquisition of domestic financial assets	694	1,794	3,344	4,164	856	2,900
Net investment abroad	−474	−628	−70	−71	−703	−1,352
Other identified and unidentified assets	661	715	1,705	1,624	1,433	395
Total uses of funds	5,566	6,110	9,718	13,961	13,523	11,353

the development of North Sea Oil is a recent example. Low profitability reduces an important source of funds, discourages the investment of what has been accumulated in the past, and reduces a company's ability to borrow any additional funds.

Before the actual profitability of a company can be determined, however, an allowance must be made for the *depreciation* of fixed assets that would have occurred when output was being produced. This erosion of the value of fixed assets is in fact a cost even though it does not involve a cash outlay, but a financial provision must be made for this depreciation and the cost of replacing items of capital at inflated price levels. Similarly, account must be taken of stock appreciation which is a measure of the increased cost of maintaining stock levels when prices are rising. Thus some of the profit earned must be viewed as immediately absorbed in meeting the higher cost of replacement.

It has been estimated that the average real rate of return on capital employed by industrial and commercial companies in the UK (i.e. after stock appreciation and after charging capital consumption at replacement cost) has been falling recently as shown in Fig. 5.11 (p. 86). Even if companies consider that they possess or can secure adequate funds the eventual acquisition of fixed

assets will be largely influenced by the general economic environment in which they are likely to be operating, and their recent experience will have helped determine these expectations regarding potential rates of return. Mr. James Callaghan, in a speech in September 1976 when he was Prime Minister, recognised that the growth of internal funds for a period of time sufficient to create more buoyant business expectations is important for gross domestic fixed capital formation in the private sector. He said:

> The willingness of industry to invest in new plant and machinery requires not only that we overcome inflation but that industry is left with sufficient funds and sufficient confidence to make the new investment. When I say they must have sufficient funds, I mean that they must be able to earn a surplus which is a euphemism for saying that they must make a profit. Whether we live in a socialist economy, a mixed economy or a capitalistic economy ...

A report written by the CBI and submitted to the Committee to Review the Functioning of Financial Institutions, set up in January 1977, contained the following comments:

> Business thrives on profitability and confidence. Companies will invest more readily when the general economic and industrial outlook

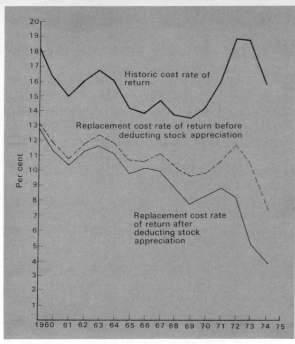

Fig. 5.11

appears settled and confidence is high, but will naturally be less inclined to do so when the prospects are less certain. With the experience of a period during which profit margins have been under severe strain and profitability has fallen well below target, and with many companies trading at a loss in real terms, it would be hardly surprising if companies were not cautious of committing themselves to ambitious investment programmes. If there is to be a sustained improvement in industrial investment in the UK then companies must be able markedly to improve their earnings.

In particular, the CBI was concerned about the need for greater stability and consistency in government policy. For example

> ... since 1950 there have been 33 changes in the form, rates or coverage of purchase tax or VAT and 19 changes in HP controls. Similarly, pay and price controls were introduced in 1966, ended in 1970, re-introduced in 1972, ended for pay in 1974, effectively re-introduced in 1975 and radically altered in mid 1977 ...

Companies operating in an inflationary climate cannot be sure what policies the government may introduce or about the level and scope of more direct intervention in business activities. Thus increased profits will not necessarily lead companies to acquire more fixed assets, as they must be confident that there is an acceptable degree of per-

manency associated with an increase in demand that will justify any long-term capital expenditure. At the same time they need to be convinced that profits are not to be eroded by a failure to control inflating costs and by higher company taxes and price controls.

Review of the Importance of Capital Investment
The reader may be either currently employed or considering a career in an organisation that utilises resources to produce capital goods which are then used to produce goods and services to meet consumer demand. The last sections have shown that this type of productive effort plays a vital role in maintaining living standards and over a period of time actually raises them. The acquisition of capital funds by firms and their transformation into real capital assets not only determines the future prosperity of firms themselves but also whether or not the economy remains largely underdeveloped or takes off into a period of sustained growth.

Fig. 5.12 highlights the problem facing an underdeveloped economy and the reader should attempt to reconstruct this illustration, but start with a *high* level of household income. This exercise will show how firms acting in their own interest can then add momentum to a 'virtuous circle of prosperity'.

External Sources of Finance
Table 5.4 shows external sources of funds divided between bank borrowing and share issues. The Committee to Review the Functioning of Financial Institutions was asked to determine the extent to which the investment plans of companies were inhibited by a shortage of external funds. The CBI asked a sample of industrial companies to give their opinion of the services provided by the banks and other financial institutions and in particular they sought the views of smaller firms which may have a greater need for external sources of finance. The CBI reported the results of their questionnaire: 'The clear conclusion of an overwhelming majority of our members is that it has not been a shortage of external finance that has restricted industrial investment but rather a lack of confidence that industry will be able to earn a sufficient return.'

Although the debate will doubtless continue, it would seem that the ability of companies to influence the allocation of resources in favour of the output of capital goods and their eventual acquisition by these companies, is not essentially restricted by a shortage of funds to supplement their internal sources. Personal savings as a percentage of total disposable income (i.e. after tax, national insurance, etc.) increased from 8·6 per cent in 1971 to 14·7 per cent in 1976—despite rapid inflation for much of this period that makes some forms of saving relatively less attractive.

It should be noted that the data provided in Table 5.4 concerning the levels and various sources of finance does not permit conclusions regarding the supply of funds for different purposes, as the total meets various needs. The pool of finance must provide working capital to finance, for example, stocks of raw materials, work in progress and goods awaiting sale. Funds will also be necessary for the acquisition of subsidiaries' financial assets, capital expenditure abroad, as well as the major items that make up gross domestic fixed capital formation.

The acquisition of joint stock capital

Although a large part of a company's fixed capital formation for expansion is financed from internal sources, the normal way in which joint stock companies supplement this is to issue shares or obtain loans by the issue of debentures. The company will first decide upon the total to be raised by debentures and preference shares and the total raised by ordinary shares. The eventual decision will depend upon how the company views its current 'gearing'—this is the ratio between the existing amount of preference shares and debentures and the amount of the ordinary shares. When the proportion of prior claimants (holders of preference shares and debentures) to equity capital (holders of ordinary shares) is high, the capital structure of the company is said to be high-geared. When this proportion is low, then the capital is low-geared. The capital gearing of the company is important from the point of view of the company itself and the potential investor.

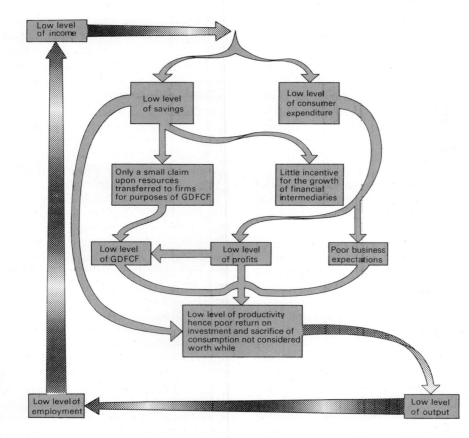

Fig. 5.12: The vicious circle of poverty

Table 5.5 depicts two companies: Company H is high-geared and Company L is low-geared, and this table can be used to show the implications for the more speculative investor holding ordinary shares.

Table 5.5

Company H

Distributed Profits	Payments on Debentures £100,000—6%	Payments on Preference shares £80,000—8%	Return on Ordinary shares £40,000 (%)
£14,000	£6,000	£6,400	4
£16,000	£6,000	£6,400	9
£18,000	£6,000	£6,400	14

Company L

Distributed Profits	Payments on Debentures £40,000—6%	Payments on Preference shares £30,000—8%	Return on Ordinary shares £150,000 (%)
£14,000	£2,400	£2,400	6·1
£16,000	£2,400	£2,400	7·4
£18,000	£2,400	£2,400	8·8

Company H

As the level of distributed profits increases ordinary shareholders will experience a substantial increase in their return because of the fixed nature of the payments made to holders of debentures and preference shares. The increased profits that remain after the prior claimants have been paid is distributed among a relatively small quantity of ordinary shares. The nature of the risk involved, however, is that at one period their dividend was as low as 4 per cent but they received 14 per cent when distributed profits increased. Such a high-geared company will be an attractive investment during a period of rapid growth and general prosperity, but less so if there is a recession in business activity. Company H will find it easier to raise additional funds from the issue of ordinary shares with this dividend record and avoid issues with fixed payments. In doing this, however, it will have to take account of the effect upon its original high gearing, which initially gave rise to the high dividends as profits increased. But in a period of very low profits it may find its fixed payments a heavy burden which may create financial difficulties as well as making it less attractive to potential holders of ordinary shares.

Company L

From the point of view of investors, this company does not offer substantial increases in dividends to ordinary shareholders when profits are growing, but this is compensated by the greater security provided when there is a downturn in profits. Dividends fluctuate from approximately 6·1 per cent to 8·8 per cent. This record during a period of expansion may make it a less attractive proposition if it is competing for capital with high-geared companies. As profitability falls, however, it will find fixed payments less of a problem compared with Company H, as well as making it a more secure investment for ordinary shareholders.

The different capital gearings will also influence the scope which exists for retaining profits for self-financing additional fixed capital assets, as dividend payments that prove acceptable to investors may act as a constraint. What actually constitutes an acceptable gearing to a company will vary according to such matters as its current and expected financial position.

The New Issue Market

There are various methods by which companies can place new issues of shares so that those seeking to raise capital in this manner are brought into contact with those individuals and institutions that are willing to supply capital.

1. *Invitation by Prospectus.* In this the company deals direct with the public and details of the issue are sent to potential investors via their banks and stockbrokers. The information is contained in a prospectus which must conform with the Companies Act 1948 requiring the disclosure of certain factual information regarding the company's activities, and stating the minimum level of capital that needs to be subscribed by the public when shares are taken up in order for the venture to be viable. Failure to raise this minimum sum implies that the company would not be able to pursue its project and existing subscriptions to the issue would have to be refunded. Companies can avoid this by arranging for the issue to be underwritten by financial institutions which receive a commission, but the underwriters are then obliged to buy shares in the event of the subscribed capital falling short of the minimum required by the prospectus. Dealing directly with the public in this way can prove a very costly operation, and the costs are likely to be disproportionately high for small companies. Companies may also use the service of an **Issuing House** which is an institution that

specialises in making issues to the public on behalf of public limited companies. Issuing Houses tend to specialise in certain types of issues and may use their own funds to underwrite some of the issue.

2. *Offer for Sale*. This method involves the sale of the complete issue to Issuing Houses, stockbrokers or other financial institutions who then sell the issue to the public at a higher price through an 'offer for sale'. The original prospectus must still provide information regarding the company's activities and the minimum subscription necessary to make the venture viable. Again the issue will be underwritten to avoid this possibility of raising insufficient external capital. This means of financing is particularly suitable for companies which are too small to warrant a quotation on the Stock Exchange.

3. *A Stock Exchange Placing*. This is another method of obtaining capital that is suitable for small companies. A stock exchange introduction is arranged in co-operation with institutions such as insurance and investment trust companies, who agree to purchase a block of the shares. Issuing Houses and stockbrokers may be involved in an arrangement whereby they 'place' their purchases with clients.

4. *A Rights Issue*. This may prove the least costly method of raising finance for those companies that have existing shareholders. Intermediaries and other fees are avoided as direct contact is made with shareholders who are given the 'right' to take up new shares. Shares will be offered in proportion to their existing holdings and this option may be made on favourable terms. Shareholders may then sell their allotted quota if they wish.

The Stock Exchange

Individuals and institutions are willing to purchase the wide variety of securities being offered by organisations in the knowledge that their holdings of such assets can readily be turned into cash, and then perhaps used to alter their portfolios of investments. If investment in the private and public sector of the economy involved a complete loss of liquidity because of shareholdings or cash was required before loan capital was repaid, then few people would be prepared to part with their money in this way. The Stock Exchange therefore fulfills a valuable role in that it increases the liquidity of claims on the government and companies by providing a market in which existing securities can be bought and sold. In 1980 there were nearly 6 million transactions in securities listed on the Stock Exchange and their total value was approximately £200,000 million and some 75 per cent of this total was in central government securities—the 'gilt-edged' market.

The Stock Exchange and the Allocation of Capital

It is the buying and selling of existing securities on the Stock Exchange which produces security prices, and hence rates of interest or yields. These transactions help to allocate new funds into various parts of the economy where they can be employed most efficiently in terms of supplying organisations that are seeking to expand to meet a growing demand. The current prices of their own and similar securities, as determined by the forces of demand and supply on the Stock Exchange, will indicate to potential borrowers the prospects of increasing their capital from external sources by new issues of securities. This is because changes in the relative prices of securities will determine the rate of interest or yield associated with them. If, for example, a listed company is particularly profitable in that it is benefiting from an increase in the demand for its output, its security prices will be attractive from the point of view of investors. This is not only from the point of view of the prospective dividend payments, but also the possibility of a capital gain in the future as security prices increase. The pressure of demand will eventually lead to a rise in the price of such securities to reflect the underlying strength of the company, and dividend payments—when measured against the current value of the securities—will reflect a fall in the rate of interest. The same results will be produced where securities representing loan capital are concerned. These developments will allow the company to secure additional capital on favourable terms, as expectations about its future prospects will make it attractive to potential investors.

In the case of a company competing in the same line of output but losing ground to its competitors as demand for its output falls, the price of its securities will fall as investors sell in anticipation of low dividends. Such security prices may need to fall to very low levels until their anticipated yield produces a rate of interest that proves acceptable to new holders. A company in this situation will find it increasingly difficult to raise external funds, as potential investors will need to receive a much higher return to compensate for the greater risk associated with the company's future prospects when compared with the more buoyant expectations surrounding the more successful companies.

Security prices will not only reflect the relative profitability of companies in the same industry but also reflect the situation in different industries and affect their ability to raise funds accordingly. If dealings in securities are the result of a rational consideration of the real prospects of a company, then, after allowing for the degree of risk involved, share prices will produce interest rates which perform the function of a price mechanism in allocating savings in the capital market as a whole into the most profitable uses. If relative profits, and hence return on capital, are a reflection of the changing pattern of consumer demand then the more profitable companies involved will be able to exert a greater influence in acquiring items of fixed capital when compared with the less profitable firms in the same industry. Similarly, the relative profitability of industries themselves will be operating to determine the broader allocation of capital as a factor of production. The re-allocation of resources should come to an end when what are regarded as 'normal' profits are established in those parts of the economy originally affected by the change in the relative strength of consumer demand. It is the price mechanism which contributes to the eventual mobility of capital in that it produces not only a re-allocation of capital funds but also a change in the nature of the overall capital stock.

The Stock Exchange plays an equally important part in providing liquidity to holders of public sector securities, particularly for those who hold very long-term or irredeemable stock. The buying and selling will produce prices for various types of government securities. This will indicate the rates of interest which the government will have to pay on new issues of various periods of maturity if it is to raise funds to repay securities that are maturing, or cover additional expenditure. Similarly local authorities will be aware of the likely cost of raising finance for their activities.

The Stock Exchange and the Acquisition of New Capital

The Stock Exchange also helps to raise new capital for industry, commerce and the public sector. This includes the large number of limited liability companies whose shares and other securities are listed on the Stock Exchange. Of about 16,000 public companies in the UK at the end of 1980 some 3000 were listed on the Stock Exchange. A public company does not have to make a public issue of securities but it has the right to do so if it wishes. An application for a listing will not normally be considered unless the expected (initial capital) market value of the company's securities is at least £500,000, and the expected market value of any one security for which quotation is sought is at least £200,000. The company is required to make available to the market a portion of the securities which are to be listed. In general, at least 35 per cent of the ordinary shares must be made available to the public while the proportion for the fixed interest securities is 30 per cent. The Stock Exchange also maintains strict regulations regarding the details contained in the company's prospectus whenever securities are offered to the public. In 1980 the total new issues on the Stock Exchange, excluding central government securities and those guaranteed by the government, amounted to about £2,000 million, of which just over £900 million was for listed companies, and virtually all of this was in ordinary shares.

Government financial support of industry

The government not only hopes to create an economic climate conducive to investment by the private sector but also to provide financial assistance with various types of investment projects. Thus the total pool of finance available to a company can be supplemented by taking advantage of government measures, changes in which could influence the funds available to a company. The main forms of government support have taken the form of:

(a) the tax allowance for investment in plant and machinery;

(b) assistance under Section 8 of the Industry Act 1972;

(c) finance from the National Enterprise Board;

(d) the assisted areas scheme, including Regional Development Grants, Regional Selective Financial Assistance (under Section 7 of the Industry Act 1972), the Scottish and Welsh Development Agencies, the provision of factory buildings through the English Industrial Estates Corporation, special assistance to industry in Northern Ireland, the Northern Ireland Development Agency;

(e) government support for research and product innovation, via, for example, the National Research Development Council. There is also the Development Commission and the Council for Small Industries in Rural Areas.

Capital expenditure in the public sector

Public Corporations

In 1980 capital funds available to public corporations amounted to £7,657 million of which approximately 43 per cent was borrowed. The largest single source of external finance was borrowing from the central government which totalled £3,358 million. Borrowing from banks and other financial institutions abroad was at one time a common feature of public corporations. For example, the British Gas Corporation raised 40 million dollars in 1976 by issuing securities abroad, the British Steel Corporation has received loans from the European Investment Bank, and the British National Oil Corporation also raises funds from overseas sources. This was in accordance with the government's aim that this part of the public sector reduce its demand upon domestic savings. The total borrowing from abroad in 1976 amounted to over £1,800 million.

The more commercial approach to the nationalised industries in recent years requires that they reduce their reliance upon the exchequer for funds, and are increasingly expected to earn a return which allows them to finance a larger part of their capital expenditure from their own sources. As with the private sector, some funds are of a short-term nature to finance stocks and work in progress but in 1980 the gross domestic fixed capital formation by public corporations was £7,657 million.

Local Authorities

In 1980 these authorities obtained capital funds totalling £4,680 million, of which approximately 65 per cent was borrowed. They borrowed £1,300 million from the central government, while a further £1,795 million was in the form of advances from banks, sales of local authority bills of exchange, and the issue of other securities with varying periods of maturity. Their combined domestic fixed capital formation was nearly £4,000 million.

Central Government

The gross domestic capital formation by the central government in 1980 was £1,679 million,

but in addition assistance was also provided in the way of various grants and loans to local authorities, public corporations and companies in the private sector for the purposes of financing fixed assets. The central government, therefore, is obliged to borrow not only to finance its own capital expenditure, but also some of that undertaken elsewhere in both the public and private sectors, and in 1980 the borrowing requirement was £11,156 million. However, when the borrowing by local authorities and public corporations from sources other than the central government is added, the total public sector borrowing requirement in 1980 was just over £12,200 million. Of this total less than 8 per cent was financed directly from overseas sources. The total public borrowing requirement has increased in recent years, as the central government's sources of revenue have not even covered its current expenditure over a year as a whole.

Short-term finance is obtained by the central government by the monthly issue of treasury bills which are purchased largely by the discount houses. As with local authorities, however, the vast majority of this borrowing—some 80 per cent—is financed by the sale of longer-term securities of various periods of maturity. Thus the activities of the government at both central and local level leads to the issue of securities in the form of stocks, whereby the loan to these authorities is for a fixed period and at a fixed rate of interest. These are known as 'gilt edged' as they carry a minimum risk regarding the payment of interest and repayment when they mature.

In 1980 the issue of government and government-guaranteed securities produced over £10,692 million, while some £3,600 million of existing securities were redeemed. For example, one such issue in that year was '15 per cent Treasury Stock 1985' which means that the stock will be redeemed in 1985 and until then the holder receives a fixed rate of interest over this period of 15 per cent per annum. Government stocks are issued in units of £100 and this rate of interest will be paid regardless of the price paid by the current holder, as it is paid on the nominal value of the stock. If, for example, the stock is bought at a price which amounts to £90 a unit, the actual rate of interest received by the new holder will be approximately 16·6 per cent i.e. $\frac{15}{90} \times \frac{100}{1}$ in addition to the capital gain received when each unit matures at its value of £100.

Over the years, as the extent of government involvement in both the public and private sector increases, the government has found it necessary to raise large sums of money to finance its activities. Thus securities must be issued to repay not only those that are maturing, but also to finance the additional creation of capital assets in social services, and to provide assistance to public corporation as well as to some companies in the private sector. This results from the fact that taxes would have to be raised to very high levels if the total revenue was to cover all such expenditure. Rather than forcing the community to 'save' by imposing higher taxes, the government competes for voluntary savings with other sectors of the economy.

This expenditure in excess of revenue has given rise to what is known as the National Debt. Interest has to be paid on it, but it does mean that in future years those that benefit from the services resulting from current gross domestic capital formation do make a contribution to the cost. The alternative would be to impose the entire burden of such capital expenditure on present-day taxpayers, rather than future beneficiaries of such services. Moreover, if living standards steadily improve, the future burden of taxes is correspondingly lessened. This is because the creation of more wealth in the economy will allow the government to acquire a claim upon resources via taxes, while still leaving individuals with a higher disposable income. By 1980 the National Debt had reached over 100,000 million.

The capital market

The previous sections have shown that both the private and public sector need to supplement their own sources of funds from a wide variety of external sources. There is thus a demand for medium- and long-term funds, but until a source of supply exists a market cannot be established. A capital market does, however, operate in that a supply of loanable funds is forthcoming from institutions which, along with individuals, are prepared to purchase shares, debentures and stocks in exchange for cash. It is difficult to draw a clear line and stipulate that certain individuals and institutions are part of the supply of this capital market. This is because savings may be channelled through more than one institution before they are actually exchanged for a financial asset that permits an organisation to influence the use of resources in favour of producing the capital goods which they

Table 5.6: Distribution of shareholdings by category of registered and beneficial holder, 31 December 1975

	£m	%
Persons	17,047	38·3
Charities and other non-profit-making bodies serving persons	925	2·1
Stockbrokers and jobbers	134	0·3
Banks	300	0·7
Insurance companies	6,911	15·5
Pension funds	7,261	16·3
Investment Trust companies	3,033	6·8
Unit Trusts	1,857	4·2
Other financial companies	1,064	2·4
Non-financial companies	1,823	4·1
Public sector	1,585	3·6
Overseas sector	2,620	5·9
	£44,560	100

require to expand their activities. Apart from those savers who maintain their funds in cash or items which they regard as 'investments', such as paintings and other works of art, the remainder—knowingly or not—will be contributing to the supply of funds on to the capital market. Table 5.6 shows the distribution of shares as at 31 December 1975 between the main categories of shareholders, and it will be noted that the major beneficiaries are those to which a large part of the community make a contribution.

Compared with the position in 1963, there has been a fall in the proportion of shares owned directly by individuals, from 54 per cent to 38·3 per cent. This has largely been balanced by increases in the holdings of insurance companies, pension funds and unit trusts which rose by 6 per cent, 10 per cent, and 3 per cent respectively over the same period. The table also shows that non-financial companies themselves may use some of their undistributed profits to invest in other companies. The reader will by now be familiar with the majority of the institutions listed in Table 5.6. The various financial intermediaries and other suppliers of funds also include: investment trust companies, unit trusts, finance companies, Finance for Industry (owned by the English and Scottish Clearing Banks and the Bank of England), Equity Capital for Industry Ltd. (ECI), the public sector, and the National Savings Bank and Trustee Savings Bank.

Government Influence in the Capital Market

As with many other markets in a mixed economy, there is a degree of intervention on the part of the government in the capital market. Because of a combination of political, economic and social motives the government has sought through some of the institutions just mentioned to channel funds into certain areas of economic activity. These firms and industries would not, by the workings of free market forces, necessarily have attracted capital in the amounts and on the terms which the government considered necessary in the light of its overall political, economic and social strategy.

These government motives include supporting industries which it believes play a strategic role in the economy and whose decline through a shortage of immediate financial assistance threatens their long-term future. The government will take a much longer-term view of the situation than the capital market is probably prepared to do. The government approach will be reinforced if such industries provide a major source of employment in Development Areas, or overall unemployment in the economy in increasing. Thus the pursuit of certain non-commercial objectives, which has been a recurring feature of the running of nationalised industries, is now given expression via financial assistance in the *private* sector. However, the government may eventually be obliged to strike an acceptable balance between these strictly non-commercial policies and the need to rationalise an industry if it is eventually to survive as a viable concern without the need for continuing government support. The government has also been made increasingly aware of the value of small firms to the economy and the possibility that their future may be inhibited by a lack of finance for further growth. Whether this is the problem, or whether their growth requires an easing of taxation and other government policies which may have a disproportionately large impact upon small firms, is a continuing debate.

Finally, there is the importance of government expenditure itself which makes a very substantial demand upon the nation's savings. The government's ability to raise funds is not necessarily impaired by relatively high rates of interest and may thus command a very substantial influence over the acquisition of real capital. The creation of social capital makes a very important contribution to general welfare, but a growing debate surrounds the extent to which such a command of scarce resources may be partly at the expense of the manufacturing sector in particular.

The acquisition of raw materials and commodity markets

In the 1970s there was an increased degree of uncertainty at various times concerning the labour costs which a company was likely to incur because of periods of rapid wage inflation. Raw material prices, however, have often been subject to volatile and wide fluctuations in their prices. Unlike other costs, however, they have moved in both directions. Changes in the prices of commodities (used here as the collective description for a wide range of raw materials and basic foodstuffs) will affect the costs of production—and hence the final prices—of a wide range of products, depending upon the percentage of total costs accounted for by these commodities. A rise in these costs will not only have a direct impact on prices but the resulting rise in the cost of living will provoke wage claims which, if not offset by a rise in productivity, will add further to the momentum of inflation.

World Food Prices

Fig. 5.13 (p. 94) shows that the world price of some important foodstuffs and beverages on commodity markets fluctuated a great deal during the relatively short period of time covered. On the assumption that the developed part of the world exerts the greatest influence upon the demand for these products, and the demand for them does not alter significantly with changes in household income, the conclusion can be drawn that changes in such prices were essentially due to factors operating on the supply side.

Many agricultural products are susceptible to large and unplanned changes in total supply because of such factors as weather conditions, crop diseases or political disturbances. A brief analysis of the foodstuffs in Fig. 5.13 will help to illustrate the importance of these various factors.

(i) *Sugar* The meteoric rise in the price of sugar in 1973–4 was due to the exceptionally poor beet crop in Western Europe because of poor weather, leading to a very strong demand for cane sugar. Recovery in output was such that in 1977 it was estimated that stocks amounted to about 25 per cent of annual output.

(ii) *Wheat* In 1976 world wheat production was above the previous record year of 1973 which led to a marked fall in price. Advances in agricultural techniques contributed to a long-term rise in productivity. Many producing countries control both output and prices.

(iii) *Maize* The exceptional crop in the USA—a major producer of the maize—in 1976 placed a downward pressure on prices. Maize is an important feed requirement for livestock but

Fig. 5.13: Prices of selected commodities   *Index numbers in $ terms 1968–70=100*

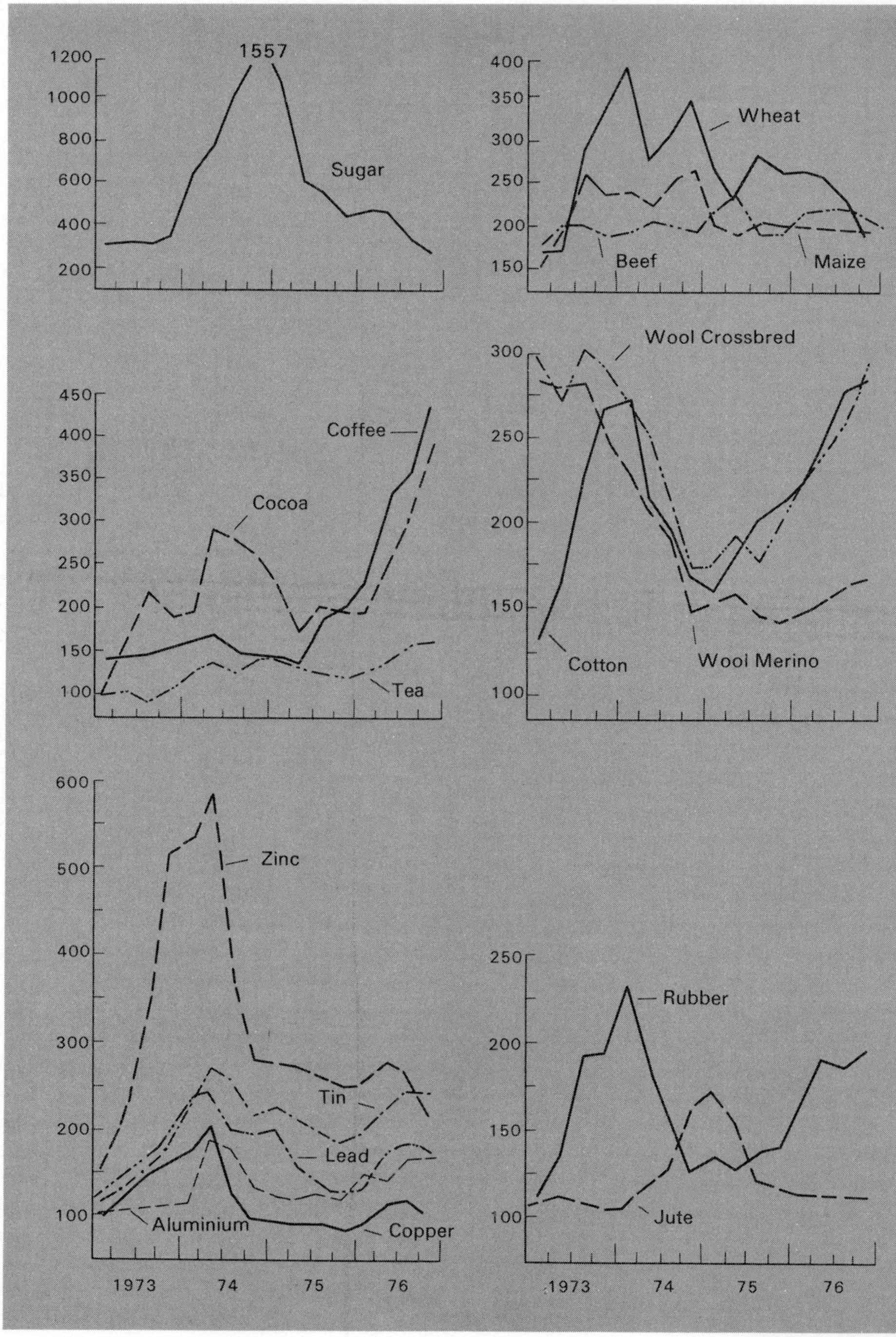

the demand slackened in 1976 due to the enforced slaughtering of animals through widespread drought.

(iv) *Beef* The supply of beef may be expanded by increased slaughtering because of higher feed prices, or because of drought, or by exceptionally large supplies from Argentina.

(v) *Coffee* The price increases in 1975 were caused by frost which damaged or destroyed 75 per cent of Brazil's coffee trees, by severe flooding in Columbia and by the civil war in Angola.

(vi) *Cocoa* The original price rise was connected with speculative buying. The output of cocoa actually fell in 1976 and this then kept prices at a relatively high level.

(vii) *Tea* Tea drinking has been declining continuously in the UK which is the largest market. Tea prices improved in 1976 because of adverse conditions in India and Sri-Lanka and the rise in the price of coffee also stimulated the demand for tea.

The EEC and the Prices of Agricultural Products

The previous examples serve to indicate the factors which can exert an influence upon some important commodity prices. Some price movements can be of a purely speculative nature and to some extent companies in the UK buying products covered by the Common Agricultural Policy are not necessarily affected by movements in world prices. If the world price of an agricultural product is lower than the EEC price, a company will have to pay an import levy on the same product from a non-EEC country. Similarly, if world prices increase, a tax is placed on the export of the product concerned and greater availability of the product at a lower price can ease the situation. This also provides the authorities with an opportunity for reducing those stocks acquired during previous years.

If there is a long-term tendency for world food prices to increase, both consumers and producers in the EEC will be sheltered from these effects to some extent, as guaranteed prices can help maintain agricultural output and export taxes will prevent their supply on to the world market when a higher price could otherwise be achieved. If, however, the relative decline in world food prices—which has been a trend over many years—continues, the level of guaranteed prices in the EEC may again exceed those on free markets in the rest of the world. Thus companies in the UK do not necessarily operate in a free market

when purchasing many items of foodstuffs. Intervention prices exist whereby the EEC authorities maintain demand at the guaranteed price by purchasing for stocks rather than allowing an excess supply to depress prices. As far as the market mechanism is concerned, this may allow the least efficient producers to survive and perhaps encourage overproduction, particularly if the guaranteed price is kept too high.

Commodity Agreements

Companies will be affected by world price movements for agricultural products not grown in the EEC. Here again free market forces may be subject to a degree of intervention. The long-term improvements in productivity may have operated to prevent an increase in the average price of coffee, cocoa and tea over a number of years. When there is a stable consumption, producing countries relying heavily upon these products can expect no significant increase in their export earnings while the prices of their imports of manufactures continue to rise. Producing countries, therefore, are increasingly forming Commodity Agreements such as that relating to coffee, whereby producers in the member countries are obliged to export via their respective government agencies at a fixed price. These agreements can help to keep prices above their free market price, but the temptation always exists for some members to leave the agreement in the knowledge that they can sell much larger quantities if they were to undercut the agreed price. Even if the agreements hold, there is the problem of allocating both production and sales quotas for member countries. Political differences between producing countries may also inhibit their formation, but developing countries may be encouraged by the success which OPEC achieved in manipulating oil prices.

Other Commodities

As far as the prices of natural fibres and metal ores are concerned, the market demand is largely influenced by the level of industrial activity in the consuming countries. The demand for natural fibres can also be influenced by changes in tastes and preferences, the weather affecting output and the prices of synthetics. Table 5.7 shows that in 1972–3 there was a marked increase in the level of industrial output in manufacturing economies and this placed a very large demand upon important commodities whose supply cannot respond in the short run because of the conditions surround-

Table 5.7: Industrial production (excluding construction)

Index numbers 1970=100

	EEC[1]	Canada	United States	Japan
1971	102	105·6	102·0	102·3
1972	106	113·0	111·0	110·2
1973	115	123·5	120·4	127·4
1974	115	127·4	119·9	123·5
1975	108	121·3	109·3	110·4
1976	115	127·4	120·4	125·4

[1] Excluding Denmark.

ing growing or extraction. Some pressure may be eased initially by sales from stockpiles but a large upturn in world demand can soon exhaust these. A recession in industrial output occurred in 1975, whereas 1976 saw a moderate recovery to 1974 levels and this is reflected in the prices of certain commodities.

(i) *Cotton*   The USA is the dominant producer and influences the supply side of the market, while higher incomes and tastes and preferences influence demand. Cotton has for many years been less competitive than man-made fibres but it was helped by the rise in the price of oil which also increased the costs of producing synthetic fibres.

(ii) *Wool*   Prices are very much influenced by the availability of supplies from Australia and the extent to which government agencies are prepared to release stocks to moderate price rises. As with cotton, wool has increasingly been losing ground to synthetics and price rises may reduce demand in the long run, though preferences may be moving in favour of wool as a textile. The later period in Fig. 5.13 shows that wool prices were influenced by the European drought but the world price was moderated to a certain extent by the devaluation of the Australian dollar.

(iii) *Jute*   Increased control over output by producing countries led to a price rise in 1974 but this soon fell back to a lower level because of increased penetration by synthetics into jute's main market of carpet-backing and upholstery.

(iv) *Rubber*   The output of rubber and metal ores is not susceptible to such large unplanned fluctuations in output, and therefore prices are more strongly influenced by changes in the demand from industrial countries which in the case of rubber is in turn affected by the prices of synthetics.

(v) *Metals*   All the metals show a similar movement closely correlated with the level of industrial demand in consuming countries. Commodity Agreements exist for many metals while in other areas the US can exert a large influence upon prices by the accumulation or release of its very large stocks of essential metals.

Spot and Future Markets

Although some large manufacturers have expanded vertically to secure the sources of supply of essential raw materials many manufacturers and independent suppliers of raw materials can be susceptible to the vagaries of commodity price fluctuations.

Markets which deal with commodities for immediate delivery are known as spot markets. Future markets, however, deal with commodities that are bought and sold but scheduled for delivery some months in the future. Future markets play an important role for both producers and users in that by stabilizing the prices of commodities they allow revenues and costs to be estimated with greater confidence, and future transactions alleviate the immediate impact of price changes upon their current positions. Production by suppliers, and manufacturing output using commodities, can then be adjusted in the light of new commodity prices, and futures will continue to play their part because of the unpredictability of these prices. Future markets are a form of insurance, and as with insurance the purpose is to mitigate losses rather than make a profit for the parties involved in commodity deals. This is illustrated in the following examples.

Producers

A cotton grower knows that his cotton will be available for sale in, say, September and he can either sell his crop at the ruling spot or hold on to it in anticipation of a favourable movement in prices at a later date. This, however, is a very risky business and he will also have the costs associated with the cotton crop which he must meet.

The cotton producer, however, can be expected to spread such risks by relating his revenue to prices over a period of time which, by balancing each other out, can provide a more secure revenue. When growing his cotton, he will wish to insure against the risk of a slump in the spot price when he needs to sell cotton in September. He may enter into contracts in May to sell at an agreed price a quantity of cotton which he considers will be the anticipated size of his crop (or at least a sizeable part of it) for delivery in December. If, when the crop is available for sale in September, the spot price has fallen, he can then buy back his futures relating to his December contracts at this low spot price. He has regained the ownership of cotton and made a profit on the transaction which will help compensate for the lower price when the crop is sold in September. He has thus used the futures market to 'hedge' against a price fall. If, however, the spot price in September had risen, he would not have made a profit when buying back his futures, but he will not suffer from lower prices when the crop is actually sold in September.

Buyers

The manufacturer using raw materials will similarly 'hedge' against a price rise when planning output of his final products. If a textile manufacturer purchases vast stocks of cotton to cover a very long period of time this will tie up a great deal of capital, even though he may feel secure against price rises. If, however, raw material prices fall, this will make his competitors—perhaps buying at a later date—more competitive in terms of the prices they can charge for the same textile products. The appreciation of stocks because of price rises can also be subject to company taxation.

A manufacturer can purchase cotton in May at the spot price for immediate delivery, in order to maintain output of cotton textiles expected to be put on to the market in the later period. He can also sell cotton futures for delivery at about the same time. If the spot price of cotton as a raw material falls, when he sells his cotton textiles he will receive a lower price than the one upon which his estimate of profits was made. He has, however, the futures which he can buy back at the current spot price, and the profit on this transaction will help compensate for the loss on the sale of cotton textiles. Had the spot price of cotton increased, then he would have received a higher-than-anticipated profit on his sales. But he is committed to selling cotton on his futures, which he must meet by buying cotton at the higher spot price for sale

at the lower price governed by the futures contract into which he had entered. This loss of futures will offset the gain on textiles sales.

Speculators and Commodity Markets

Futures markets are thus a means of reducing risk, and this will encourage both producers and users to engage in their respective activities and produce more stable prices and output for consumers of final products. A ready market exists for futures in that there are dealers in the markets who are prepared to use their financial resources to buy and sell with a view to making a profit. There will always be users prepared to buy a futures contract that promises a certain quantity in the near future, and the dealer hopes to make a profit for himself on the transaction. Similarly, they may be prepared to buy futures from those seeking a more immediate revenue or 'hedging' operation. These dealers hope to make a speculative gain and such activities can help to stabilise prices.

This stabilising effect occurs to the extent that speculators will buy futures when prices are falling in the hope of selling at a higher price in a later period, while being prepared to sell when prices are rising in the hope of buying back at a lower price in a later period. Such buying and selling activities will moderate price rises and falls. The skill of the speculator depends heavily upon what is considered to be a realistic price for the commodity after taking account of developments in both the demand and supply aspects of the market. Ill-founded speculation can lead to unjustified price fluctuations, but the final situation will be determined by the buying pressure and supplies coming on to the market both in the current situation and in the future. After a period of unstable prices the market prices will again reflect the real market situation.

The analysis of the fluctuations in Fig. 5.13 has sought to demonstrate the importance of fundamental market forces rather than those of a purely speculative nature caused by individuals with no interest in the physical properties of the commodities involved.

6. The Legal Implications of an Organisation's Use of its Resources

Land

The Crown is the owner of all land in this country. As far as individuals or business organisations are concerned, their only claim to ownership is in the form of a **legal estate**. The estate measures what interest an individual has in a particular piece of land, i.e. for how long is the land held?

The law relating to land based on the old feudal system introduced by William the Conqueror had become extremely complicated. Therefore in order to rationalise the whole process of land administration, conveyance and succession, several Acts were passed in 1925, notably the Law of Property Act 1925.

Freehold Land

The Law of Property Act 1925 reduced the number of legal estates which can exist over land to two:

1. a fee simple absolute in possession;
2. a term of years absolute.

A fee simple absolute in possession is **freehold land**. This rather technical term can be broken down:

(a) fee simple—this means that the estate is capable of inheritance to the general heirs of the grantee.
(b) absolute—this signifies that the grant will continue for ever.
(c) possession—the owner is entitled to immediate possession of the land. The meaning of possession also includes any rents and profits that may accrue to the land.

The owner of freehold land is in complete control, including the space above and below the property. There is no danger of eviction from the land unless the owner fails to make the repayments on a mortgage, or the land is compulsorily purchased by the government or a local authority.

There are other constraints and restrictions on the use of freehold property. There are controls exercised through local authorities which necessitate planning permission for most development. Various statutory controls prevent the owner of property from creating a nuisance or causing pollution. There are also remedies in common law for victims of acts which constitute a nuisance. The use of freehold land may be further constrained by the sale agreement which includes restrictive covenants.

Leasehold Land

As a result of the legislation of 1925, the only legal estate in land other than the fee simple absolute is the term of years absolute—**leasehold land**. A lease is a document which entitles the owner to an interest in land for a fixed duration of time. A **lessor** is the person who grants a lease to the **lessee** and he retains a right of reversion. A lease is often interchangeable with 'tenancy', although the latter relates to short-term interest whereas a lease is longer term.

The creation of a lease

A major feature of any lease is that it creates an agreement between the landlord and tenant. It also enables the tenant to exclude all others from the premises. A lease is usually created under seal, which means that all the terms of the contract are in writing. Leases for less than three years have to be in writing to be enforceable. If a lease did not fulfil the above requirements it was regarded as void at common law. **Equity** (natural justice), however, takes a different view and in some cases will insist that the lessor executes a proper lease. If a tenant registers the agreement under the Law of Property Act 1925, then all subsequent purchasers of the legal estate are deemed to have notice of the lease and the written lease will now be as virtually secure as an actual lease. This remedies the defect in equitable leases which meant that third parties purchasing the estate without notice of the estate could turn out the lessees.

Types of leases

Leases can be made for any fixed period of time

as long as this is clear before the lease is signed. The lease generally automatically terminates when the fixed period expires.

A yearly tenancy can be created which none the less carries on indefinitely until the party either terminates through proper notice, dies or assigns his share of the interest. A yearly tenancy will be created impliedly in those circumstances where the lessee is in possession lawfully of the land, and rent is assessed on a yearly basis. Such tenancies can be determined by mutual agreement or, in the absence of this, by half-yearly notice. Tenancies of other lengths, e.g. weekly or monthly, can be created in the same way, either by express or implied agreement, the difference being that notice of termination is the length of the tenancy period and not a half period.

A **tenancy at will** is where permission is given to the tenant to occupy property and the arrangement is that either party can terminate the tenancy by giving notice. If no agreement is reached as to the payment of rent, but rent is paid on a regular basis, then the tenancy becomes a periodic tenancy in line with the intervals between rent payment.

Where a tenant remains in possession of the land after his lease has expired, against the landlord's will, then this is known as a **tenancy at sufferance**. The tenant is not exactly a trespasser because he had the basic right to come into the land in the first place. The landlord can give notice to quit at any time, and the tenant will have to pay compensation in the form of mesne profits, which is calculated at double the annual rent or land value.

Implied duties of a landlord and tenant
In the majority of cases the lease will contain a number of express duties which govern the relationship between the landlord and tenant, but the courts also recognise a number of implied duties.

The main duties of the landlord are that he must ensure that the tenant gets 'quiet enjoyment' of the land, and that the landlord will not commit nuisances, i.e. using the neighbouring premises in an unreasonable manner, continually entering the land and interfering with the tenant's enjoyment of his land.

The tenant also has a number of implied duties, which are usually incorporated within the lease. The major duties are that the tenant must pay his rent and any rates which accrue. Also he must not use the property in a way which will damage the reversionary interest.

Determination of tenancies
There are many ways in which a lease can be terminated and the principal means will be dealt with briefly:

1. *Expiration of time* This automatically determines the lease, but certain statutory provisions (discussed later) may give the tenant security of tenure.

2. Yearly, weekly, monthly and other periodic tenancies can be determined by notice, subject to a tenant's statutory protection, as we have already seen. Leases for fixed periods cannot be terminated by notice, but the agreement will often contain an express provision allowing for termination after a set number of years.

3. *Forfeiture* Most leases will contain an express number of conditions or covenants, the breach of which may lead to the lease's forfeiture. The most common covenants will be: the duty to pay the rent, not assign or sub-let, to take out insurance, or to make repairs. Forfeiture will be granted if there is a serious breach of the tenancy agreement, but the courts will normally not grant repossession unless the tenant has received a solicitor's letter pointing out the defect in the operation of his tenancy and giving the tenant opportunity to correct the breach. With regard to rent arrears, no notice has to be served and possession can be applied for from the court immediately. This will usually be granted unless the tenant has paid all arrears before the court hearing. At any court hearing consideration is taken of the general conduct of a tenant. A tenant persistently in breach of his agreement will be made to forfeit the tenancy.

There may be occasions where the owner of the premises simply requires the premises back from the tenant for his own use. A **notice to quit** can be served according to the length of notice specified in the agreement. But unlike forfeiture, the serving of such a notice merely brings the contract of tenancy to an end, but the tenant is entitled to retain possession. A proper notice of eviction has to be served giving the tenant at least six months' continuing residency, and requesting the tenant to state within two months whether he is going to vacate the premises voluntarily. If the notice to quit is challenged, then the court will have to approve or disapprove the tenancy. A new tenancy will be granted unless the owner can convince the court otherwise. There are several grounds: that the tenant has not maintained the tenancy under the terms of his agreement, that he has persistently failed to pay the rent, or that there have been serious breaches in his obligations.

The courts will also accept that the owner may wish to use the premises for business himself. Also, a case may be made that where a tenant is letting only part of a building, dispersal of the whole of the building is a better financial arrangement for the owner. The court will also be keen to see that reasonable alternative accommodation has been offered to the tenant. In any event, compensation will be payable in all cases other than breaches of the tenancy agreement. A tenant may, in some circumstances, be able to prevent any prospective loss of his tenancy. The Leasehold Reform Act 1967 may allow the tenant the opportunity to purchase the freehold.

Compulsory Purchase
If a private individual or company wishes to buy a property, the owner can refuse to sell, whatever the sellers are prepared to pay. But if the government, local authority or certain other public bodies wish to buy a property, then the owner may be compelled to sell by the issuing of a compulsory purchase order. Compensation based on current market values is of course payable.

Methods of objection are limited, but the order can be challenged on the basis that the whole scheme is unsound, impracticable and likely to cause unnecessary disruption and harm. These objections are heard at a public inquiry conducted by an inspector appointed by the responsible minister. Public opinion carries weight at such inquiries. The inspector will, after listening to the objections, make a report and recommendations to the minister, who will make the final decision.

Restrictions on the use of Premises
The Town and Country Planning Law requires planning permission for any **physical alteration** of the character of the land, e.g. constructing new buildings, and also if the use of the premises is to undergo **material alteration**. Planning permission will not be granted by local authorities if the plans infringe building regulations which lay down standards of construction, with emphasis on health and safety, e.g. the construction of staircases, the installation of drains, the provision of toilets, and adequate safety systems to deal with outbreaks of fire.

Once an organisation has been given planning permission for any development or change of use, it must make sure that a nuisance is not being caused by excessive smells, noise, vibration or heat; any unreasonable interference can be compensated by damages or prevented by an injunction.

There are also a number of statutory controls concerning the abuse of business premises, and Parliament has passed a number of Acts imposing criminal penalties. The Clean Air Acts of 1956 and 1968 control the emission of 'dark smoke' and delegate authority to local councils to prevent excessive pollution by creating smokeless zones. Harmful emissions are also further controlled by the Control of Pollution Act 1974, which restricts the usage of furnaces unless they are fitted with approved plant to prevent pollution.

Parliament passed the Control of Pollution Act 1974 to further and expand provisions with respect to pollution. The major points in this legislative measure are:

1. The local authority is responsible for ensuring that there is a system of adequate disposal of controlled waste.
2. It is an offence to pollute waterways (including sewers) or to impede their flow, and it is necessary for organisations to obtain permission from water authorities for the right to discharge effluent.
3. Local authorities have an overall responsibility for the control of noise and investigation of complaints about excessive noise.
4. The local authorities also have an overall responsibility for keeping a check on atmospheric pollution.

Finally the common law has developed a criminal offence of public nuisance where the lives of the public or a section of the public are endangered or interfered with by some unlawful act or omission. The police usually bring a prosecution on indictment but in the more serious cases the Attorney-General can bring a prosecution on behalf of the public. (If any individual member of the public suffers special damage as a result of a public nuisance a tortious action can be taken.)

Capital: the non-payment of debts

It is now essential to examine the consequences of an organisation failing to pay its debts, and how the law enables such an organisation to free itself from its financial difficulties, and at the same time ensure that the creditor obtains the best possible financial arrangement.

Insolvency

Insolvency in business is where an organisation is unable, temporarily, to pay its debts. Many of today's organisations, whether large or small, can suffer from this ignominy. It may be for many reasons, such as mismanagement of its working capital, a strike at the plant causing loss of much-needed revenue, principal debtors stalling in payments, seasonal fall-off in orders, a downturn in the economy, or a loss of an expected tender or contract.

There are, therefore, many contributory factors to temporary financial embarrassment. Usually the company can recover by reallocating resources, cutting back in production, rationalisation, redundancies. Financial support may be obtained. An overdraft or a loan from the bank may be enough to tide the firm over its difficulties until further revenue is obtained. Short-term finance may be obtained—a 'bail-out' loan from a director or a partner or even a moneylender. Bills of Exchange help to delay payments. Suppliers of stock and raw materials may be prepared to extend credit in more serious cases, and when a priority firm is in danger of financial collapse, a rescue operation may be mounted by the government under the auspices of the National Enterprise Board.

However, if the inability to pay current debts is a reflection of more fundamental problems within the organisation, then the firm must face the prospect of ultimately ceasing trading. But before this drastic action is taken, there may still be an alternative course to follow. A meeting could be arranged with creditors and the full facts of the firm's instability spelt out. A **composition agreement** may be worked out whereby the creditors agree collectively to accept less than what is due, rather than force the company to cease trading completely. In the event of bankruptcy or liquidation the creditors may receive even less than promised under the composition agreement. Individual debts, if relatively small, could be paid by instalments after a judgment debt has been enforced at the county court. The small man might find it worth while seeking an Administration Order.

Administration Orders

Established by the County Courts Act 1959, an Administration Order enables a debtor, whose indebtedness does not exceed £2000, to have all his debts dealt with together. The effect is that creditors cannot enforce their debts without leave of the court. (It does not, however, prevent them from petitioning for bankruptcy.) The administration order normally provides for the debts to be repaid by instalments over a period not exceeding ten years.

There may be other ways that a firm in difficulties can resolve its troubles. A take-over by another firm is one answer. A **Receiver** could be appointed at the insistence of one or several of the creditors, who may manage the business as a going concern, although in the interests of the creditors.

If insolvency is a future prospect, then a firm can **voluntarily dissolve** before insolvency is reached. A company has the statutory right to wind up voluntarily. A partnership can dissolve by mutal agreement or by one of the partners applying to the court for an order of dissolution, when he feels that the firm can be carried on only at a loss. A sole proprietor can simply put his business up for sale.

Bankruptcy

The process of bankruptcy is where the state takes over the property of a debtor and appoints an officer to distribute the assets fairly to the organisation's creditors. This will occur when the insolvency is more than a temporary situation. Bankruptcy also enables the debtor to be rid of his liabilities and make a fresh start. The bulk of bankruptcy law is contained in the Bankruptcy Act 1914, supplemented by Bankruptcy Rules and the recent Insolvency Act 1976. (Bankruptcy does not apply to companies which are wound up; these are controlled by different legislation.)

Bankruptcy is not possible unless the debtor has committed an act of bankruptcy. A creditor can file a bankruptcy petition where the debtor owes a liquidated debt of at least £200 and which indicates that insolvency has reached the stage that creditors would not be paid if all demanded payment at the same time. Within three months the creditor may present a petition to the court asking for a **receiving order**. An Official Receiver will be appointed whose task is to investigate thoroughly the financial affairs of the debtor. Meetings with creditors will be arranged and if possible some method of repayment by instalments may be agreed upon. If this cannot be arranged, then the court will make an order adjudicating the debtor as a bankrupt.

After this order has been made, all the debtor's property passes over to the control of a **Trustee in Bankruptcy**. The purpose is to sell off as much of the debtor's property as possible and to distribute it to the creditors. The property included are all goods, chattels, papers, documents, plus freehold and leasehold land. The limitation is that the trustee only has title to property which the bankrupt possessed. Also the trustee will allow the bankrupt the tools of his trade, plus clothes and bedding for himself and his family, to the value of £250, and personal earnings are permitted to maintain the bankrupt and his family.

The debtor himself may present his own bankruptcy petition if he feels this is the only way out of his difficulties. In all cases of bankruptcy, the debtor submits to the Official Receiver an affidavit containing a statement of affairs. This has to be within three days of his own petition or seven days after the creditor's petition has been received. The statement of affairs will contain a full list of assets and liabilities, with the names and addresses of creditors. It may be necessary for the debtor in the light of the disclosure of his affairs, the amount of his debts or a regard for the public in general, to undergo a public examination by the registrar under oath, which means that no question put to the debtor may be answered untruthfully. Failure to attend such examination may lead to the debtor's arrest.

If no arrangement can be made with creditors, and a trustee in bankruptcy is appointed, then the proceeds of the debtor's assets will be distributed to the creditors. There are priority claims, for instance, the expenses of the bankruptcy procedures are paid first, as also are any rates or taxes due to the Inland Revenue. Employees' pay, holiday pay, National Insurance, and redundancy payments are also a priority claim. With the exception of landlords, who may seize the debtor's goods in lieu of unpaid rent (only six months' rent is recoverable if he distrains after the bankruptcy proceedings), all other creditors' debts are deferred until these are paid in full. In any case, no creditor is entitled to a share of the assets until the Official Receiver has received an affidavit proving his debt. Some creditors may be paid before others if they can establish that the debt is secured, i.e. with a mortgage charge or lien.

The bankrupt is now in a position to make a fresh start, although this is subject to certain specific limitations—for instance he needs the court's leave before becoming a director of a company. Also he must not obtain credit over £50 without disclosing that he is an undeclared bankrupt. It is possible to apply for a discharge of the **adjudication order,** effectively releasing him from bankruptcy. Before granting the discharge, the court will take into account the conduct of the bankrupt before and during the bankruptcy, and also how much has been distributed to creditors—the court prefers at least 50p in the £. The Insolvency Act 1976 gives the undischarged bankrupt a further opportunity. The court can order an absolute discharge (if satisfied with the conduct of the bankrupt), after five years of bankruptcy have elapsed, upon the receipt of an application from the Official Receiver. Basically, a discharged bankrupt is free from his former liabilities and is free to enter business again.

Liquidation

Companies are not subject to the law of bankruptcy but if they become insolvent they can be **wound up** by one of three methods all of which are legal processes, governed principally by the Companies Acts of 1948 and 1967.

1. A company can be compulsorily wound up by the court if it is insolvent. There are similarities with the bankruptcy proceedings in that creditors have the power to apply for an order where a creditor is indebted in excess of £200 which has not been paid within three weeks of request, or a judgement cannot be satisfied on the company's property.

2. The petition is not restricted to creditors. The company itself may pass a resolution deciding upon winding up.

3. The right is also given to dissatisfied shareholders.

The court, if it accepts the request to wind up the company, appoints an Official Receiver. He acts as a provisional liquidator, usually until a **liquidator** is appointed. As with the Trustee in Bankruptcy, he must dispose of the company's assets and satisfy creditors. He works from a statement of affairs prepared by the directors of the company and draws on any unpaid capital owing by shareholders. Shareholders who have been members within the previous twelve months can also be called upon to contribute (only up to the amount of unpaid capital) if the current members fail to meet the debts. Creditors must again prove their debts, and they receive proceeds in the same order of priority as in the law of bankruptcy.

A company faced with difficulties in trading may pass a special resolution to be voluntarily wound up. The members can supervise the winding up if the company states that its debts can be absolved within one year. A general meeting will appoint a liquidator who will dispose of assets to pay off creditors. The members will be kept closely informed of the liquidator's activities. After a general meeting at which a full statement of the distribution of assets is made, a return is made to the Registrar of Companies and on the expiration of three months the company is legally dissolved.

If the directors have not made a declaration of solvency within the twelve-month period, then it is the creditors who will be responsible for winding up the company. The procedure is similar to winding up by the members, with the exception that the creditors may be prepared to accept some compromise of the debts rather than see the company face liquidation. However, if this is impossible, a liquidator will be appointed by the creditors who will operate on the same lines as members when they deal with the winding up. The creditors may appoint a Committee of Inspection to supervise the operations of the liquidator.

Court supervision
The court has additional powers to appoint a further liquidator to supervise the voluntary winding up of a company if, for example, a creditor feels that the liquidation by voluntary means cannot be completed fairly.

Industrial property—its protection

Patents
If an organisation has spent time and money researching and developing a new product or design, then it is only right that it should be able to protect its invention from competitors. Such protection is contained in the Patents Act 1977. This largely replaces the Patents Act 1949 with the intention of streamlining patent law, increasing the protection given to UK inventors and also harmonising the law with that in force in Europe.

For an invention to be patentable several criteria must be satisfied: namely that the invention is new and unique, and that it is capable of some form of industrial application. A patent will not, however, be granted for pure scientific discoveries or mathematical methods and equations. Also excluded are schemes which present management information, including computer software. This latter exclusion follows the recommendations of the Banks Committee, but has caused some protest from the computer industry—understandably so, considering the vast sums of money spent on developing computer programs and software. No patent will be granted to any invention which is potentially undesirable, in that it could encourage or lead to 'offensive, immoral or anti-social' behaviour.

It is possible for applicants to have a preliminary search and investigation of their invention which may save them the time and expense of submitting a detailed specification for a substantive examination in the Patent Office. This also serves as a warning to alert any interested third parties.

If a patent is granted, then the protection given is for twenty years, which is an increase on the previous law under the Patents Act 1949. This is another example of harmonisation with Europe, but it is also a recognition that increasingly sophisticated technology makes inventions harder and more time-consuming to develop.

Any infringement of the patent can be challenged either by taking the action to the Comptroller of Patents or to the newly established Patents Court in the Chancery Division. The remedy available in both cases is damages, but the Patents Court has also the power to grant an injunction which can include the return or destruction of any infringing material. Infringements can also be indirect in that damages or an injunction can be awarded against anyone who, though not necessarily directly using a patent, is nonetheless receiving some benefit from it.

The rights of the employee are now statutorily protected under the 1977 Act. Ownership of any invention is given to the employee unless the invention was part of the normal course of his duties. Similarly, the employee will have to give up an invention to his employer if it is reasonably expected that his job entailed contributory actions towards new discoveries and development, e.g. *British Soda Syphon Co. v. Homewood* (1956), where the defendant developed a new syphon out of his own interests. None the less, he was a technician at the plaintiff company, and he had to forfeit the invention rights.

However, an employee can claim compensation from the Comptroller of the Patents Court where his invention has been a substantial success for his employer. This right to further compensation exists even where the employee has transferred his invention by assignment and the invention has been of benefit to the employer not anticipated at the time of assignment. As a further enhancement of employee's rights, the Act makes unenforceable any terms in an employee's contract of employment which diminish the statutory rights of the employee to claim his own inventions or a share of them.

The Patents Act 1977 refers only to the United Kingdom and if an inventor wants world-wide protection then he must seek a patent in each country where competition might exist. However, the European Patent Convention provides for the establishment of a European Patent Office, which will have the effect of a national patent in any of the contracting countries that he wishes, including non-member states of the EEC.

Copyright

It would obviously be wrong for a business, after spending time and effort researching and developing a variety of literary material, only to see it taken and used by competitors. Therefore the Copyright Act 1956 protects organisations who produce original literature in a variety of forms, e.g. drawings, maps, plans, charts, reports, etc. They cannot be reproduced, either exactly or as a near imitation, without permission.

This means that original literature cannot be sold, let or hired out for trade or distributed as part of a trade venture, nor can it be used in any way which might be construed as prejudicial to the original owner's copyright. The production is implied, without any formality—it is not even necessary to put the owner's name and address on copyright material.

Any owner of a literary work who feels that his copyright has been infringed has the right to an action in the courts. An injunction can be granted to prevent the offender continuing the breach of copyright. Damages will also be awarded unless the defendant can prove that he had no reasonable grounds for suspecting that copyright was being infringed. Damages will be based on the seriousness of the infringement and the benefit the defendant may have received from the use of the copyright. Usually compensation is the aim of the award of damages, but if the court feels that the

infringement has been particularly flagrant, then punitive damages will be awarded as a future deterrent. The owner also has the additional right of claiming any of the material that constitutes the infringing copy.

A breach of copyright constitutes a criminal offence and a fine not exceeding £50 can be levied for a summary conviction. For serious and persistent breaches an unlimited fine is possible, or a term of imprisonment for the offender not exceeding two years.

Goodwill

Goodwill has often been described as difficult to define, but basically it is the benefit arising from a firm's business reputation and connections. It suggests that custom will continue to be attracted in the future. Its source is not always easy to pinpoint but it usually originates from such areas as:

(i)   the reputation of the owners of the business;
(ii) the respect given to the quality of the firm's products;
(iii) the monopolistic advantages gained by a business's particular location or site;
(iv) the overall growth prospects;
(v)   the possession of patents or trade marks.

Goodwill is an asset and therefore in the case of a sole trader he may sell his business and pocket the goodwill which is the reward for his business expertise and skills. With regard to partnerships, the Partnership Act 1890 lays down a number of rules which apply unless the partners themselves agree otherwise. Any retiring partner is entitled to the value of his share of goodwill. Equally, on dissolution of the partnership, every partner is entitled to have the goodwill sold for their collective benefit.

The purchasers of the goodwill are buying for themselves the right to conduct business in the name of the existing firm and to solicit all the established customers. Because the purchase of goodwill can be expensive, its saleable value has to be protected. Purchasers will sensibly include in the contractual agreement a covenant preventing the vendor from setting up a competing business in the vicinity. He can be prevented from soliciting the business of old customers in any case, but a restraint will have to be enforced if it is to bar him from the vicinity. The courts recognise the saleable value of goodwill and therefore are more sympathetic towards such restraints than they are with similar restraints against employees. As long as they are reasonable and not against the public interest leading to a monopolistic situation then they will be enforced. The restraint will, however, have to be expressly contained in the contract of sale, otherwise the courts will rely on the precedent established in *Tregor v. Hunt* (1896) where L. MacNaughton L.J. said 'a person who sells the goodwill of a business is under no obligation to retire from the field'.

Labour

It is now necessary to examine the enormous legal framework surrounding the use of labour as a factor of production. That there are so many rules and duties is a reflection of the type of resource being used. It is easy to examine it in pure economic terms and forget that labour has very human qualities.

An Employer's Responsibilities to his Employees

Common Law duties

There is a basic duty owed by all employers to their employees of reasonable care not to subject them to any unnecessary risk. This principle is based on the case of *Donoghue v. Stevenson* (1932), which imposes a duty of 'reasonable' care upon us all—but it is not an absolute duty as is the case with some statutes, i.e. the Factories Act 1961. This means that the courts will take into account several conflicting factors, but if an employer fails to observe this duty, the injured employee may have an action for damages in negligence. However, not all successful cases against an employer in negligence will result in his having to pay fully, for the law of contributory negligence will serve to reduce a victim's share of the damages if he has not taken reasonable care of himself.

Of course an employer must take steps to prevent injury occurring from obvious risks, but it must be recognised that some jobs have a higher risk factor than others, e.g. steeplejacks, oil-rig workers, etc. The courts will also take some account of the difficulty of providing a safety system, the costs involved in installing it and its subsequent maintenance, but the financial consideration will be outweighed if the risk of injury is high and the consequences serious.

The Health and Safety at Work Act 1974 imposes a similar criminal liability on employers and if there is a serious breach of safety in the opinion of the factory inspector, a firm's operations can be curtailed or suspended by means of an Improvement or Prohibition Notice.

General duties

Independent of the contract of employment, or any statutory intervention in the field of employment, it has become recognised that the employer owes his employee a number of duties.

Safe system of work   The employer must take all steps to ensure that the operational tasks within his organisation are undertaken with all risks and hazards reasonably minimised. Employers will achieve this by a combination of training, supervision (including discipline where necessary) and the provision of safety facilities. Again the duty revolves round the test of reasonableness. Obviously an employer cannot watch and supervise his employees all the time (*McWilliams v. Arrol* (1962)), but it is expected that account is taken of dangerous activities, or those operations undertaken by inexperienced employees, where the risk of injury is obviously higher. Where there are particularly hazardous risks, then it is expected that the employer will take greater steps to warn his employees (e.g. by providing safety goggles where there is a risk of eye injury) (*Bux v. Slough Metals* (1974)) and by introducing a rigorous safety campaign (*Crookall v. Vickers Armstrong* (1955)). However, the employer is not expected to warn employees where commonsense should have warned them of the risk.

Safe plant, equipment and premises   Generally the statutory obligations, plus the level of care in industry and commerce, provide for an acceptable level of safety. The real danger occurs when accidents happen through familiarity. Therefore, the courts will penalise any employer who does not take appropriate measures where the risk of injury is apparent.

Obvious dangers are where there is a risk of infection, if there is contact with oil or dust, where there is excess noise, where there is a danger of cuts from sharp edges, where there is a risk of injury from badly maintained equipment (*Bradford v. Robinson* (1967)). The employer will be liable if these dangers could reasonably have been eliminated. The employer is also expected to keep abreast of health and safety developments, certainly that information which has become part of general public knowledge.

It should be noted that the safety of the employee is regarded as paramount and Parliament passed the Employers' Liability (Defective Equipment) Act 1969 which holds the employer strictly liable for any *hidden* defects in plant and equipment used in the course of employment. This is an obvious departure from the common law principle of reasonable care, but the result is more satisfactory. The employer does at least have the resources to bring an action against the supplier of the equipment.

Safe employees

We have seen under the principle of vicarious liability (page 49), the employer must also select his employees carefully and see that they are adequately trained and supervised. Obviously, particular care must be taken over the general supervision of young and inexperienced workers; also special attention must be paid to the giving of clear, unambiguous instructions to immigrant workers. The question of discipline can cause problems. The employer must ensure that employees are protected from skylarking and bullying from fellow employees. They need take disciplinary steps only to prevent abuses of rules which are recognised, but they must remove all obvious hazards, i.e. where an employee has a known reputation for bad behaviour (*Hudson v. Ridge Manufacturing Co Ltd* (1957)).

Responsibility to visitors

We all have a duty towards each other to try to avoid injury and loss, but it is recognised that there is a special responsibility towards visitors to business premises because they are in unfamiliar surroundings and probably unaware of any dangers and hazards. Even if visitors are on business premises under a contract it is rare that their safey is mentioned.

The basis of the civil law relating to the protection of visitors to land or premises is contained in the Occupiers' Liability Act 1957. A person is an occupier if he is in immediate occupation or control of the land or premises. This means that the occupier is not necessarily the owner, and can be a visiting contractor who temporarily occupies part or the whole of some business premises. The Act establishes 'a duty to take such care as in all the circumstances of the case is reasonable' to see that the visitor will be *reasonably* safe 'in using the premises for the purposes for which he is invited or permitted to be there' (s. 2 (2)). The term 'visitor', has proved troublesome in distinguishing lawful persons and trespassers. *British Railways Board v Herrington* (1972) has established that there is some duty owed to trespassers, although it is the lower duty of 'common humanity'.

Liability for visiting contractors

The occupier is not generally responsible for the risks that an independent contractor and his employees experience within their own trade or for any harm they may cause to third parties. This is because the occupier does not, as a rule, have any direct control over the actions of the contractor. If he does, however, adopt a supervisory role, then he will be liable under the principle of vicarious liability. But this liability is only for general tasks, because the occupier of premises rarely instructs a hired, skilled tradesman on how to do his job!

The occupier will be liable for any hazards which are not purely occupational hazards, but are peculiar to his premises, or which pose a particular danger to the public at large.

Criminal Liability

The Health and Safety at Work Act 1974 extends the employer's and occupier's criminal liabilities. Section 3 of the Act obliges the employer to take reasonable care for the safety of those not his employees who may be affected by his undertakings; and Section 4 lays down a general duty for any occupier to make his premises safe for those using them, though they are not his employees. Failure to discharge either of these duties may lead to a fine of up to £1000 on a summary conviction, or an unlimited fine if a conviction is secured at the Crown Court.

Exclusion of liability

The 1957 Act allowed the occupier to escape liability by warning notices which, if clearly written and visible, protected the occupier against all actions including his own negligence. The Unfair Contract Terms Act 1977 improved the situation for visitors to business premises. An occupier can no longer exclude or restrict liability for death or personal injury resulting from negligence. The occupier also cannot exclude or restrict other loss or damage unless it is 'reasonable' to do so, and the onus of proof rests on the occupier.

Extract 6.1

Women in the Civil Service

Despite legislation, women do not always have equal opportunities in practice, Lady Young, minister in charge of the Civil Service Management and Personnel Office acknowledged to a YWCA audience last month. In April 1981 women's average earnings were only threequarters of those of men. And despite many individual achievements, most women remained concentrated in a limited range of jobs. They tended to restrict, or be restricted in, their choice of occupation and work, mostly in education, welfare and health, clerical work, retailing, catering and hairdressing. Even highly-qualified women tended to be biased towards public sector employment and under-represented in industry and commerce—particularly in those occupations requiring a high technical and scientific background. . . .

'Despite training, women will still not find equal opportunities to rise to the top unless employers also adapt personnel policies and practices to women's needs as well as men's. I am thinking particularly of the assumption that the normal family has two parents, one of whom is the principal breadwinner with an uninterrupted career to offer his employer. This assumption underlies almost every aspect of the average employer's personnel system: pay, promotion criteria, appraisal of performance and potential, training needs, working hours and pensions. And women, who are assumed not to be offering a sustained career at work, find their abilities discounted and their promotion prospects lessened as a result.'

Source: *Department of Employment Gazette* August 1982, HMSO.

An Employer's Implied Statutory Duties

Discrimination

Recent years have seen a trend towards intervention by the legislature into the area of employment. This trend is likely to continue as governments attempt to achieve a more balanced society according to their political ideologies. Some of the legislation is by our standards radical and is seeking to compel people not to discriminate. This first step may lead to a change in attitudes for, if the law seems acceptable to the majority then perhaps some of the prejudices may be removed.

Let us consider this legislation.

Sex Discrimination Act 1975   The purpose of this Act is to prevent unfavourable treatment of persons because of their sex. The Act applies to both sexes, although principally it is aimed at women perhaps to allow them to penetrate business organisations where men have dominated in the past. It is designed to eliminate discrimination that is *direct* and by its nature intentional. Also covered by the Act is the more subtle or unintentional *indirect* discrimination by setting standards that have the effect of preventing more women than men from applying for an employment vacancy (*Price v. Civil Service Commission* (1978)). Acts of *victimisation* against those who are attempting to enforce or pursue the rights established by the discriminatory laws are also unlawful.

There is no discrimination if the presence of one sex is a genuine qualification, e.g. (i) the need for authentic male characteristics such as physical strength and stamina; (ii) where decency or privacy must be preserved; (iii) where the employer has communal sleeping arrangements and sanitary facilities, and it cannot be expected that he provide alternative facilities, e.g. oil rigs can probably be male dominated for reasons (i), (ii) and (iii). Furthermore, the need for a particular sex is desirable in institutions where care or supervision is required, such as prisons and mental institutions. It would be justifiable to appoint a male, for instance, in a mental institution entirely devoted to males. It is worth noting that there still remain restrictions on the hours women can work (Factories Act 1961) and employment of women underground (Mines and Quarries Act 1954).

It is unfavourable treatment if the employer discriminates against a woman in terms of employment opportunities and also opportunities for advancement, including promotion, training and transfer. The discriminatory dismissal of a woman is also unlawful. Employers are not permitted to discriminate purely on the grounds that customers prefer one particular sex, nor can they discriminate on the grounds that the job is unpleasant or dangerous. If discrimination is suspected then a complaint can be made within three months of the discriminatory act to an industrial tribunal. This has the power to declare the rights that the complainant possesses, award compensation against the employer up to £6,250 and recommend that the employer takes steps to remove the discrimination in the future.

Some women may not feel like personally taking action against their employer, and in recognition of this fact, the **Equal Opportunities Commission** was established by the Act, and this may intervene on the complainant's behalf. Their objective is to work for the elimination of discrimination and they have wide powers to conduct formal investigations to the extent that any person may be requested, and if necessary compelled, to give information. The Commission can issue a non-discriminatory notice against any employer, and this will be sufficient to obtain the necessary improvements. For those stubborn enough to resist the notice, an injunction can be obtained to enforce the relevant measures in the notice.

An interesting case was that of *Peake v. Automotive Products Ltd.* (1977) reminding us that the Act applies to both sexes. Mr Peake maintained that he had been unfairly discriminated against on the grounds that the women employees were allowed to leave five minutes earlier to prevent jostling whilst leaving the factory. The Employment Appeal Tribunal agreed with Mr Peake but in the Court of Appeal it was decided there was no unlawful discrimination, Lord Denning pointing out that the statute was not designed to obliterate all differences between the sexes or remove the last vestiges of courtesy!

The need for legislative action is clear from the fact that despite an increase in the number of women now prepared to go to work, the sexual division of Labour continues to be reinforced.

Equal Pay Act 1970   The basis of this legislation as amended by the Sex Discrimination Act 1975 is, as the title suggests, the attempt to eliminate irregularities in pay between men and women who are doing broadly similar work. Sometimes in the past the differences in pay between male and female employees was quite substantial, even though they were performing the same tasks and often producing at the same rate and with the same effort. This gap in pay is no longer socially acceptable. It is demeaning to the female sex and the Act therefore declares that it is unlawful. A complaint can be lodged with an industrial tribunal at any time whilst still employed in the job, or within six months of the contract being terminated. The tribunal has the power to award up to two years' arrears of remuneration as damages (*Electrolux Ltd v. Hutchinson* (1976)).

Racial Discrimination   Any legislation on this topic obviously has to be carefully drafted so that

intolerance and prejudice is not further stimulated and yet at the same time balancing the need for complete equality in the field of employment. The Race Relations Act 1976 which replaces the 1965 and 1968 Race Relations Acts reflects the cautious approach by the government to this topic. This new Act does not signify confusion within parliamentary circles, but is simply an improving piece of legislation based on experience gained over the years.

It is unlawful to treat a person less favourably in the field of employment (the Act also relates to housing, education, goods, services and facilities) and not to grant them equal opportunities for advancement because of their nationality, citizenship, ethnic background, race, colour or national origin. Such unlawfulness will extend to indirect discrimination, e.g. the request that an employee has a good command of English when the job does not warrant this qualification. It is worth noting that there may be the occasional grounds for 'racial discrimination' – it will be lawful to request a Chinese waiter for a Chinese restaurant. That there is a need for positive non-discrimination can be seen from Table 6.1.

Table 6.1: Differences in job distribution by skill category between white and minority group employees

		(Percentage)
	All men	Men from minority groups
Non-skilled manual	37	67
Skilled manual	21	19
Non-manual	42	14

Source: PEP, 1974, p. 39.

The enforcement of this Act is in the hands of the newly formed **Commission for Racial Equality** (CRE). It has wider powers than the old Race Relations Board which it replaces, in that instead of merely handling the complaints of aggrieved parties, it has the power to instigate its own formal investigations into cases of suspected discrimination. (Note that its powers have been to some extent harmonised with the other legislation dealing with discrimination.) It has the new power of issuing non-discrimination notices. For example, it may discover that a firm offering a wide variety of employment opportunities has substantially less of a proportion of other races within its work force than is reflected in the community. The Commission can insist that the employer keeps the Commission informed of any changes in policy that it has been required to make. An injunction can be obtained if necessary to enforce the notice.

The individual no longer has to wait for action to be carried out on his behalf. He has the power to bring his own action to the County Court, who can: (i) make a declaration of the rights of the individual, (ii) award damages including a figure for injured feelings, (iii) issue an injunction. An alternative action is through an industrial tribunal, where the remedies are: (i) a declaration of the rights of the individual, (ii) financial compensation up to £6,250, and (iii) recommendation of a course of action designed to remedy matters.

The contract of employment

This is covered, firstly, by Section 1 of the Employment Protection (Consolidation) Act 1978. It requires that no later than the end of the thirteenth week from the commencement of employment, the employer must give to the employee a written statement containing the following:

(a) an identification of the parties, specifying the date when the employment began, and stating whether any employment with a previous employer counts as part of the employee's continuous period of employment with him and, if so, specifying the date on which the continuous period of employment began;

(b) the scale or rate of remuneration, or method of calculating remuneration;

(c) the intervals at which remuneration is to be paid (e.g. weekly, monthly, etc.);

(d) terms and conditions relating to hours of work;

(e) any terms and conditions relating to holiday entitlement, including public holidays, holiday pay and accrued holiday pay;

(f) details of sick pay (if any) which is payable;

(g) details of pension rights (if any);

(h) the length of notice the employee is obliged to give and entitled to receive to determine the contract;

(i) The title of the job which he is employed to do.

Instead of giving such details, it is permissible to make reference to a document which contains this information (in most cases this will be a collective agreement), provided that the document is reasonably accessible.

In addition every such statement shall include a note:

(a) specifying any disciplinary rules applicable to the employee, or referring to a document reasonably accessible to him which specifies such rules;

(b) specifying a person to whom he can apply for the purpose of seeking the redress of any grievance relating to his employment and, where there are further steps consequent on such application, explaining those steps or referring to a document which is reasonably accessible to the employee which explains them. This does not apply to rules, disciplinary decisions, grievances or procedures relating to health and safety at work.

Written particulars need not be given to employees who work less than sixteen hours per week, registered dock workers, merchant seamen, Crown employees (including National Health Service employees—see *Wood v. United Leeds Hospitals*), an employee who is the husband or wife of the employer, and employees who usually work outside Great Britain.

It must, however, be remembered that the statement given by virtue of Section 1 is not necessarily a contract and helps to establish what those contractual terms were, and also a failure by an employer to provide such a statement may well lead an industrial tribunal to take the side of the employee. Any change in the terms of employment must be notified to the employee within one month, but again reference must be made to a reasonably accessible document. Therefore, if an employer does not provide the written statement under Section 1, or if it is incomplete, the employee may apply to an industrial tribunal to determine what particulars ought to be included in such a statement.

Further major statutory protection owed to an employee by an employer is as follows:

1. An employee has the right to belong to a union, without fear of dismissal, or other discriminatory tactics against him, such as the loss of privileges, promotional opportunities, training, etc. He also has the right to time off to participate in and carry out trade union duties.

2. The employer must provide insurance cover up to £2 million under the Employers Liability (Compulsory Insurance) Act 1969, against claims by other employees.

3. The employer must pay the agreed wages in coin of the realm (Truck Acts 1831–1940), unless there has been an express written agreement to the contrary between the employers and employees (Payment of Wages Act 1960). This enables payment to be made by cheque or by a direct debit into the employee's bank account. Payment is subject to recognised deductions—i.e. to trade unions, PAYE, etc.

The Wages Councils Act 1979 provides for the establishment of a Wages Council for a particular industry which has the power to issue an order fixing pay, conditions and other suitable terms of employment.

The Employment Protection (Consolidation) Act 1978 also provides for a guaranteed payment of up to £8.75 a day for five days in a three-month period if the employee is laid off because production is affected by actions of other workers in unrelated industries.

4. The Employment Protection (Consolidation) Act entitles a pregnant employee (with two years service) to six weeks' pay after the eleventh week before confinement. She is also entitled to reinstatement after giving three weeks' notice within twenty-nine weeks of confinement. If her job is not available, she is entitled to redundancy or compensation if the dismissal is unfair, depending on the employer's reason for not keeping the job open.

An Employee's Implied Duties

The employee owes his employer a number of **common law** duties, which are implied in all master and servant contracts. These duties have been developed by the courts themselves in recognition of the special relationship which exists between an employer and his employees, based on trust and confidence in each other.

Obedience

An employer could not possibly run an efficient organisation if his lawful orders and requests were constantly ignored or challenged. Therefore, if an employee wilfully refuses to obey an order of his employer, he may place his job in jeopardy (*Pepper v. Webb* (1969)). Obviously a refusal of a trivial request is not serious, but if, for example, the employee refuses to work contracted overtime, or walks out from the job, this may constitute grounds for dismissal. One particularly difficult area is the 'go slow' or 'work to rule'. There is no disobedience if an employee withdraws his good-will, slows his output, but yet is still working within the rules of his contract. But the courts will not be too sympathetic with an employee deliberately taking too long to accomplish his tasks with the object of disrupting his employer's production. For example, every employee has a duty to check that his machine is safe to operate before commencing work, but to check three or four times before commencing each cycle of work may be construed as wilful disobedience (*Secretary of State v. ASLEF* (1972)).

An employee may be lawfully dismissed if he is objectionally rude, but it is possible for him to escape dismissal if there is a justifiable reason why he should refuse a lawful order. He must be given the opportunity of explaining why he is not complying with his employer's instructions. It is also right for an employee to refuse to obey orders which are unlawful (*Morrish v. Henleys Ltd* (1973)). Obviously an illegal order can be disobeyed without fear of recrimination, e.g. for an operative to work a machine without a safety guard, if the employer is attempting to boost production. The difficulty courts have in construing the lawful and unlawful orders, suggests that many of the disputes could be avoided if a clear job description is given to each employee. An employer has the right to change an employee's terms of employment if job requirements and needs alter, and as long as this is not contrary to his contract of employment, but it is reasonable to expect that the employee or his union are consulted beforehand.

Competence

If an employee does not perform his duties with the competence expected of his position, then he may be dismissed (see p. 113 for precise grounds for dismissal). The standard of competence will be much higher for professional workers or those accredited with a high level of skill, e.g. accountants, architects (*Alidair Ltd v. Taylor* (1978)); examples of incompetence are slowness, persistent lateness, theft, inefficiency or illness. The incompetence does not have to be wilful or even 'a regular feature of the man's work'. For instance, one mistake by an employee may have such serious consequences that dismissal is acceptable, such as a man careless with a discarded match in a storeroom of inflammable liquids.

Of course, it is not necessarily a serious breach of contract if an employee is ill (even for a length of time) and this fact is recognised by many firms by the provision of generous sick pay schemes. But if an employee's personal presence is vital for the continuation of the job, then his illness may be grounds for dismissal.

Faithful service

One of the fundamental obligations of an employee is the duty to conduct his employment faithfully on behalf of his employer. He must work with honesty and integrity and not do anything which is in conflict with the employer's interests, apart from accepted areas of strife through union activities. An employee must not compete against his employer, accept gifts, take bribes or make secret profits, even if the employer has not lost profits nor suffered damage. The principle that the courts maintain is that the employee must not be allowed to keep any financial reward. To avoid the possibility of employees being susceptible to corruptive influences many employers safeguard their interests by expressly forbidding them to take gifts, i.e. expensive lunches, bottles of whisky, free theatre tickets, etc.

Pilferage by employees has risen in recent years to alarming levels. In the distribution industry it is estimated that stealing by staff represents 1–2 per cent of actual turnover. Some employees may feel that pilferage is an acceptable 'perk' and is not necessarily wrong, but of course it is a serious breach of an employee's duty of good faith. Even the theft of some trivial item is a ground for dismissal (*Trust House Forte v. Murphy* (1977)). The courts will regard it as an irrelevant point if an employee has not gained personally from his faithless act. Dismissal will also be upheld because this employee has shown himself susceptible to the breaking of rules, and it suggests that he cannot be trusted in the future.

During the course of their employment employees will often gain information about their employer's business which would be valuable to rival competitors. An employee must not divulge this information for gain or otherwise. In certain circumstances this duty will continue even though the employee has left his job. Nothing (apart from a reasonable restraint-of-trade clause) can prevent an employee taking with him the skill and experience that he has developed within his job, even if the employer has spent a considerable amount on his training and instruction. But an injunction can be obtained to prevent the passing on of trade secrets and confidential information. One particularly contentious area of conflict is where the employee works for another employer out of working hours. The employee may be merely attempting to supplement his wages. Is the employer justified in preventing him from working in his own time? Well, if the employee is working for a similar organisation then the answer is yes, because this is a breach of his fiduciary duty. The employer has the right to prohibit any activity which may interfere with the employee's ability to perform his duties properly, or may endanger his professional position or trust—for example, if an employee was unable to work properly through tiredness, or if he was gambling excessively and held a position of trust at work. Unlawful or criminal activities outside the Contract of Employment may also lead to disciplinary action, even dismissal if the offence is serious enough to challenge the integrity and future standing of the employee (*Richardson v. City of Bradford Metropolitan Council* (1975)).

To what extent must an employee disclose information to his employer about matters which might be of concern to him? The employee has a basic obligation to tell the employer about suspected cases of dishonesty that he may encounter during his employment. Also it would be a breach of trust if he did not reveal that he suffered from some disability which would affect the performance of his job, and put others in jeopardy—for example, an airline pilot failing to report that he had begun to suffer from dizzy spells.

Most relevant information will be revealed in any case at the initial interview. If, however, the employer omits to put relevant questions then it seems that the employee will not be failing in his duty if he remains silent. One interesting development recently has been the passing of the Rehabitation of Offenders Act 1974. Those who are convicted and are punished with a sentence of less than two and a half years' imprisonment (this includes fines, probation, suspended prison sentences, Borstal, etc.) can have their conviction 'spent' after a trouble-free period of between 6 months and 10 years. They do not have to disclose this conviction even if asked, unless they are applying for certain financial or public posts.

Inventions

As we have already seen under the section dealing with patents, if an employee develops or invents some process or product which gains enormous revenue for his employer, and if this invention has been the result of his employment and the facilities and resources put at his disposal, then the employer has the right to take all the proceeds of the invention. Normally in such cases there is no contention, as either it will be clearly stated in the contract or the employee is paid a contribution from a suggestion scheme.

Dismissal

The Trade Union and Labour Relations Act 1974 and the Employment Protection (Consolidation) Act 1978 have supported, widened and consolidated the initial protection against dismissal laid down in the Industrial Relations Act 1971. This is now incorporated in the Employment Protection (Consolidation) Act 1978. Unlike the pre-1971 Act position, where the employer could dismiss for any reason or for *no reason at all*, every employee has the right not to be unfairly dismissed. Even where sometimes the employee is in breach of one of his implied duties, the current legislation will still protect him to the extent that his dismissal will only be fair if all circumstances connected with the termination of the contract have been fully considered. The protection covers both types of dismissal—with or without notice.

What is dismissal?

Dismissal without notice

This type of summary dismissal is used only in exceptional circumstances, because employers recognise that even an outrageous act may have some reason behind it, or at least a contributory element, which might help the employee's case if a proper investigation is carried out.

A dismissal without notice could be for reasons of gross misconduct (e.g. some act of immorality, theft, drunkenness, skylarking, mouthing obscenities); gross neglect (e.g. seriously damaging employer's property and the disobeying of lawful and reasonable orders—this could include a breach of express regulations, e.g. of a safety rule not to smoke in a prohibited area). These grounds for instant dismissal have been established over the years, but it must be remembered that each case must be assessed on its own merits. The courts will examine each set of facts, taking into account standards of behaviour and attitudes inside and outside the organisation. For example, a senior employee is expected to carry out his duties with more care and diligence.

Proof

If an employee is to claim that he is unfairly dismissed, he must also prove that he has been dismissed. If an employee resigns of his own accord, this is probably not a dismissal. But it can constitute a dismissal if an employee is asked for his resignation—a measure often employed to save the employee the indignity of being sacked.

Usually an employer makes it absolutely clear that an employee is dismissed, but sometimes confusion may reign because of misunderstandings. There have been many cases and debate, for instance, over the strict interpretation of various expletives! *And* whether such abuse from a person in an authoritative position constitutes a dismissal.

Termination of the contract of employment can be indirect—known as 'constructive dismissal'. For instance, the employer may make the employee's position intolerable by demoting him, or unilaterally changing the terms of their agreement to the severe detriment of the employee. Discrimination or victimisation pressurising the employee into giving up his job can entitle the employee to regard himself as unfairly dismissed. The only question to be decided in these cases is whether there really are grounds for complaint, and it is not just bad feeling on the part of the employee because his prospects and advancement have not progressed at the rate he would have expected.

Fair or Unfair Dismissal?

Every employee, states the Trade Union and Labour Relations Act 1974, has the right not to be unfairly dismissed. What is regarded as fair or unfair is determined basically by the Act. Two further considerations are:

(i) the Employment Protection (Consolidation) Act 1978 lays down minimum periods of notice which each party must give the other.

The statutory notice is for all employees who are under contract for more than sixteen hours per week (with certain exclusions, e.g. fishermen, seamen, dock workers). After four weeks' and up to two years' employment, notice to the employee must be:

(a) one week.
(b) plus one week for each subsequent year of continuous employment, up to a maximum of twelve (e.g. if an employee had been continuously employed at a company for twenty years, then the statutory notice he must receive is still twelve weeks). The court, however, may extend the notice if the judge thinks it is reasonable to do so.

The employee must give a minimum of one

week's notice after four weeks of employment (more may be required by contract).

(ii) The Advisory, Conciliation and Arbitration Service (ACAS) has produced a practical guide for industry in the form of a Code of Practice. It is suggested that the Code is worth adopting in the business world, for it may certainly improve industrial relations, and its contents, although not followed to the letter, are closely considered by the Industrial Tribunal.

The Employment Protection (Consolidation) Act 1978 as amended states that apart from a few notable exceptions, all dismissals are regarded essentially as unfair. The burden of proof has, however, been shifted from the employer by the Employment Act 1980. The burden has been 'neutralised', with directions given to industrial tribunals to take into account 'the size and administrative resources of the employer's undertaking' in determining the fairness or otherwise of a dismissal.

Grounds for Dismissal with Notice

(i) *Incapacity*   However efficient an organisation's selection process, there will be circumstances where an employee is unsuitable for a job (irrespective of his qualifications). He may not show the drive and flair for a responsible post. His attitudes and general behaviour may continuously cause conflict with other employees, or perhaps he just does not seem to be able to perform the job with any measure of skill.

An employee must be able to do the job he was employed to do, but inability does not mean automatic dismissal. In fact dismissal is the last resort. In order to prove that the employer is acting reasonably and fairly there should be an investigation of the alleged incapacity. Perhaps the training or instruction were insufficient or inadequate. Does the employee have a job description with which to relate and compare? Is there suitable supervision of his tasks? What general support and facilities is this employee offered? It is important that in all cases of dissatisfaction, sufficient 'warning' should be given. It is only just that failings in an employee should be discussed, so that opportunities of improvement are made clear, and also any complaints from the employee can be heard.

Vague statements about incompetence will not be sufficient: specific grounds of incapacity must be proved by the employer.

A man's continuing illness and absence could be a reflection on his ability and capacity to do his job. But illness is no longer an automatic ground for dismissal. If anything, the employer must try to keep his job open for as long as possible. Regular absenteeism may show that the employee is not fit for the job, but his dismissal is justified only if the man holds a key position which is difficult to fill. If a temporary replacement can be obtained, then the firm may have to carry the sick personnel—certainly as long as any sick pay scheme. It seems that tribunals will also expect employers to find lighter work for employees if this proves to be necessary. A good practice is one where an employer also places those with long-term illnesses on a form of 'reserve' list so that they can be given the chance of fresh employment if full fitness is achieved again.

(ii) *Misconduct*   It is one of the basic duties of an employee that he must conduct himself properly. This is a broad requirement and as we have already seen its neglect can take several forms, e.g. disobedience, rudeness, lack of good faith and criminal conduct. As most of these areas have already been discussed under the subject of employee's duties, only the major issues which could result in a dismissal will be mentioned here.

With problems stemming from disobedience of employer's orders, a better understanding could usually be achieved if a written job description is given to the employee. However, flexibility is to be expected and the practice by some unions of interpreting the terms of their contract too literally is discouraged by the tribunals and courts. An employer's unilateral alteration of the terms of the contract is not acceptable, but many areas of work, such as methods and techniques of completing a task, are really the province of the employer and not strictly terms of the contract of employment. The difficulty arises where the two areas overlap. It is best for general industrial relations if consultation in all matters is carried out wherever possible. Not all disobedience of orders requires dismissal. Employers should take account of the Code of Practice, and in some cases administer a smaller penalty. Obviously some rules are more important than others and a breach does not always warrant dismissal.

Other grounds for dismissal by misconduct could be lateness, absence without leave, going on strike, working to rule and refusal to work contracted overtime. Dismissal would probably not be justified on any of these grounds if warnings had not been given, particularly if the breach was not a regular incident.

Dismissal for striking is usually a difficult issue and most employers will try to avoid such drastic action if the consequences are likely to be full-scale industrial action. Inefficiency, carelessness and general rudeness are, as has already been noted, serious breaches of duty and dismissal is a consequence. But again it must be stressed that proper disciplinary procedures must be followed.

An employee suspected of criminal conduct, e.g. theft or violence, will usually find himself dismissed, often summarily. However, there may be mitigating circumstances and many employers find it sensible to wait for the outcome of criminal proceedings before contemplating dismissal—often suspending the employee. There should be consultations with any union involved.

(iii) *Redundancy* Redundancy is acceptable under the Employment Protection (Consolidation) Act 1978, and a form of compensation is made for loss of a particular job. Redundancy payments do not affect re-employment, unemployment pay or any other benefits, and are available to all employees as a right, with a few notable exceptions, e.g., government employees, National Health Service employees, those who work abroad, the self-employed, those over retirement age, etc.

Perhaps the most frequent and easily definable reason for redundancy is where the employer stops work completely in a particular area or location. Problems may arise in distinguishing between the reorganisation of the existing work situation, using the employee's same skills and competence, and an alteration in job description which is a redundancy situation.

Alternative employment
An employee may lose his entitlement to redundancy if his employer, within four weeks of terminating his contract of employment, offers suitable alternative employment. Whether it is 'suitable' depends on the facts of each case, which must be examined on their individual merits. The job does not necessarily have to be exactly the same, but if the employee refuses it, he has to act reasonably in doing so. Basically it is recognised that in all cases of redundancy the 'last in, first out' principle is the most equitable. But the longer an employee has worked for a business organisation it seems

that the employer owes him a moral duty not to make him redundant.

Redundancy pay
Payment is made by the employer who can claim back 41 per cent from the **Redundancy Fund,** controlled by the Secretary of State for Employment and made up from contributions by both employees and employers. Claims should be made to an industrial tribunal within six months of the termination of employment. The claim is based primarily on the employee's past record of continuous employment and his age. In the event of the employer not being able to pay, the Department of Employment will still satisfy the claim.

Basically the employee must have been continuously employed for two years or more, and be over the age of eighteen. Continuity still exists even if the business has been the subject of a takeover and the employee has been re-engaged on similar terms. The calculation also excludes time off through sickness, holidays, lay-offs, short-term working, and even pregnancy, as long as the time off was within the statutory limits.

The amount due, which must be shown in writing to the employee, is determined in the following way:

Age	Pay
18–21	$\frac{1}{2}$ week
22–40	1 week
41–64	$1\frac{1}{2}$ weeks

This is subject to a maximum of twenty years' service and a maximum pay at present of £80 per week ($20 \times 1\frac{1}{2}$ weeks' pay at £130 per week will give £3,900—the maximum redundancy payment). The sum paid to the employee is tax free, and does not affect the claimant's right to unemployment benefit. The week's pay is calculated on the normal rate of pay for the employee's last full week in employment (for a piece-worker it is the average of the last twelve weeks' pay) and does not include any overtime or any other benefit, unless this is regarded as part of normal pay.

Aids to Good Industrial Relations

(1) *The Code of Practice*
The ACAS has produced a **Code of Practice** to help promote good industrial relations. It is not given statutory force but, in the event of any dispute appearing before a tribunal, failure to recognise it would be taken into account.

The Code of Practice firmly places the responsibility of maintaining good industrial relations on the management. It stresses that membership of trade unions should be encouraged and recognised to give a firm basis for consultation and bargaining. The management should be a responsible management, respectful of their employees, but above all trained and capable of managing their responsibilities. At the same time, the trade unions are also expected to act responsibly by assisting employees in establishing procedures for bargaining and settling disputes. Enough shop stewards should be appointed to keep regular contact with the management and they should be adequately trained and aware of their duties.

The Code seeks to prevent potentially unfair treatment of employees by placing on management the burden of developing through consultation effective procedures on all disciplinary matters. For instance guidelines might be considered on a progressive scale ranging from an informal oral warning through written warnings, transfers or suspension leading to the ultimate sanction of dismissal.

It is expected that organisations will consult with the employees on all matters likely to affect their conditions of work, and agree methods and levels of consultation, with suggested solutions for resolving disputes. A grievance procedure should be outlined for all employees with the emphasis on a speedy and fair settlement of the grievance. It is to be suggested that the procedures for settling disputes should be followed by both parties, and drastic action—such as lock-outs and strikes—should be only a last resort. Full usage of schemes for consultation and arbitration should always be made.

Many disputes could be avoided if the employees were clearly aware of the rules and regulations of the organisation, particularly with regard to suspension and dismissal because of misconduct. The Code states that care should be exercised before serious action is taken against an employee guilty of misconduct, to ensure that sufficient verbal and written warnings have been given. There should be no dismissal for a first offence unless there has been gross misconduct.

(2) *Advisory, Conciliation and Arbitration Service* (*ACAS*)

The ACAS was established by the Labour Government in 1974, and given statutory recognition in the Employment Protection Act 1975. The objective was to provide an arena in which labour disputes could be discussed. More specifically, it attempts to bring about:

1. The voluntary settlement of disputes.
2. The observance of procedures for dealing with disputes.
3. The recognition of agreements made between employers and employees.
4. The provision of Codes of Practice for particular industries.

The service, which is an independent body containing members from the CBI and the TUC, can deal with any dispute by way of arbitration. This is only possible, of course, if both parties to a dispute agree to this attempt to solve their difficulties. Alternatively, the issue can be handed over to the Central Arbitration Committee (CAB). This body consists of members experienced in industrial relations, who are appointed by the Secretary of State and the ACAS. The ACAS will also attempt to provide conciliation before the dispute has to resort to arbitration.

The ACAS can deal with claims by trade unions for union recognition for the purposes of collective bargaining. It may also investigate any protracted or serious labour dispute, mainly as an exercise in obtaining the facts about the dispute and upon doing so, focusing public opinion.

The ACAS does not have any powers of enforcement, but it must rely on recommendations and the weight of public opinion.

The Objectives of Organised Labour

Each trade union in this country has its own individual framework of organisation supported by the statutory provisions of the Trade Union and Labour Relations Act 1974. They would all claim to have a variety of objectives which reflected their individuality, but nonetheless several objectives are prevalent in all trade unions.

One of the most important objectives of any trade union is to secure for its members the maximum real wages. Many unions anxiously compare their position in relation to 'league tables' of other similar working groups, and an eye is also kept on the average incomes of the nation and their members' position in relation to this. However, the striving to maximise pay is not always an arbitrary action by trade unionists, but is often closely linked with a careful consideration of the increasing cost of their labour. The continued full employment of their members is obviously a strong factor in any negotiation with employers.

No union wishes to see its membership depleted by redundancies and dismissals, and will strive hard for the protection and security of the workers under its control. An efficient, strong union will use a variety of methods in fighting any employer who attempts unilaterally to remove a worker's job security. Such methods are strikes, going slow, working to rule, overtime bans, etc. But of course unions do not always resort to the more extreme measures when attempting to resolve a problem or dispute and much negotiating and consultation goes on within organisations today. Moreover, much of the discussion between employers and unions is not antagonistic or hostile, but reflects the power of the trade union movement today to be heard and to carry their opinions and grievances to all levels of company management.

Apart from the threat of redundancy, the unions also concern themselves with other aspects of job security and status. There may be an interest in improving the holiday entitlement for employees, and the actual number of hours worked in the week may be reduced as part of a productivity package offered to the management. There is a growing realisation that increased leisure time is an important improvement in working conditions to be aimed at. Progress has been slow, with many people receiving only three weeks' paid holiday and still working a forty-hour basic week.

Many unions will assist their members in obtaining any benefits due to them as a right, e.g. compensation for an injury at work or social security benefits, and will often represent them at tribunals, such as those established to investigate unfair dismissal. Attention will be given to the status of their members' employment. Pressure will be applied to improve working conditions, often to limits beyond the basic needs necessary to ensure the job is within the protection of the Health and Safety at Work Act 1974. (It is not unknown for firms to provide baths, showers and saunas for workers involved in dirty operations.)

The individual is in a very poor bargaining position with his employer, and it is only through the collective action of the trade union (even stronger when a closed shop is in operation) that the bargaining imbalance is redressed. The threat of strike action is perhaps the ultimate sanction a union can use to support a claim, and it is through this collective action that the individual employee has gained the respect of the employer.

As an overall objective and policy, above the skirmishes within the organisation, each union will be seeking to promote itself, to establish a stronger identity, and to ensure its continuing development. Many seek to do this by a closer involvement in national and international organisations. There are union representatives, for instance, on such bodies as the Monopolies Commission, the Road Safety Committee, the UK Committee of UNICEF, the Workers' Educational Association and the International Labour Organisation.

The unions have also forged a position in society where they are recognised as a political force and are a leading party in tripartite industrial discussions with the CBI and the government, and no government would now attempt to introduce economic policies and restraints without adequate consultation. The unions have also not hesitated to involve the highest authorities in any disputes. Cabinet ministers, and even the Prime Minister, are often personally involved in employer–union squabbles, particularly where the national economy itself is seriously threatened.

The Legal Status of Trade Unions

The Trade Union and Labour Relations Act (TULRA) defines a trade union as an organisation consisting wholly or mainly of workers of one description whose principal purpose is the regulation of industrial relations with employers or employers' associations. The Employment Protection Act 1975 provides for a system of registration by a Certification Officer. Any trade union can apply for a certificate which may be refused if the Certification Officer is of the opinion that the trade union is not an independent body.

To an extent, trade unions have immunity from certain legal actions. For instance, it is justifiable to order a member to go on strike and to agree with an employer to establish a 'closed shop' without either of these being an unreasonable part of trade or interfering with a man's right to work. The TULRA also confers on trade unions a wide immunity from actions in tort. Immunity is granted in cases where trade union members induce another to break his contract, i.e. requesting a member to go on strike, or perhaps persuading a supplier to break his contract of supply. Such immunity is granted only if it is in furtherance of a **trade dispute**.

Picketing is recognised nowadays as an acceptable method of bringing to the attention of employers, suppliers and members of the public the existence of a grievance. Trade unionists are given statutory protection to engage in the peaceful obtaining or communicating of information, or the peaceful persuading of any person to work or abstain from working. However, the picketing must be peaceful. The police will take preventative action if there is likely to be a breach of the peace or an obstruction of the highway, and action will be taken if the police are obstructed in the carrying out of their duty. Furthermore, the Employment Act 1980 has introduced legislative restraints on 'secondary picketing'.

Collective agreements

The TULRA settles the issue of whether collective agreements between employer and employee are legally binding. The answer is that there is no legally enforceable contract unless the agreement is in writing and there is an express provision to that effect.

Trade union rules

Each trade union has its own individual rules of procedure, but generally they follow similar lines. Admission to a union is often quite simple, requiring merely a proposer and seconder. (Craft unions, however, normally require the serving of an apprenticeship.) Members must pay a subscription and obey union rules. Members in breach of union rules can be disciplined by fines, suspension or even expulsion. The courts tend not to interfere in union procedures if they are correctly followed.

Trade union institutional framework

Each trade union differs in its structure as there are no formalised rules of constitution. But nonetheless there are a number of similarities in the operation of union affairs and of the officers controlling and running them.

Shop stewards

Members are commonly represented in the working situation by shop stewards. Their main responsibilities are the registration of members and collecting or supervising contributions. But by far the biggest responsibility is the handling of localised grievances and (where possible) negotiating pay structures and terms of employment. They act as linkmen for their branch and district committees and their duties are principally honorary.

The branch

The branch usually consists of a chairman, secretary and treasurer (honorary positions) and generally meets regularly to deal with correspondence and issues raised by members in the locality. Many decisions affecting workplace disputes are handled at branch meetings but if the problem seems to be beyond their control it can be passed to a higher authority within the union. (The activities of the branches are co-ordinated and stimulated by district organisers appointed by the members of the executive.)

Executive committees

The formation and execution of policy is handled by the executive committee, who are elected members based on regional and other sectional interests. The members can hold full-time or part-time appointments, and they include a general secretary, a full-time paid official. He represents the union at all its important meetings, and is generally responsible for the administration of the trade union headquarters and staff. Unions supplement their activities by holding an annual conference which delegates can attend to discuss motions submitted by the branches in advance. The idea is to harden policy and suggest plans for future action. It is also an opportunity to change union rules.

Trades Union Congress

This is the national centre of the trade union movement. Its major objective is to promote the welfare and conditions of its members and most of the trade unions are affiliated to it. An annual congress of delegates is held where issues concerning the trade union movement are voted upon. The voting power of the delegates is proportionate to the membership of the union.

Throughout the rest of the year, the trade union movement is represented by the General Council of thirty-eight unpaid members elected by the whole Congress who hold regular meetings and conduct most of their business through committees. Their decisions are not binding on the unions, but their value is in influence and recommendations, including advice in industrial disputes. It can also intervene in industrial disputes if requested by the affiliated union. As a representative of the unions it has considerable powers of consultation with the government and the CBI.

7. The Customer's Needs and the Changing Nature of the Market Environment

The role of market research as a means of identifying customers' needs

Consumers tend to associate market research with the activities of companies which gather information from them regarding their opinions on goods and services, through the completion of a questionnaire usually aimed at establishing their pattern of expenditure. This, however, is known as **consumer research** and is only one aspect of the scope of **market research,** which has been defined by the British Institute of Management as 'the objective gathering, recording, and analysing of all facts about the problems relating to the transfer and sales of goods and services from producer to consumer'. Market research is therefore concerned not only with the investigation into the consumer market for products, but also the original concept of a new or improved product, the analysis of existing or new methods of distribution, the sales organisation, advertising and other promotional activities.

Market research is also a two-way process in that it can originate with changes on the product side, continue through to the analysis of consumer demand, or stem from consumer demand itself. A change in any of the aspects of marketing, for example, is likely to have repercussions on related activities, and they may need investigation. Again market research is usually associated with the eventual purchase by consumers of final goods and services, but producers themselves constitute a market in that they are customers for plant, equipment, components, raw materials and a range of services. Thus producers of these inputs, which assist in the production of consumer goods and services, will also be concerned with investigating the market which in their case comprises the firms to which they sell their output. When this wider concept of market research is taken into account, it is possible to identify several areas which may prove valuable subjects for investigation and analysis.

(i) Product research

New or improved products will be put forward on the basis of information derived from other research activities and will then be subjected to a series of tests.

(a) These tests may be aimed at such features as design, materials or ingredients, colour, durability, ease of handling, fitness for purpose, reliability, operating capacity or any other factor likely to be considered by the final user.

(b) They will also be analysed from the point of view of the extent to which they will meet other demands of a psychological nature. This is because consumers can be motivated in their selection of purchases by the status or prestige which they believe the good or service confers upon them, and even the brand name given to an item can be important in this respect.

(c) Similarly tests will be directed at the way in which the product is finally presented to the consumer in its container or package, as several factors can be important, such as material, design, labelling, robustness, weight and ease of storage.

(d) Comparable tests may be run on competitors' products to highlight any advantages or deficiences in certain areas of the new or improved product.

(e) Testing of both the product and packaging may produce features which prove to be superfluous and provide scope for greater standardisation in production.

(f) The company may also be concerned with ensuring that it has a sufficient range of output to allow it to compete in all areas of the market that may prove profitable.

(g) After-sales service records may indicate areas for improvement or means of raising the quality of the service provided.

(ii) Sales organisation and distribution research
Opportunities may exist to reorganise the sales force both to make it more effective and to eradicate wasted effort.

(a) Greater efficiency may be achieved by altering the sequence of calls by sales representatives, and by comparing the number of calls with the corresponding number and size or orders. Sales figures from various areas when compared with the sales force employed may provide useful information particularly when some areas supposedly had the same market potential. New markets may also require a review of the most efficient way of organising the sales force.

(b) Existing methods of distribution, such as selling direct to the customer, using a wholesaler or independent retail unit, may leave scope for improvement or alteration in the light of changes in consumer habits or other marketing activities. Different methods of distribution and the performance of individual units may be investigated in order that strong areas are built upon, while unprofitable products and services, customers, orders and territories, may be eliminated.

(c) Contact with those purchasing on behalf of distributive outlets or trades will provide useful opinions on the company's marketing techniques when compared with those adopted by competitors.

(d) Sales staff will generally be operating under some form of incentive scheme and new schemes may lead to greater effort on the part of those actually seeking orders from customers or distributors, and the most effective incentive scheme will be a subject of research.

(iii) Communication research
(a) This can help to establish the effectiveness of advertising material and the media used, such as television, press, periodicals, trade journals, and posters.

(b) The sales force will also use advertising material, and after consideration of its effectiveness descriptive brochures may need to be reviewed.

(c) Companies may also organise exhibitions and demonstrations, and their contribution to sales will be indicated by the number of enquiries and eventual orders placed as a result of these special events.

(d) Not only do companies wish to introduce their products to the market but also to create a favourable image in the eyes of the public that could help foster future sales. Thus public relations and image-building exercises will be related to any change in the general opinion of the company held by both consumers and the public in general.

(iv) Economies and business research
(a) The activities of the company will be influenced by the general economic climate and forecasts concerning the general level of economic activity, and this will require analysis of key economic indicators.

(b) Data relating to sectors which are closely connected with the prospects of the company concerned will be a subject of investigation. In particular, a company will be interested in any information which it can gather concerning the activities of its competitors, suppliers and trade customers.

(c) The economic and business climate in which the company operates may be influenced by the government's economic policy in terms of its approach to managing the level of demand in the economy, policies dealing with company taxation, investment and the extent and nature of government intervention in the form of legislation dealing with consumer protection and other business activities. A change of government may produce a different emphasis in areas such as these, but even during the lifetime of the same government attitudes may change.

(d) Research will also take account of social and demographic trends. For example, growing consumer awareness and consumer organisations are developments that will influence company policy. Similarly, changes in living, working and leisure habits all contribute to a changing life style that will be reflected in patterns of demand. Such research means that social cults and fashions can be identified and perhaps related to profitable business activities.

The political, economic and social environment is never stable and will have an impact upon the business community which in turn can be a factor contributing to changes in this environment.

(v) Consumer or user research
A company must accurately identify and assess the needs of a consumer in the context of changing tastes and preferences.

(a) This aspect of market research applies not only to consumer goods and services, but also to capital goods and other inputs which assist in production. This is because the demands placed upon such items by user industries may necessitate accommodating changes in specifications, technical requirements and other features associated with such inputs.

(b) As with other objectives of market research that aimed at consumers or users, this must be an ongoing activity in order that the company is aware of market trends as soon as they develop, and the implications which they have for their products and other aspects of marketing.

(c) Research into final markets will allow the producer to assess the potential for new, improved or existing products. Such research should provide information relating to such features as design, quality, price, convenience, size and other physical characteristics of products and packaging which the consumer may consider before selecting a final purchase.

(d) The company will also wish to know the background of consumers in terms of sex, marital status, family size, social class, income group and other elements that are important in product development and promotional activities.

(e) There are also the less easily identifiable factors which influence the behaviour of individuals as consumers, and hence their pattern of expenditure. These relate to the individual's psychological make-up which leads to a certain expression of attitudes, opinions, reactions and other areas where scope may exist for the expression of personality when a purchase is made. Special surveys aimed at these psychological factors will have to take account of images, social standing, standards of value and other aspects as they affect consumer behaviour.

(f) The company will wish to discover from what type of retail outlet certain purchases are made and also when they are generally made.

(g) Sales will also be analysed from the point of view of the total market share and the share of sales among certain types of consumers.

Consumer research techniques

Subsequent sections will concentrate upon the methods employed by producers of consumer goods and services rather than user research in the field of capital goods and other inputs. This is not to imply that the latter is less important, but the nature of this type of production is such that the problems which need to be investigated are largely different from those which arise in the field of consumer goods and services. Producers of capital goods, for example, are often involved in a highly technical and specialised market where there are relatively few customers but with whom in many cases close contact exists. Buyers of such products will be motivated by factors which are readily identifiable in terms of technical capabilities, working capacity, reliability and price, rather than the more subjective factors that influence the tastes and preferences of consumers which constitute a larger and more impersonal market. This is reflected in the fact that consumer goods manufacturers allocate a much larger proportion of their total expenditure to various forms of market research than producers of industrial inputs. In particular, the proportion spent on consumer research is much larger than that spent on user research by industrial producers. The latter, however, do spend vast sums on research and development of products and processes of a technical or scientific nature.

Independent Market Research Units

The highly specialised nature of industrial production is also reflected in the relatively small part of market research work allocated to outside organisations, whereas the demands of consumer goods producers can more readily be catered for by independent agencies.

(a) Independent market research organisations can provide facilities for large-scale consumer research, and this is often required by those companies dealing with mass-produced consumer goods.

(b) The research staff will be highly specialised and experienced in dealing with consumer research projects, and they will employ specialists on psychological influences upon consumer choice and the methods of assessing and analysing these.

(c) The agency will have developed research techniques using highly trained analysts and statisticians, assisted by specially developed data-processing systems using computers.

(d) An independent organisation allows the client the advantage of not making a company's research objectives known to its competitors and can also take an unbiased approach when reporting direct to the client company at management level. This will be important if some of the company's marketing activities are eventually shown in an unfavourable light. If such research was conducted by an internal unit it could produce an emphasis in the results which hides the deficiency in the company's marketing department.

Why Consumer Research is Possible

The following description of consumer research highlights the main techniques employed. Some problem areas will be identified, but these may be of less concern to the specialist research organisation because of the techniques it has developed over a long period and the data which it will have accumulated and is continually updating.

Information which both contributes to, and results from, consumer surveys can be a valuable guide to assessing the buying habits and life style of those who make up the market. This is possible because both economic and social developments have led to a greater uniformity in certain aspects of human behaviour. The raising of the lower levels of income, combined with the ability to place larger numbers of people into fewer income groups, and social groupings on the basis of class, as well as the general improvement in real incomes, have all contributed to this greater uniformity in consumer behaviour. These developments—along with mass productions—have led to the mass consumption of many products, with the result that a very large part of the population has experienced a wide range of consumer goods and services. It is thus possible to accept the results derived from a survey of a cross-section of the market as being a fairly reliable guide to the characteristics of the market as a whole. All this, of course, is on the assumption that the research techniques, the analysis of results and final conclusions are conducted on a correct basis.

Some Constraints upon Marketing Activities

Before actually attempting to discover where the market lies, and the relative strengths of various influences upon the consumer, there are some constraints imposed upon the producer which will already be known to him.

(a) These constraints may be imposed by legislation relating to consumer or environmental protection that prevent the company from embodying certain features in its product or packaging.

(b) Such legislation may also control other aspects of marketing, such as advertising or promotional tactics, and actually oblige the company to incorporate certain characteristics into its products and advertisements.

(c) However, some constraints may be imposed, for example, by the physical properties of dwellings and the existing stock of consumer durables to which the product may be complementary. The design of a refrigerator, for example, will have to take account of the kitchen space available in those households which are likely to form a large part of the market, while producers of perishable foodstuffs will have to pay attention to shelf space and the dimensions of refrigerators.

Desk Research

The first stage of any research will be the gathering of factual information from existing publications. A useful range of publications stems from the **Government Statistical Service.** This provides data on broad aggregates in the economy such as national income and expenditure, industrial production, investment, international trade, prices, demographic and social trends; these are then broken down into a more detailed presentation to provide more specific information. Such is the quantity and scope of this statistical service that an official guide to statistical sources is also provided to assist the researcher in discovering certain facts and figures. *The Annual Digest of Statistics, 1977* contained nearly 700 tables on various aspects of economic and social signficance in the UK, while during the year there are regular up-to-date publications such as *Economic Trends, Financial Statistics* and *The Monthly Digest of Statistics.*

Trade publications are produced on behalf of firms that constitute an industry or particular trade. These journals will contain data, information and articles on subjects and developments of relevance to the industry as a whole. They will contain informed opinion of how political, economic and social trends can be expected to affect the product or service around which the industry's activities are concentrated.

There are also journals of a more general nature produced by various institutes and professional organisations, in addition to the weekly review published by the Department of Trade and Industry which contains key economic indicators and articles of interest to various sections of industry and commerce. A researcher can also make contact with a specific organisation to seek certain types of information, and directories exist which can be used for this purpose. For example the *Directory of British Associations* (published by CBD Research Ltd) deals with 'interests, activities and publications of trade associations, scientific and technical societies, professional institutes, learned societies, research organisations, chambers of commerce and trade, agricultural societies, trade unions, cultural, sports and welfare organisations in the UK and Northern Ireland'. There is also Kelly's *Manufacturers and Merchants Directory*, and publications such as these can provide the initial contact for researchers seeking information and possible outlets for advertising material.

The company's own records of past sales may provide valuable data for research purposes as, for example, establishing a connection between the company's own performance and outside influences identified as possible reasons for fluctuations in sales. The results of economic and business research previously described will also be available for further analysis.

Field Research

When all existing sources of information have been tapped, it will then be necessary to supplement general trends and influences on sales with a more detailed analysis of the factors that eventually lead the consumer to select purchases from the choice available. It is at this stage that field research must be undertaken and is the means by which the company seeks to be customer orientated in its marketing activities. Some form of contact will be made with consumers and generally a questionnaire of some form will be employed. The vast majority of people do not intentionally distort their answers to a questionnaire, but the final conclusions drawn from research will not prove reliable if the consumer sample selected is not a representative cross-section of the market under investigation. The market, or **universe,** as the researcher calls it, is first determined and then a number is decided upon to constitute a sample. If this sample is too small it will not be a useful guide, whereas if it is too large it will mean an unwarranted use of money and effort. Ideally, the sample should be a microcosm of the universe in that it is selected to reproduce exactly the characteristics of the universe itself. This means that in the sample there should be the same proportion of people with certain characteristics that form particular sub-groups in terms of sex, age, marital status, income groups, and so on. The group to be interviewed should be a scale model of the universe whose opinions are sought.

The larger the number of sub-groups that a researcher wishes to identify, then the larger the sample required. If, for example, the universe is estimated at 1 million and the consumer sample is to be 3,000, while a sub-group of the universe is 2 per cent then this will make up only 60 of the sample. It may be that from the statistician's point of view such a number is too small to give a reliable indication of opinions held by those in the universe where they number 20,000. In this event, the number in the sub-group could be increased and this disproportionate number taken into account when analysing the results. If the number of such sub-groups is relatively high, the sample will need to be correspondingly larger and this will raise the cost of the research. This demonstrates one of the problems facing the researcher: the less uniform the universe and the greater the number of sub-groups he wishes to identify, the larger the sample must be. Having decided upon the size of the sample, the researcher will select a method of making up the sample and its constituent parts that readily lends itself to contacting the types of consumers involved.

(i) *The probability system*

This involves obtaining a list of the universe to be researched. Sources of names and addresses may be available from trade and telephone directories, electoral registers and subscribers to journals and professional organisations. Although names and addresses may be available from many such sources, it is not always possible to identify them as falling within the universe or a particular sub-group. This will depend very much on having access to relevant lists, which even then will often not indicate enough of an individual's personal background to allocate them to a specific sub-group.

The researcher will select the sample by taking perhaps 1 name in 30 from lists and allocating them to interviewers who must then adhere to their quotas, otherwise their own bias in terms of the people they would like to interview will not make the results representative. This selection and interviewing will have to continue until the various sub-sections are complete, and this will not necessarily be at the same time that the number of contacts reaches the number prescribed by the sample. This is because lists themselves may not be a cross-section unless they were selected on the basis that they were essentially the whole universe or a uniform part of it.

(ii) *The random selection system*

This involves contacting households selected largely on a random basis, rather than allowing the interviewer to make a conscious choice. The interviewer may select contacts by requesting co-operation from passers-by, perhaps asking every tenth person until a contact is established. Any such random selection would be more acceptable than the interviewer being allowed to decide because of personal preference entering into the exercise. This may be predetermined to a certain extent by basing the random selection upon homes which are capable of being placed into sub-groups. For example, areas may be placed into categories in terms of region, rural or urban location, and types of dwelling, from which random selection is then made. This will be particularly advantageous when the sample is to contain sub-groups based upon such characteristics.

(iii) *The quota system*

This can be a more clearly defined method and is a very popular means of consumer research. Once the size of the sample is decided upon, the sub-groups are defined and interviewers are allocated a quota of individuals which they must contact according to certain characteristics of the sub-groups. For example, an interviewer may be required to trace and interview a certain number of households in an urban area which are owner-occupied, with two children of school age, and both parents working. With the probability and random methods, the interviewer was obliged to contact those listed or adhere to a uniform random selection basis, such as every tenth house, if the representative nature of the sample was to be achieved. With the quota system, however, the interviewer is not obliged to adhere to such a process of selection as long as the respondent meets the requirements of a sub-group. Thus the interviewer is not obliged to call again on those who were not at home when first called upon and can have greater flexibility in selecting alternative contacts.

(iv) *Consumer panels*

A continuous flow of information can be derived from households which agree to report on certain items which form a part of their pattern of expenditure or living habits. This will allow the researcher to identify trends in their early stages and possibly relate them to fluctuations in demand or suggest new markets. A cross-section of households is requested to make up a panel designed to be a representative sample of the market. They are asked to submit details of their spending or other information on a regular basis, dealing with such matters as products, their prices and sizes, place and time of purchase or allocation of leisure time between various alternatives. Such panels are expensive to establish and may require continuous attention if they are to be maintained for a sufficiently long period to make the results from participants worth while. Results from a panel with a large turn-over will not give an accurate impression of longer-term trends, and hence changes in the pattern of expenditure and living habits. The longer a household remains on the panel, the more accustomed they become to making returns. They may then become less self-conscious when making purchases and not continuously consider the implications which their spending will have on their report. They may then act more naturally in accordance with their personal tastes and preferences, and for these reasons the information submitted to the researcher will be more valuable.

Interviewing techniques

The information which the researcher is seeking is usually derived from the answers which consumers are willing to give to some form of questionnaire. It is therefore important that the actual contact with the respondent takes a form which makes full use of the questionnaire and permits as much accuracy as possible.

(i) **Personal interview**

This is generally the most successful method in that it achieves the greatest response. A personable and experienced interviewer will acquire a technique which not only encourages participation in the questionnaire but generally leads to more complete and accurate answers. The interviewer's approach can be adapted to put the respondent at ease, the value of their participation explained in the light of the researcher's objectives, and any difficulty in interpreting a question or areas of response can be dealt with by verbal alternatives. Where the quota system is employed, the interviewer will gain experience of certain types of households and more readily identify areas where they can be located. The interviewer may become accomplished in identifying other general characteristics concerning the individual or household and therefore submit information that could not be obtained from questions since they would have to be of a more personal nature.

Personal interviews are expensive, however, in terms of salaries and travelling costs, particularly when the probability and random systems means that they must re-call on people who were originally not at home, as substitutes would destroy the nature of these techniques. Even in the quota system, a sub-section may contain a group with characteristics which it proves very time-consuming and difficult to trace within a particular area, and this will add to travelling expenses. Interviewers themselves may subconsciously allow bias to enter into their choice of respondents and any assistance which they may provide in completing the questionnaire. Moreover, if questionnaires are completed in face-to-face situations the respondents may try to give the answers expected of them, or those which they believe will create the best impression on the interviewer.

(ii) The discussion group technique

In this case a group of people representing a cross-section of the universe is invited to participate in a discussion to express their tastes and preferences in relation to certain goods and services or give their views on household activities. The chairman of the meeting will be an experienced researcher who will be able to create an atmosphere in which the participants will feel free to express their opinions. The chairman will introduce topics and guide the conversation in the desired direction. The whole exercise can be recorded and analysed at a later stage and the tone of conversation will also help indicate the strength of certain opinions and attitudes. This may prove a limited exercise because the more vociferous person will play a disproportionately large part and the shy and more retiring person will not be well represented.

(iii) Postal surveys

Mailing questionnaires to households will be less expensive than the personal interview, but this may be partly offset by the number which must be sent out to achieve a sufficient number of replies and the extra literature which must be enclosed to describe the purpose of the research. The questionnaire must be expressed in simple terms and readily understood as the questionnaire must be completed without assistance. The answer technique should be of a nature that reduces the amount of effort involved on the part of the respondent. They must therefore be of the *yes/no* type, or boxes which require ticking, one of them

covering the respondents' activities and opinions. Such postal communications must be made as attractive as possible so that they are not immediately discarded.

(iv) Telephone interviews

In 1980 telephones were possessed by only 70 per cent of the population. This would not present a problem if it were not for the fact that such households are not likely to provide a representative sample in terms of important sub-sections, as telephones may be heavily concentrated in a narrow range of households. It may prove a relatively cheap method of contacting respondents, but the subscriber may be unwilling to provide essential information to an unknown caller for reasons of security.

Questionnaires

Having decided upon the area to be researched, the questions must be designed so that the answers allow respondents to be classified into the desired sub-sections of the universe.

(a) The initial questions will seek facts about the person being interviewed such as sex, age, marital status, family and occupation.

(b) Some of the early questions, in fact, can be designed to arouse the participant's interest in the survey and create an impression that his contribution will play an important part in the research.

(c) Other questions of a more personal nature, necessary to identify sub-sections in terms of income and important items of personal expenditure, may follow at a later stage when the respondent has become more relaxed.

(d) The researcher may also need to design questions which seek to gain information concerning not only patterns of expenditure but also related household activities, and to gain opinions on certain features of goods and services.

(e) Although the majority of people will have no reason for giving false information, the possibility of this happening does arise with questions where the participant might hesitate to give an answer that would affect his personal standing and show him in an unfavourable social light. Where such questions are necessary, they can be checked against control questions included in the questionnaire with the intention of obtaining the same information using a different style of question. If control questions indicate contradictory answers then it can be supposed that for personal reasons the answers provided are not a true reflection of the individual's activities or opinions. The questionnaire can then be omitted from the sample used in the eventual analysis. The need for control questions in sensitive areas can be avoided if the question is constructed in such a way that issues of guilt or social standing do not arise.

(f) Questions should not be too exacting and should follow logically upon one another, not changing direction. The sentence construction and choice of words should avoid ambiguity and be of a nature that strikes an acceptable balance between the vocabulary and powers of expression of various groups of the community. Similarly, answers should not make great demands upon the respondent's ability to communicate orally.

(g) The easiest question for both parties, and the analyst, is the one which simply demands a *yes/no* response. In areas which do not lend themselves to such answers it is possible to give a range of responses which can also help to remind the participant of the choices available. For example, the question may be: 'If you were to buy a newly built home what type of central heating would you prefer?' The following responses could then be contained in boxes one of which could be crossed through: 'oil, gas, solid fuel, storage heaters, under floor, warm-air'. This multiple response is also useful where the respondent cannot be expected to give a precise answer but an approximate indication would prove acceptable. In this case the individual selects an answer which most closely reflects his or her activities or views.

(h) Some questions may be open-ended in that they allow the respondent greater scope in the answer, but they are more time-consuming for both respondent and interviewer. They are also more difficult to process using computer techniques as they require analysing before being given a code. Personal judgement may have to be used in allocating some such open-ended answers to certain codes. The interviewer may assist by writing a summary of the answer but again this leaves scope for personal interpretation of the respondent's remarks.

(i) The interviewer must also take care that the question is posed in such a way that the tone of the voice does not create undue emphasis on certain words or parts of the question.

(j) Questions can be designed and used to obtain factual data on the characteristics of consumers and what they regard as important influences in their selection of products. The important

aspect of *why* they hold these opinions, or are influenced by certain features of a product, is a much more complex area of investigation that enters more deeply into the field of psychology. It is far more difficult to research into **consumer motivation** in selecting between alternatives for expenditure and between various retail outlets, and into what influences the timing of expenditure. Consumer motivation research seeks to identify the features that should be incorporated into the product, packaging and other marketing activities in order that a consumer will select in favour of the company concerned. The choice of a brand name and advertising are areas where there is often an attempt to appeal to the inner feelings and emotional make-up of consumers. Some such attempts may be obvious to the consumer but others may be of a more subtle nature.

These aspects of research are more difficult to deal with in the form of a questionnaire as consumers are less willing to discuss their inner motives and desires, even if they are conscious of them. Specialist research units will concentrate upon this aspect of human behaviour and then relate it to consumer behaviour and marketing activities.

(k) A problem may arise if the potential respondent wishes to know both the name of the company sponsoring the research and further details of the purpose of the investigation. If the identity of the company is disclosed, this may prejudice answers—they may be deliberately flattering or very critical, rather than a rational assessment of opinion. If the activities of the company become known to competitors, it may lose some initial advantage and provoke early competitive reactions.

(l) Again, if too much detail of the purpose of the research is revealed, this can create a bias by influencing answers in a particular direction which the respondent believes will assist the researcher.

Test marketing

When a large capital investment is involved in the development of a new or improved product, some form of test marketing will generally be an important pre-condition for a national sales effort. Test marketing applies not only to the product itself, but also to all the marketing activities supporting the product—the sales organisation, the distribution system, advertising and promotional aids. It allows the company to experience the realities of competitive pressures in a market, to make accommodating changes in the product, and to discover any deficiencies. Test marketing has a very impressive record: products launched on a national scale after having been corrected in the light of test market findings have a success record of about 90 per cent.

The Characteristics of the Test Area

(a) The test area selected must be representative of the universe in order that results can be a reliable guide for the basis of a national campaign. Thus the residents of the area must be a cross-section in terms of their personal characteristics, and all other factors must be typical of those elsewhere. Thus the quality of the marketing force, and the strength of competition, must be typical of that which exists in other areas. Even the level and type of employment should approach that which exists in the economy as a whole.

(b) The size of the test market is also an important factor. If the product by its very nature is not expected to sell in vast quantities, the area selected must be sufficiently large to produce sales that can be used for statistical purposes. It must also take account of the market share which the firm believes will make the product a viable proposition. If, for example, the company anticipates that 10 per cent of a market of 1 million will be viable, then an area yielding sales in the region of 10,000—but not less—will prove a workable basis for a test.

(c) The area must also be typical as regards the organisation of sales and distribution networks. For example, the selection of an area that is too large for the prospective sales organisation may produce disappointing results that are not due to deficiencies in the product itself.

(d) If advertising is to be tested, the area for the product test should as far as possible coincide with the coverage of the media being used. The area for the test should also be considered from the point of view of retail outlets using point-of-sale promotions and demonstrations, as they will have certain catchment areas. If national advertising is likely to play an important part in the total market, the area selected to test such media must be one where, for example, regional television or editions of national newspapers are available. This will allow a test of the anticipated advertising media.

(e) Producing output for test purposes and setting up a marketing network for new products can be a costly exercise, as the company will not yet be geared to high levels of output in terms of the type and size of productive capacity. The unit costs of the product may thus be very high and the company will be particularly keen to deal with a test market that is small yet practical. A large area does run the risk of a substantial financial loss if the test is unsuccessful, but such a loss may be justified if the company reduces the risk of launching a national sales effort on the basis of statistical evidence taken from such a small area. Moreover, the larger the area selected for the test the more difficult it becomes for a competitor to obscure the results by engaging in concentrated competition in that area.

(f) Test marketing should not attempt to test too many factors at the same time in the same area. If, for example, an advertising technique is being tested, then altering other factors—such as special offers and packaging—will not allow the researcher to assess the relative importance of any single factor on sales. The response of competitors must be monitored, as this may not necessarily be a type of competition which a rival could be expected to maintain on a national scale.

(g) If test marketing is used for what is considered to be an improved product or a more effective marketing technique, the results should be compared with those in a similar area in order to identify changes in sales peculiar to the test area itself. A similar yardstick can be obtained by an initial consumer research in the test area and then repeated at a later date to assess changes in tastes and preferences.

(h) If test plans are changed it may be a wise precaution to change the test area, as results of new factors introduced into the original test area will be distorted by those that may still be working their way through.

(i) The company must take care that the total effort which it exerts in the area is one which can be maintained on a national scale, otherwise conclusions drawn from the test area results may be unduly optimistic.

(j) The actual length of the test market period should be long enough to cater for all the possible seasonal fluctuations in demand and perhaps confirm the trends which have been identified in consumer research. The test area should be kept under continuous scrutiny even after the national launch has commenced and has been running for some time. This monitoring process will give an early indication of trends as they develop and lead the company to check them on a national scale. Moreover, the initial response of consumers to new or improved products will not be a true indication of future spending habits on a more permanent basis. The initial purchase may have been on a promotional offer to encourage a consumer to make the first purchase, or simply curiosity on the part of the consumer. The test period must therefore be sufficiently long to allow changes of a more permanent nature to show themselves as the consumers eventually place the product within their scale of tastes and preferences.

(k) Test marketing is largely concerned with consumer goods rather than, for example, capital goods. To produce a quantity of machine tools for test marketing purposes would prove very costly! Users would not be keen to introduce a machine in their factories for test purposes because of the dislocation which might arise in other production processes to which it might not be geared. So here it is essentially a problem of persuading users to operate them on an experimental basis to assess them in the light of actual production. A capital good is likely to be put through intensive trials by the producer as results of experimental projects may best be kept confidential. Customers are likely to be more widespread and dealt with on a more personal basis, as close liaison with them will allow the producer to assess their technical needs and the use to which such capital goods are to be put. The testing of advertising may be less urgent as it is likely to be informative rather than purely persuasive and the choice of media restricted essentially to trade journals. Many millions of pounds are often involved in developing new capital goods and during the stages of research and development continuous reference will be made to the users' requirements.

The factors that influence demand

The following sections identify important economic factors which, if they were to change, can be expected to influence the demand for goods and services. Whenever one of these factors is being analysed it will be assumed that all the remaining factors remain unchanged in order that one can attribute subsequent changes in demand to this single factor.

(i) Demand for a product in relation to its price
In the vast majority of cases the demand for a product is inversely related to its price. As the price

of a product increases, it becomes more expensive relative to possible substitutes and the demand for it can be expected to fall. The relationship between the demand and the price of cotton shirts, for example, can be shown by the use of a demand curve as in Fig. 7.1.

Fig. 7.1

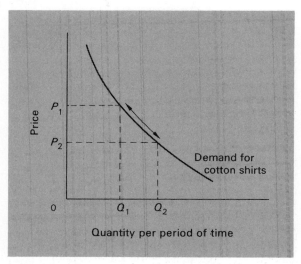

This demand curve shows the quantity of cotton shirts which the total market is prepared to purchase at different price levels. If, for example, the price of cotton shirts was OP_1 then the market would be prepared to purchase the quantity of shirts as shown by OQ_1. However, at a lower price of OP_2 consumers would be prepared to purchase a quantity of shirts totalling OQ_2. In order to register the quantity demanded at various price levels, it is necessary to describe demand in the context of a particular period of time—per month or per year. Demand is a flow, and the absence of a time period over which this flow is measured would not allow an estimation of the strength of demand.

Perhaps the rationale behind this relationship between the price of a product and the demand for it can usefully be explained. Consumers always seek to maximise the level of satisfaction or well-being which they can derive from using their income in various ways. The consumer is said to be in equilibrium when buying less of some products in order to release income for other uses is not considered worth while. The reaction of a consumer to a fall in price can be analysed in the light of the law of diminishing marginal utility (satisfaction or well-being). The amount of extra utility which a consumer derives from additional purchases of a product falls and thus total utility does increase, but by progressively smaller amounts.

Whenever consumers contemplate a change in their patterns of expenditure between existing products or to include new products, they ask themselves 'Is it worth it?' The eventual decision is then taken on the basis of how much a move will affect their own level of satisfaction. The aggregation of these individual decisions regarding changes in relative prices leads to their combined expression, via the market demand for a product in relation to its price. The extent of the reaction to a price change among individual consumers will differ according to the marginal utility they attach to purchases of different products within the constraint imposed by their respective incomes. The impact upon demand of a change in price is known as the 'substitution effect'; a change in price will also have an 'income effect' (see section (iv), page 129).

This inverse relationship between prices and the quantity demanded exists with the majority of products but there are some areas where a perverse relationship may exist. This arises with products associated with the 'demonstration effect' whereby some consumers derive increased satisfaction from a product because it actually increases in price. Consumers are expected to behave rationally and reduce by various amounts their purchases of products whose relative price has increased. If some consumers, however, are observed actually to increase their demand for a product when it increases in price, they are not acting irrationally. This is because one assumes that consumers always seek to maximise their satisfaction. Producers have discovered that in certain cases if a product is re-launched at a higher price, supported by advertising and promotional activities that seek to raise its image, sales increase. This does, however, raise the question of whether one is still dealing with the same product. If the producer succeeds in up-marketing the product, this increase in sales may be largely due to the campaign which seeks to influence tastes and preferences in favour of the product. Thus another factor likely to influence demand—tastes and preferences—has not remained unchanged, and this influence on demand is described in section (v) (page 132).

This 'demonstration effect' does exist, but the conclusion should not necessarily be drawn that a fall in price will lower the demand. Any reduced purchases by those who feel the product no longer has sufficient exclusiveness or prestige may be more than outweighed by those who would be keen to buy for the first time now that the price is reduced to within their reach and the product still possesses a favourable image.

There are some markets where the reason for a perverse relationship is more readily identified. In markets such as those for securities, foreign exchange and commodities, there is always the element of speculative trading present. An increase in market prices may provoke speculative buying in anticipation of further price rises which may produce a capital gain when sold at a higher price. Similarly, if prices in such markets start to fall, then speculative pressures may lead to a fall in demand. The holding of cash may be seen as preferable, thus avoiding any capital loss if an unforeseen need for cash forces the holder of such assets to sell when market prices are even further depressed.

(ii) The demand for a product and the price of substitutes

Although there are a large number of items competing for the consumer's income, there are some markets where this competition is particularly strong—where the consumer's need can be satisfied from a range of products which can be substituted for each other. In this case the demand for a product will vary directly with the price of a substitute, and this will be particularly apparent when products are very close substitutes. For example, the demand for margarine is closely associated with the price of butter, and between 1970 and 1972 in the UK the consumption of margarine per head rose from 2·86 oz per week to 3·52 oz per week, whereas over the same period the consumption of butter fell from 5·99 oz per week to 4·79 oz per week. This was also a period when there was a relatively large increase in the price of butter. The fall in the price of butter by 1975, however, produced margarine consumption of 2·60 oz per week and butter consumption of 5·61 oz per week. Similarly, if there was a change in the price of timber, the demand for products such as plastics would be influenced, as scope exists to employ either of them in some aspects of building and furniture-making, for example.

Fig. 7.2 shows this expected relationship between the demand for a product and the price of a substitute. This diagram refers to paint and wallpaper, which compete for the income of those consumers who regard them as possible substitutes. When the price of wallpaper is at OP the demand for paint is OQ_1, but when the price of wallpaper rises to OP_2 the demand for paint increases to OQ_2.

Fig. 7.2

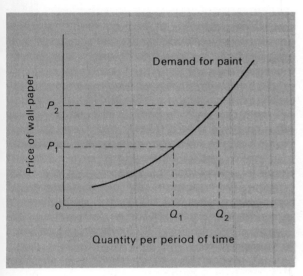

Quantity per period of time

Fig. 7.3

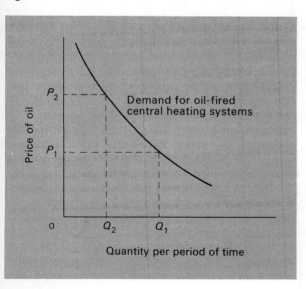

Quantity per period of time

(iii) The demand for a product and the price of complementary products

The description 'complementary products' is given to those products which must be used in conjunction with each other so that a particular need can be satisfied. For example, cameras and film are complementary products, as are gas appliances and gas. Fig. 7.3 shows such a relationship by suggesting how the demand for oil-fired central heating systems is influenced by a change in the price of oil. When the price of oil is OP_1 the demand for this type of heating system is OQ_1, but it falls to OQ_2 when the price of oil rises to OP_2. In 1976 in the UK less than 50 per cent of households had central heating, which suggests that a significant rise in the price of oil would reduce sales, both to the first-time buyer and those replacing an obsolete or inefficient system, by firms engaged in manufacturing oil-fired central heating systems.

(iv) The demand for a product and the level of household income

The effect of a change in income upon the demand for a product will depend upon the product in question and the level of income that existed before the change. The assumption that all other factors likely to influence demand remain unchanged is very important here, particularly that all *prices* remain constant. This is because the response of demand to a change in income depends upon **real income,** in that the change in money income does mean a change in real purchasing power and is not off-set by a change in the general level of prices.

Income is referred to in this context as **disposable income** which is the income remaining after all direct taxes and national insurance contributions have been deducted. In 1976 in the UK total personal income was £112,354 million, whereas total personal disposable income was £86,253 million; £12,597 million of this latter amount was 'disposed' of in the form of personal savings, as various forms of savings also compete for household income since these can also be a source of satisfaction.

Another important assumption when tracing possible changes in income upon demand is that the existing distribution of income between different groups of the community remains unchanged. This is because changes in the level of total income accompanied by a redistribution of income will change the anticipated pattern of consumer expenditure. Fig. 7.4 contains the demand curve X which shows that the demand for this particular product varies directly with the average level of household income. As income rises, households have the opportunity of increasing their purchase of items which will add to their total satisfaction with the obvious advantage of not having to cut the purchase of other products. The consumer will distribute an increase in income in such a way that, having regard to relative prices and the satisfaction derived from various products, a new equilibrium will be reached and satisfaction again maximised within the budget imposed by this higher income.

Fig. 7.4

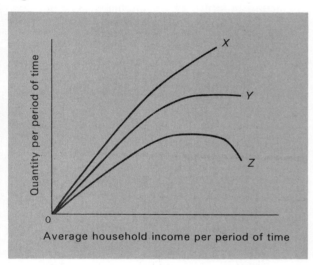

where demand increases at first, and then actually remains constant at a certain quantity per period of time despite further increases in income. Table 7.1 shows this to be virtually the case with items of food, suggesting that once incomes have reached a certain level these needs are completely satisfied. The consumer may, however, alter the composition of food consumption in favour of those items which could not be purchased on a lower income.

There is also the possibility, as shown by demand curve Z in Fig. 7.4, that the demand for some products may eventually fall once incomes reach a certain level. This will be the case when the higher income allows the consumer to replace some existing purchases with what are regarded as superior substitutes. Table 7.1 shows, for example, that coal and coke have experienced a decline in domestic demand as households have been able to afford superior means of heating. Books, newspapers and magazines, however, seem to have lost ground to other forms of leisure activities, and in fact over the same period the volume of sales of indoor games and sports equipment rose by over 100 per cent. Similarly, although expenditure on floor coverings has increased, the demand for linoleum has fallen by an average of 7 per cent a year, whereas the demand for carpets and rugs has increased by over 10 per cent a year over the same period.

In the long run, virtually all products are replaced by superior substitutes, and this is the driving force which helps to maintain the momentum of industrial and commercial organisations. Research and development produces new materials and technologies which are incorporated into new or improved products. Producers will then inform the market of the superior nature of these products through advertising as higher incomes widen the market for them. Fig. 7.5 shows the life cycle of monochrome television sets. On the assumption that income is not evenly distributed, there will be some televisions demanded at a low average income as the better off will be able to purchase them. As average household income increases, a larger number of households will have reached a level of income which allows them to purchase a television set, while perhaps some of the higher-income households will purchase a second set. Eventually a position will be reached when the demand is completely satisfied. In order to maintain sales, producers may restyle the sets to make them more attractive and to induce households to

Table 7.1 gives an indication of the likely areas where consumers will direct this increase in spending power. Although figures in Table 7.1 have been adjusted to take account of inflation, it is possible that some of the changes in expenditure in various categories may have been due to changes in relative prices, but the magnitude of some of the changes in consumer expenditure would suggest that increases in real income were a major influence on the pattern of expenditure that emerged over the period covered. Various forms of alcoholic drinks, consumer durables, chemists' goods, and goods and services associated with recreation and entertainment, were major areas where expenditure increased.

Demand curve Y in Fig. 7.4 shows the case

Table 7.1: UK consumers' expenditure at 1975 prices (selected items)

	1970	1980	Percentage increase
Total personal disposable income	63,745	84,847	+33·1
Food—Total	12,041	12,651	+5·1
of which Bread and cereals	1,658	1,597	−3·6
Meat and bacon	3,408	3,609	+5·9
Sugar, preserves and confectionery	1,295	1,273	−1·7
Dairy products	1,504	1,565	+4·1
Fruit	728	763	+4·8
Beverages	674	956	+41·8
Alcoholic drink—Total	3,668	5,367	+21·4
of which Beer	2,265	2,721	+20·1
Spirits	880	1,553	+65·1
Wines, etc.	547	1,093	+99·8
Fuel and light—Total	2,782	3,073	+10·5
of which Coal and coke	658	279	−57·6
Electricity, gas and others	2,127	2,794	+31·3
Clothing—Total	4,635	6,247	+34·8
of which Footwear	752	972	+26·6
Other clothing	3,883	5,275	+35·8
Durable goods—Total	3,987	6,337	+58·9
of which Motor cars and motor cycles	1,759	2,381	+35·3
Furniture and floor coverings	1,335	1,800	+34·8
Radio, electrical and other durable goods	954	2,156	+126·0
Books, newspapers and magazines	979	930	−5·0
Chemists' goods	793	1,071	+35·0
Miscellaneous recreational goods	1,263	2,088	+65·3
Entertainment and recreational services	834	1,543	+85·0
Catering, insurance and other services	6,414	7,038	+9·7

replace their existing models. Any additional increase in sales may then require the development of a set which is a very superior product, which higher incomes allow households to purchase as a substitute for their existing models, and this will be the case with colour television sets. In 1976 nearly 96 per cent of households in the UK possessed a television set, and the market had been virtually saturated for many years. The development of colour sets, however, gave fresh impetus to sales as there was a substantial increase in the replacement demand. In 1969 colour sets accounted for 15·5 per cent of total sales, whereas by 1974 they were 74·4 per cent of sales.

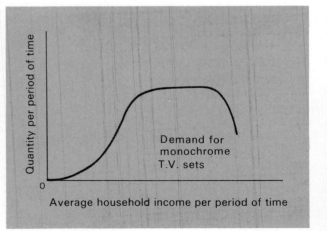

Fig. 7.5

The life-cycle of many products can be identified although in some cases the fall may eventually be arrested and even off at a lower level. For example, as incomes increase the demand for bread may fall, but some bread will still be consumed because of the advantages which bread may possess in terms of food value, convenience and versatility in its uses.

Real incomes, and hence real purchasing power, may be affected by changes in the general level of prices or by price changes for those products which form an important part of household expenditure. If money incomes remain unchanged, or rise at a slower rate than prices, this produces a fall in real income as was experienced in the UK in 1976. Real incomes increase if the economy succeeds in raising its overall productivity. This is because increased output per head will not only mean that more is produced with an economy's limited resources, but the higher income generated will provide the means of purchasing this increased output. It is conceivable of course that real incomes could be increased by a *fall* in the general level of prices, while incomes remained unchanged or fall at a slower rate. This is unlikely, however, in an economy such as in the UK where the prices of most products tend to be rather inflexible in a downward direction. Occasionally, the rise in the cost of living may be arrested by the seasonal fall in some prices, or by improved production techniques that allow a producer to reduce a price in order to increase sales. In the absence of measures that would overcome inflation completely, increases in real incomes are mainly the result of income increases in excess of the general rise in prices.

Section (i) dealt with a change in price which led to what was termed the 'substitution' effect. If the change in price, however, relates to a product which commands a large part of the consumer's expenditure, then a noticeable 'income' effect may be produced. A marked increase in the price of petrol, for example, may lead to a slight fall in demand but to purchase this reduced quantity will involve transferring expenditure from other products. Similarly, if the price of petrol were to fall this will release some purchasing power for other products.

(v) Demand and tastes and preferences
This factor influences demand despite the important constraint imposed by income and the prices of various products remaining unchanged. Tastes and preferences is an area upon which producers seek to operate by the use of persuasive advertising suggesting that greater satisfaction can be achieved by purchasing a particular product rather than its alternatives. There may be certain features of the product that make it superior and attractive as incomes rise, but it is assumed here that tastes and preferences may stem directly from consumers and be expressed in a change in the pattern of expenditure.

For example, there are many ways of filling leisure time and increased preference for sporting activities would be reflected in the increased demand for sports equipment and sportswear. Eating habits may also change, as has occurred in the UK with the increased popularity of foreign dishes. The consumption of food may also be influenced by factors which cause consumers to be more discriminating between alternatives on the basis of calories or cholesterol content, and ingredients of a health food or nutritional nature. This influence on demand can also be seen in the market for consumer durables as, for example, the popularity of hatch-back cars and cassette players. Male toiletries have also been a rapid growth area in recent years, as men have shown a greater interest in various lotions and talcs which previously were in minority use. Fashion is an important element in some purchases and this may give rise to an increase in the demand for denim, cheesecloth and leather at the expense of other materials from which clothing is made. An important feature of tastes and preferences is that although some may seem to have led to permanent changes in demand, trends may eventually develop that reverse the process and traditional products can regain their popularity.

Other important economic factors that influence demand, which are not explained in detail, are the size and structure of the population and the distribution of income.

The elasticity of demand

As one factor that influences demand alters, producers will be concerned about the repercussions of this change upon the demand for their products. The producer may be aware of the direction of this change in demand but will be equally concerned about its expected magnitude. The elasticity of demand is used to determine the size of this change as it measures the extent to which the quantity demanded responds to a change in one of the factors that influence demand. If a value can be attached to these elasticities, the producer may be able to estimate the total effect upon demand of one or more of these factors changing at the same time.

(i) The price elasticity of demand

This is a means of measuring the extent to which the demand for a product responds to a change in the price of that product. Figs. 7.6 and 7.7 show demand curves relating to two different products X and Y. It will be noticed that when the prices of the two goods are raised from OX_1 to OX_2 and OY_1 to OY_2 respectively, the demand for good X is much less sensitive to this price change than is the demand for good Y. The percentage increase in price is the same in both cases, but the percentage fall in the demand for good X is much smaller than the percentage fall in the demand for good Y. Similarly, if one starts at the prices OX_2 and OY_2, and then lowers them to OX_1 and OY_1, respectively, the percentage increase in the demand for good X is much smaller than the percentage increase in the demand for good Y. As far as the price change in Fig. 7.6 is concerned, the demand for X does not prove to be very sensitive and is said to be inelastic in that the percentage change in price is met by a smaller percentage change in the quantity demanded. In Fig. 7.7, however, the demand for Y shows itself to be much more sensitive and is said to be elastic as the percentage change in price is met by a larger percentage change in the quantity demanded. A numerical value can be given to this **price elasticity of demand** (E^d) by the following formula:

$$\text{Price } E^d = \frac{\text{percentage change in the quantity demanded}}{\text{percentage change in price}}$$

An example will help to illustrate this means of determining the E^d. When the price of petrol is raised from 80p to 90p a gallon, the demand falls from 10 million gallons to 9·5 million gallons per period of time. The rise in price amounts to an increase of $12\frac{1}{2}$ per cent whereas the percentage fall in the demand for petrol is 5 per cent. Using the above fomula, this produces a price E^d for petrol in this price range of 0·4. For every 1 per cent increase in the price of petrol there is a 0·4 per cent change in the demand, and as long as the formula produces a value of less than one, then demand is said to be inelastic within this price range. Another example can be used to illustrate the case where

Fig. 7.6

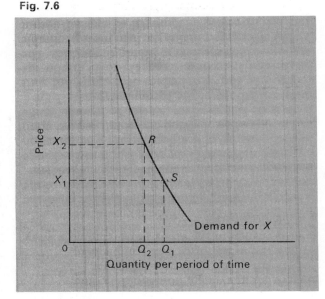

Fig. 7.7

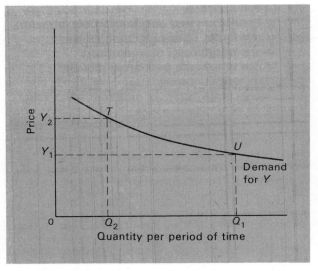

demand proves to be elastic with respect to a change in prices. When the price of lager is increased from 32p to 38p a pint, the demand for lager falls from 5 million pints to 3·5 million pints per period of time. The rise in price amounts to an 18·75 per cent change, while the fall in the quantity demanded is a 30 per cent change. The formula for the price E^d produces a value of 1·6 per cent for lager within this price range, and for every 1 per cent change in price there is a 1·6 per cent change in demand. As long as a value greater than one is achieved, then demand is said to be elastic.

It should be noted, however, that the value of the price E^d in both of these examples does depend upon the direction of the price change. If, for example, one starts with a petrol price of 90p and then lowers it to 80p, this amounts to a 9·1 per cent change, while the increase in the demand from 9·5 to 10 million gallons produces a percentage change of 5·26 per cent. Although demand is still inelastic, the value will be different. Thus a producer will need to know the price E^d with respect to price movements in both directions. The main importance of the price E^d from the producer's point of view, however, is what reaction he can expect if the current price is altered by a certain percentage.

The fact that our numerical examples produced different values according to the direction of the change is of less importance as long as the producer has some idea of what the response is likely to be. This is because a change in price will affect the producer's total revenue earned by sales according to the price E^d within the price range considered. If demand is inelastic, then an increase in price will raise the producer's revenue, while a reduction in price will reduce total revenue. This can be seen in Fig. 7.6. If the price is OX_1 then the total revenue earned from sales is the price OX_1 multiplied by the quantity which consumers are prepared to purchase, which is OQ_1. This can be represented by the area OX_1SQ_1. If the price is raised to OX_2 then the total revenue is represented by OX_2RQ_2. Since OX_2RQ_2 is greater than OX_1SQ_1 then the producer has succeeded in raising total revenue because, although sales have fallen, this is more than outweighed by the higher price obtained from each of the units still being sold. If one starts at OX_2 then total revenue falls from OX_2RQ_2 to OX_1SQ_1, since although sales have increased this is more than outweighed by the lower price which was necessary to induce a greater demand. Similarly, if demand is elastic, as in Fig. 7.7, then a fall in price will raise total revenue from OY_2TQ_2 to OY_1UQ_1 as the reduction in price does not have to be substantial to attract greater sales which are large enough to outweigh the lower price received per unit sold. Similarly, if the price is raised in Fig. 7.7, then total revenue falls from OY_1UQ_1 to OY_2TQ_2, as the rise in price is more than outweighed by the fall in demand. As far as producers are concerned when contemplating a price change, they are primarily interested in whether or not demand is likely to prove elastic or inelastic. There are certain areas of elasticity of interest to the student of economic theory, but the descriptions elastic or inelastic will suffice to deal with the majority of cases when dealing with the response of demand to a change in price.

The value of the price E^d will vary according to the current position of price and demand in relation to the market demand curve and possible changes in the slope of this demand curve. In Fig. 7.8 the initial price is £9, as a result of which consumers are willing to purchase 12 units. Although this part of the demand curve is very steep, this does not necessarily imply that demand is inelastic, as a fall in price to £8 is a relatively small percentage change when compared with the percentage increase in demand which this price reduction produces. Thus a price of £9 produces a total revenue of £108 while a price of £8 produces an increase in total to £120, as shown in the table attached to Fig. 7.8. If, however, the price is lowered further from £8 to £7, this is met by a smaller percentage increase in demand as total revenue falls from £120 to £112. As one moves downwards along this steep part of the demand curve, the percentage fall in price is increasing while the percentage increase in demand is falling. Thus the demand is becoming increasingly inelastic, and if this demand curve were to continue this steep decline, the percentage reduction in price would become progressively larger while the percentage increase in demand would become progressively smaller. Eventually, however, the demand for this particular product becomes much more sensitive to price reductions and it must have entered a range that makes it more attractive to a larger number of consumers working within the constraints imposed by their income and other prices, and engaging in spending which maximises their respective level of satisfaction. For example, a price reduction from £6 to £5 produces a larger percentage change in demand as total revenue increases from £108 to £130. Demand is now entering a price range where it proves elastic, and as long as this is the case, the firm will be adding to its total revenue as it lowers its price. A price in the area of £3 would seem to produce the highest revenue since additional price reductions promote significantly smaller percentage increases in demand. In fact a price reduction from £3 to £2 is a change of 33·3 per cent yet the percentage increase in demand is only 12·5 per cent. If consumers are to be persuaded to buy more, then as far as this product is concerned a large price reduc-

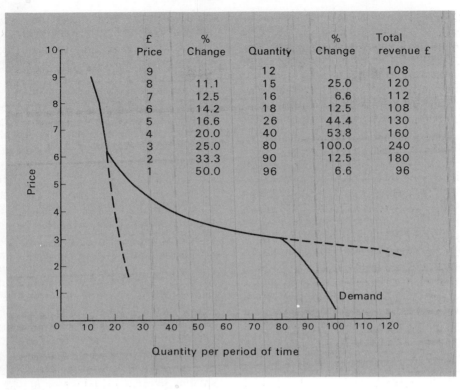

£ Price	% Change	Quantity	% Change	Total revenue £
9		12		108
8	11.1	15	25.0	120
7	12.5	16	6.6	112
6	14.2	18	12.5	108
5	16.6	26	44.4	130
4	20.0	40	53.8	160
3	25.0	80	100.0	240
2	33.3	90	12.5	180
1	50.0	96	6.6	96

Fig. 7.8

tion is necessary. The diminishing marginal utility which they derive from extra units must be met by a large reduction in price to make such extra purchases worth while when compared with the satisfaction which must be given up elsewhere in order to finance such purchases. This reduced sensitivity of demand to further price reductions is shown by the steep nature of the final section of the demand curve, but demand would eventually have become inelastic even if the demand schedule had continued with the lower slope. This is because the fall in price as one approaches lower levels is still becoming increasingly larger, while the increase in demand is becoming a smaller percentage change, thus reducing the value of the price E^d. Therefore a demand curve which is essentially inelastic will have a price range at low levels of output where demand is elastic, while a demand curve which is essentially elastic will have a price range at high levels of output where demand becomes inelastic.

A producer will wish to know the effect upon total revenue of a price change. This can then be compared with the effect on the total costs which are incurred in adjusting output to a level to accommodate this demand. The level of output where revenue is maximised will not necessarily be the level of output where profits are maximised. The producer will have to take account of the costs involved and this may not prove to be a level of output where the difference between total revenues and total costs is at a maximum. The determination of the level of output where profits are maximised is dealt with in subsequent sections of this chapter.

The factors that influence the price E^d

The price E^d for a product will depend upon several factors:

(a) If the product has very close substitutes, a price change can be expected to create relatively large changes in demand over a wide range of prices.

(b) There is often a temptation to conclude that the demand for necessities is inelastic while the demand for luxuries is elastic. Definitions of 'luxuries' and 'necessities' will vary according to the type of consumer one is dealing with. Nevertheless, necessities can be identified from recent market evidence as products consumers are willing to purchase in quantities despite a substantial price rise, such as petrol, heating and lighting and essential foodstuffs.

(c) The price E^d for a product will also depend upon the proportion of income accounted for by the expenditure on the product. Demand may prove inelastic if expenditure is a small proportion of total income. If a product represents a large part of total expenditure, one cannot necessarily conclude that demand would prove elastic, as such a large expenditure would suggest that the product in question plays a major part in the consumer's general well-being and demand in this case would depend upon the availability of substitutes.

(d) The purchase of some products is dictated by personal habits which lead the consumer to regard them in some sense as necessities. This would include tobacco, as well as purchases of beverages and alcoholic drinks.

(e) With some products demand may prove more elastic in the long run than in the short run, particularly if changes in the prices of complementary products are involved. Demand may also have a speculative element as in commodity markets.

(ii) The income elasticity of demand

This refers to the responsiveness of demand to a change in income and is measured as follows:

$$\text{Income } E^d = \frac{\text{percentage change in the quantity demanded}}{\text{percentage change in income}}$$

If, for example, average household income rises from £50 to £75 per week and the quantity of long-playing records demanded rises from 30 million to 40 million per period of time, these amount to changes of 50 per cent and 33·3 per cent respectively. Using the above formula, this produces an income E^d of 0·6 per cent which means that for every 1 per cent rise in income the demand for records increases by 0·6 per cent. As far as this income range is concerned, demand is said to be inelastic with respect to income changes as it has a value less than one. If, however, a percentage change in the level of income is met by a larger percentage change in the demand for a product,

demand is said to be elastic. The value of the income E^d will depend upon the product in question and the existing level of income. As incomes rise from very low levels, households will increase their purchases of those products which play an important part in satisfying their most urgent needs. The income E^d for food, heating, basic items of clothing, and essential furnishings, for example, will be positive and possibly increase as incomes first rise. Once, however, a certain level of income is reached the income E^d for them will start to fall, and when demand remains constant the income E^d will be zero. Further increases in income may then lead to an increase in the demand for consumer durables, and those goods and services associated with entertainment and recreational activities, while some of the existing purchases may be replaced with superior substitutes. The availability of superior products means that as incomes rise the income E^d for those actually replaced will become negative. Fig. 7.5 (page 131), dealing with the demand for monochrome television sets, can be used to illustrate areas of income E^d. The initial part of this demand curve shows that percentage increases in income cause smaller percentage increases in the demand for such television sets. As the gradient of the curve increases, this indicates that demand is becoming more sensitive to changes in income, and eventually the income E^d becomes greater than one. The demand for monochrome television sets then becomes less responsive as sales reach their maximum and the value of the income E^d falls. When the demand curve levels off, the income E^d has reached zero, and then displays an increasingly larger negative value when it starts to fall. If, for example, the income E^d at higher levels of income is −1·5, a 10 per cent rise in income will produce a 15 per cent fall in the demand for monochrome sets.

The income E^d is important for a producer, as sales will depend not only upon their relative competitive position in a market, but also upon what is happening to the total market in which the producer is selling. Those engaged in products with a low income E^d will need to direct a great deal of effort towards capturing a greater share of a stable market by persuading consumers that their particular product is superior to that of its competitors. Producers of household cleansers and foodstuffs would come into this category and can be expected to monitor tastes and preferences very closely to gain a competitive advantage. Producers of some consumer durables may also be faced with what is virtually a saturated market, and those involved in vacuum cleaners and refrigerators, for example, will attempt to increase replacement demand by developing superior products. In other cases, there will be producers dealing in products which have a high income E^d, such as domestic deep-freezes, more sophisticated furnishings and household goods and those goods and services associated with recreation and entertainment. Further increases in income may then also leave these latter producers with a saturated market and a need to develop superior products, or—like many firms—seek to diversify into new and growing areas of demand for which they see trends developing.

If incomes were to fall, however, producers of products with a high income E^d may experience a recession in their markets, as not only would sales not be maintained but the actual fall in income may cause consumers to react by reducing their replacement demand. It is the growth in income which leads to the expression of consumer demand in what are new markets, and plays such an important part in bringing about a re-allocation of resources in an economy to satisfy these new demands.

(iii) The cross-elasticity of demand

This refers to the extent to which the demand for one product responds to a change in the price of another product. This concept is particularly noticeable with products which are regarded as substitute or complementary products. For example, if the price of coffee rises from £1 to £1·50 per jar and the demand for tea rises from 1 million to 1·25 million packets per period of time, a 50 per cent rise in the price of coffee has caused a 25 per cent increase in the demand for tea. The formula for the cross-E^d would be:

$$\text{Cross-}E^d = \frac{\text{percentage change in the demand for tea}}{\text{percentage change in the price of coffee}}$$

The cross-E^d for tea, with respect to a change in the price of coffee, would thus be 0·5 and for every 1 per cent rise in the price of coffee there is a 0·5 per cent rise in the demand for tea.

The more closely that two products are regarded as substitutes the greater will be the value of the cross-elasticity of demand. If the bulk of the reduced demand for one product is transferred to another, the value of the cross-E^d will be correspondingly larger. If, however, there are a range of substitutes available, a rise in the price of one of them will result in a shift in demand which is more widely spread among the remaining products, and the cross-E^d will also be correspondingly smaller for any one of them. The value of the cross-E^d will also be smaller the less the opportunity for substituting one product for another.

The larger the cross-E^d the greater the increase in demand which a producer can expect to experience when there is a rise in the price of a substitute product, but equally important is the fact that he can expect to lose sales if the other product is reduced in price. This will act as an incentive for a producer to keep prices at a competitive level in order that an advantage can be derived from a price rise elsewhere, while hoping to minimise the loss of sales in the event of another product being reduced in price. As long as the cross-E^d is greater than zero, the producer benefiting from a switch of consumer expenditure will increase his total revenue as there will be more demand for this product at its existing price level. One of the objectives of continuing to monitor demand in a test market is to determine the effect upon a particular product of price changes in competing products, and so to be able to adjust and deal with these trends in the market as a whole.

A significant cross-E^d will also exist with products which are complements. If, for example, there was a change in the price of deep-freezes then this would have repercussions upon the demand for frozen foods designed for storage in deep-freezes. This again is a reason for continuing market research as trends in certain markets may open up profitable opportunities for products which are complementary to the product which is in increasing demand. The use of skateboards, for example, provided a market for producers of safety equipment. The research may show, however, that a complementary product is increasing in price which may lead to a significant reduction in sales and the need to seek alternative markets.

Profitability as a factor influencing supply

The following analysis of the factors that influence the supply of a product will initially concentrate upon the major influence exerted by the desire of a firm to make profits. When the objectives of organisations were discussed in Chapter 2, it was suggested that firms had several objectives, one of which was a desire to maximise profits.

Other objectives, such as maximising sales or achieving a position of security, might involve the sacrifice of some profits so that maximum profits were not necessarily obtained. A conclusion was drawn, however, that when this sacrifice of short-run profits was analysed, there was not necessarily a conflict with other objectives when a longer period of time was considered. For example, the aim of maximising sales while engaging in vertical and lateral expansion may have meant a level of profits which was not at the maximum. But the increased security derived from a larger market share and a degree of diversification would allow the firm to secure its future with a view to ensuring profits in a later period. The firm will assess the position in the market for its own output, and also developments in other product markets and those where it purchases its resources. The firm will then adopt policies in pursuit of certain objectives which in its opinion will be in its long-run interest, and then concentrate upon maximising profits while adhering to those other objectives.

The firm will conduct its activities within the business environment, as dictated by developments in both product and resource markets and by the general economic, social and political climate. The possible sacrifice of profits can be likened to a cost which the firm is willing to accept because of the return which accrues in a non-monetary form. For example, the firm may have increasingly involved itself in producing or processing its own components or materials, when strictly speaking the resulting diversification may have resulted in a loss of some of the advantages stemming from increased specialisation. In this case, the firm will have placed a value upon the increased security which control over important inputs may bring. The extra costs and effect on profits that may be incurred as a result of this vertical expansion will produce a return in the form of increased security. Similarly, accepting a lower profit margin in order to maintain or increase sales may place the firm in a stronger market position against its rivals, and this lower profit margin may be regarded as a price worth paying in order to reduce the strength of existing or potential competition. Also the firm may agree to comply with the government's current policies as they affect the company, as it may be in the interest of their long-term existence to do so.

Thus the pursuit of objectives that would seem to detract from maximum profits provides the constraints within which the firm is then able to seek maximum profits. It can be assumed, therefore, that the firm does seek to maximise profits and is prepared to accept what at first may seem non-profit-maximising activities.

The higher the price which a firm can obtain for its product the more it is prepared to supply. Different levels of output will involve the firm in various levels of unit costs, and an increase in output will only be forthcoming if the price of the product in question is such that the extra output adds more to total revenue than it does to total costs, with the result that total profits increase. The supply from a firm will be dictated by the price of the product and the unit costs of producing it, as these two factors will dictate profitability. The determination of the level of output which a firm is prepared to supply in order to maximise profits can be shown with the use of diagrams which involve revenue curves and cost curves.

Revenue Curves

It is assumed that a firm is faced with a demand curve as shown in Fig. 7.9. This curve shows that if the firm wishes to raise its prices, it must be prepared to accept a fall in the demand for its product. The important point about the market is that a firm cannot dictate both price and quantity sold. If it sets a price, it must then accept the amount which consumers are prepared to purchase at that price. Similarly, if it decides upon a level of output then the firm must be prepared to accept the price at which the market is willing to absorb that amount. Thus this demand curve provides us with

Fig. 7.9

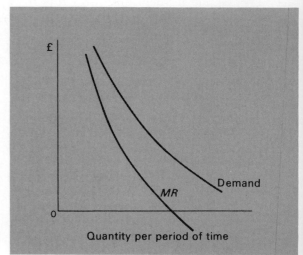

information concerning the total revenue which the firm can expect to receive from various levels of sales. As with Fig. 7.6 and 7.7 (both on page 133), any point on these demand curves is a combination of price and quantity and this was used to indicate the total revenue earned by the firm from these particular price and quantity combinations. Total revenue will differ according to which level of output is selected and it proved useful to discover what happened to total revenue as output was changed. Comparing areas is a tedious and cumbersome process but a marginal revenue curve will provide this information on changes in total revenue.

Marginal revenue (MR) is defined as the addition to total revenue as a result of selling one more unit. If, for example, a firm is selling 8 units a week at £80 each, then the total revenue earned over this period is £640. In order to sell 9 units, however, the firm may be obliged to lower the price to £78 and the total revenue is now £702. In this case, the addition to total revenue as a result of selling the 9th unit is £62 (i.e. £702 − £640). The firm gains an extra £78 by selling the extra unit, but it will have to lower the price of the existing 8 units to the same price which means that the extra £78 is partly offset by the reduced revenue from existing sales of £16. The firm is not in a position where it could charge 8 consumers £80 and the remaining consumer £78. If this same firm wished to sell 10 units, the price may have to be lowered to £75, which means that the marginal revenue of the 10th unit is £48 (i.e. £750 − £702). An 11th unit, involving a price of £70, will produce a marginal revenue of £20. Thus the marginal revenue is always below the price received for each unit sold, and in Fig. 7.9 this is reflected in the fact that the marginal revenue curve lies below the demand curve. The gap between them also widens, as not only must greater price reductions be given to attract more sales, but these price reductions must be given on an increasingly large number of units.

As long as the marginal revenue schedule is above the horizontal axis, additional sales (although at a lower price) must be raising total revenue. This is because the marginal revenue, although falling, is still positive. This section of the demand curve must reflect an elastic market demand curve within the various price ranges, as any percentage fall in price is matched by a larger percentage increase in demand, and this leads to an increase in total revenue. Where the marginal

revenue curve cuts the horizontal axis, the marginal revenue is zero and increased sales have left total revenue unchanged. When this is the case, it implies that the percentage fall in price was accompanied by an equal percentage increase in sales so that total revenue remained unchanged. At the point on the demand curve directly above the intersection of the marginal revenue curve and the horizontal axis, demand is said to be of unit elasticity (price $E^d = 1$). Once marginal revenue becomes negative, however, this means that total revenue is now beginning to fall. For this to happen, the percentage fall in price must have been met by a smaller percentage increase in demand and thus the firm has reached an area where demand for its product is increasingly inelastic.

Another relevant point is that the extent to which the marginal revenue curve lies below the demand curve will be dictated by the general nature of the demand curve. If demand is essentially inelastic as in Fig. 7.10, very large price reductions are necessary to induce even a small increase in sales. Thus the marginal revenue will fall very rapidly soon becoming negative, and this reflects the generally inelastic nature of the demand curve itself. Fig. 7.11 (p. 140), however, shows a demand curve that is essentially elastic and only relatively small price reductions are necessary to stimulate extra demand, with the result that the marginal revenue falls more slowly and the point at which marginal revenue becomes negative is postponed till much later.

Fig. 7.10

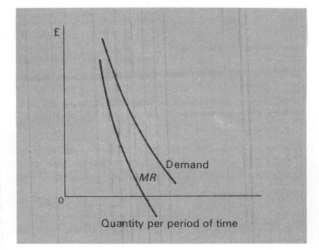

Fig. 7.11

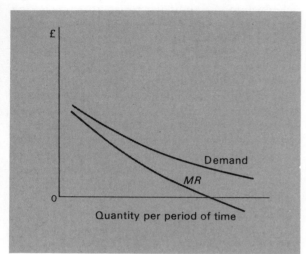

Fig. 7.12

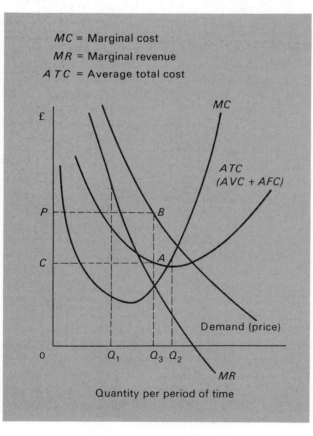

MC = Marginal cost

MR = Marginal revenue

ATC = Average total cost

This is the basic information which one can derive from demand and marginal revenue curves, and it is now possible to proceed with the determination of the output at which a firm will maximise profits. These revenue curves are combined with cost curves in Fig. 7.12 and the basic shape and direction of the cost curves facing this firm demonstrate their characteristics as explained in Chapter 5. The firm will increase production until the last unit produced adds as much to total revenue as it does to total costs. If, for example, this firm was producing OQ_1 units then this would not be a level of output at which the firm would be making maximum profits. This is because additional units of output beyond OQ_1 would add more to total revenue than to total costs, as the marginal revenue associated with extra units of output is greater than the marginal costs of these extra units. Total profits will thus increase. Although the marginal revenue is falling and the marginal cost eventually rises, extra units will still increase total profits, but of course by progressively smaller amounts. Nevertheless the essential point is that it is profitable to expand output as long as marginal revenue is greater than marginal costs. Similarly, output OQ_2 would not represent a position where the firm would be maximising profits, as it has moved into an area of output where additional units of output have added more to total costs than to total revenue. This is because marginal cost is greater than marginal revenue, and the losses made on these higher units of output will start to reduce the total profits which were made on earlier units of output. The level of output where this firm will be making maximum profits is in fact at OQ_3.

The total cost incurred by this firm at OQ_3 will be that level of output multiplied by the average total costs of those units which make up OQ_3. In Fig. 7.12 this is represented by the area OQ_3AC. The total revenue derived from selling OQ_3 units is the same quantity multiplied by the price received per unit, which is OP. As predicted in Fig. 7.9, the selling price is greater than the marginal revenue resulting from the sale of the last unit. Total revenue is thus OQ_3BP. The total profits made by this firm is therefore $CABP$. This firm is more than covering its costs at OQ_3 and within costs is an element of profit which is regarded as normal profit. This is the minimum return which the firm is prepared to accept, taking account of the risks involved in this particular line of production. This normal profit must be covered for the

Recommendations:

Main recommedation which we ~~thought~~ suggested were

1) to increase prices of cigarettes because ~~keep~~ it this would stop young people from buying cigarettes. more then they can afford. Considering most of them are either unemployed or in Further Education. Which shows that ~~they to~~ it would be difficult for them afford to buy high priced cigarettes. just to enjoy them selves.

② To stick more anti smoking posters around Schools and collages, showing the bad effects of smoking, to pervert their minds from smoking.

places where there are more young people

3) Introduce anti-smoking campaigns, advertising them in the media and showing more programmes on TV of anti smoking.

4) To ask people to give up smoking as a group so that that there is more chance of them giving it up as a whole then just by them selves.

venture to be worth while, and it can therefore be likened to a cost and is accordingly included in the average total cost curve. Since this firm is more than covering total costs, it is said to be making **super-normal profits.**

The effect of price and cost changes on supply

Profitability has thus dictated the amount of the product which this firm is willing to supply, and since profitability is determined by the revenue and cost curves, any change in these factors will influence profits and hence the supply of the product. A change in the demand for the product will be reflected in a change in the price of that product, and this will mean that the firm is faced with a different revenue situation. Similarly, a change in the factors that influence total costs will mean that the firm is faced with a different cost situation. The repercussions of changes in these two situations on the firm will now be examined.

(i) A change in demand

The demand curve with which the firm is faced shows the relationship between the price of the product and the quantity demanded, on the assumption that all other factors that influence the demand for the product remain unchanged. If the price of the product itself changes, the demand curve tells us what happens to the demand. A rise in the price in Fig. 7.13, for example, from OP_1 to OP_2, results in a movement along the existing demand curve indicating that the quantity demanded falls from OQ_1 to OQ_2. If price were lowered from OP_2 to OP_1, then again the increase in the quantity demanded is shown by a movement along the existing demand curve, indicating that the quantity demanded has increased from OQ_2 to OQ_1.

A change in any of the other factors that influence the demand for this product will cause the demand curve to shift. If, for example, there is an increase in the average level of household income and the income E^d for this product is positive, more of this product will be demanded at each price than previously. The producer can expect a percentage increase in the demand for his product at all the possible price levels. In Fig. 7.14, for example, consumers are now prepared to purchase the quantity OQ_4 at the price OP_1, rather than the quantity OQ_1; and at the price OP_2 they are now

Fig. 7.13

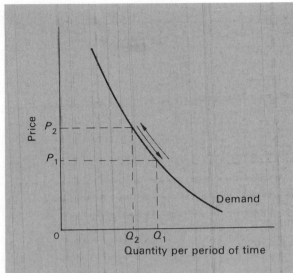

Fig. 7.14

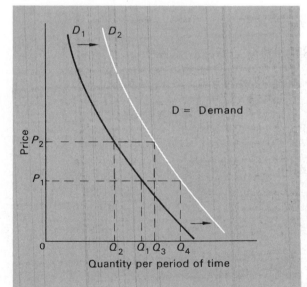

willing to buy OQ_3 rather than OQ_2. The demand schedule has shifted to the right from D_1 to D_2. If the average level of household income falls, however, then the demand for this product will be lower at each price than previously, as shown by the leftward shift of the curve in Fig. 7.15 (p. 142) from D_1 to D_2. At the price OP_1 the quantity demanded has fallen from OQ_1 to OQ_4, whereas at the price OP_2 demand has fallen from OQ_2 to OQ_3. The factors which can cause such a shift can be summarised as follows:

Fig. 7.15

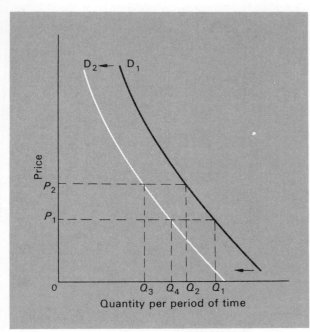

Fig. 7.16

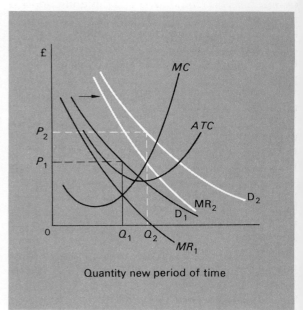

Quantity new period of time

Rightward shift of demand
 (i) A rise in average household income.
 (ii) A rise in the price of a substitute.
 (iii) A fall in the price of a complement.
 (iv) A change in tastes and preferences in favour of the product.

Leftward shift of demand
 (i) A fall in average household income.
 (ii) A fall in the price of a substitute.
 (iii) A rise in the price of a complement.
 (iv) A change in the tastes and preferences away from the product.

There are other factors that may influence the demand for a product and thus cause a shift of the demand curve, such as a redistribution of income, a change in the size of the population and a change in the structure of the population. The direction of the shift of the demand curve will depend upon how these factors affect the size or income of the different groups of the community.

Fig. 7.16 shows the effect of a rightward shift of the demand curve from D_1 to D_2 upon the amount which the firm is willing to produce. The higher price in fact makes the firm more profitable and it is therefore encouraged to expand output to make even higher profits. The cost situation and

demand curve D_1 initially produced a level of output where profits were maximised at OQ_1, as this was the level of output where marginal cost was equal to marginal revenue. The shift of the demand curve from D_1 to D_2 now means much higher profits at this level of output, as the price received for each of the units can be shown by continuing the vertical line from OQ_1 until it reaches the demand curve D_2. The difference between total revenue and total costs at OQ_1 is now much larger. There is now every incentive to expand output as the demand curve D_2 has produced a new and higher marginal revenue curve MR_2. Therefore at output OQ_1 the marginal revenue is now greater than the marginal cost, and additional units of output will mean more is added to total revenue than to total costs. The firm will continue to expand output until once again a level of output is reached where marginal revenue is equal to marginal costs. Profits will be at a maximum at the output OQ_2, and had the firm remained at OQ_1 it would have been denying itself profitable units of output. The difference between total revenue and total costs at OQ_2 will be much larger than that which existed at OQ_1. It will be noticed that by extending the vertical line to D_2 the new and much higher price that existed at OQ_1 has fallen to OP_2. This was the result of the firm expanding output to take advantage of profits from higher output, and this would involve a lowering of price if the extra output was to be absorbed by the market. This is shown by a movement downwards along D_2. The firm was prepared to accept this fall in price as extra units of output still raised total profits.

This analysis can be reversed if one starts with the demand curve D_2 and then shifts it to D_1. The initial output is now one where marginal cost exceeds marginal revenue and output will be contracted to OQ_1, where once again profits are being maximised, although at a lower level.

The conclusion therefore is that the quantity supplied is influenced by profitability and the higher the price the larger the quantity the firm is prepared to supply, and the lower the price the smaller the quantity the firm is prepared to supply. This relationship between price and supply is thus reflected in the supply curve in Fig. 7.17, in that when the price is raised from OP_1 to OP_2 the quantity supplied is increased from OQ_1 to OQ_2, while a fall in price from OP_2 to OP_1 will lower supply from OQ_2 to OQ_1. This supply curve relates to the reaction of one producer to a change in price, and a market supply curve relating to the same type of product coming from all producers involved in the market would also slope upwards from left to right, showing the relationship between the price and the total quantity which will be supplied to the market. Since firms can expect to have different cost structures because, for example, of their size and productivity, a certain price will produce different levels of output from each firm within the market as a whole.

Let us assume that the market for a particular product X is supplied by five different firms, and the quantities which each of them is prepared to supply at various price levels, so that each of them maximises its profits, is as shown in Table 7.2. The total of the individual amounts which each firm is willing to supply at each of the price levels can then be used to produce the market supply curve for the product X in Fig. 7.18. The most efficient is Firm A because it can afford to supply more at each price than the others, indicating that its marginal costs do not rise as rapidly as the others; so Firm A is thus provided with greater scope to increase output as the price increases. This is in contrast to Firm E which experiences rapidly increasing marginal costs that soon reach the marginal revenue associated with any extra units which it produces.

Fig. 7.17

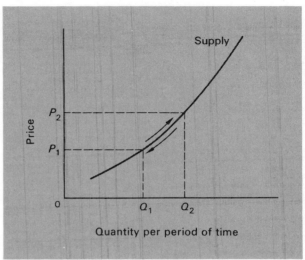

Table 7.2

| Price in £s | Units of product X supplied per period of time | | | | | Total supply |
	Firm A	Firm B	Firm C	Firm D	Firm E	
1	10	9	7	4	2	32
2	25	21	17	12	10	85
3	45	36	29	22	19	151
4	75	48	39	30	25	217
5	95	56	45	36	28	260
6	105	60	48	38	29	280

Fig. 7.18

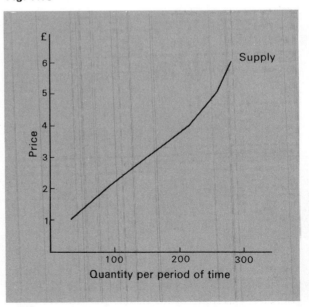

(ii) A change in costs

The quantity which a firm is willing to supply will not only be influenced by the price which it can obtain but also by changes in its costs of production. The firm analysed in Fig. 7.16 (page 142) was seen to respond to a change in price brought about by a shift of the demand schedule, while operating within a certain cost structure. If, however, the cost structure changes, output will be associated with different average total costs and marginal costs. The firm in Fig. 7.19 is initially maximising its profits at output OQ_1 where marginal cost is equal to marginal revenue. The existing cost curves are MC_1 and ATC_1 but these then change, perhaps because of advances in the technology employed in making the product. The level of output OQ_1 is no longer a level at which profits are maximised, as marginal revenue is now above the lower marginal cost curve MC_2 which reflects this improvement in technology. The firm is now in a position to increase profits by expanding output, as additional units of output will add more to total revenue than to total costs. Had the firm remained at OQ_1 it would have denied itself these profitable units of output. Profits will again be maximised at OQ_2, where again marginal revenue is equal to marginal costs, and where the difference between total revenue and total costs is now larger than that which existed at OQ_1. The firm was prepared to supply more, and to reduce the price of its product in order to encourage consumers to purchase the higher output, since extra units of output still raised profits because of the lowering of costs.

The effect of unfavourable changes in the firm's cost structure can be followed if one starts with the curves MC_2 and ATC_2 and replaces them with MC_1 and ATC_2. If this happens, OQ_2 will not be a level of output where profits are maximised, as marginal cost as shown by MC_1 will be far in excess of the marginal revenue, and the firm will contract output to OQ_1 where it is maximising profits again but at a lower level of output.

Fig. 7.20

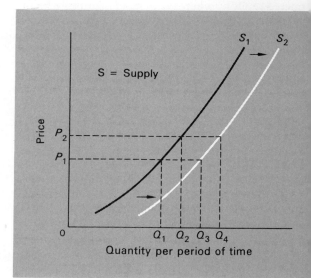

Fig. 7.19

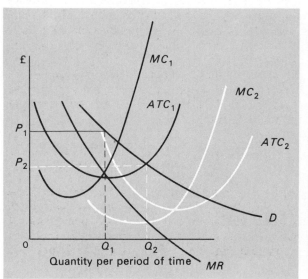

Fig. 7.21

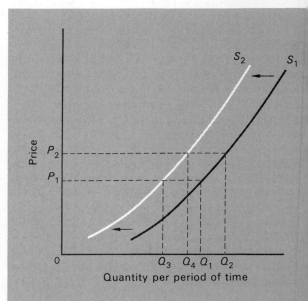

Thus another conclusion that one can draw about supply is that a fall in the costs of production will lead to an increase in the quantity supplied, while an increase in the costs of production will produce a fall in the quantity which producers are willing to supply at various price levels. This reaction of producers to changes in costs can be seen in Figs. 7.20 and 7.21. The supply curve S_1 shows the relationship between price and the quantity supplied in a market for a product, on the assumption that all the other factors that influence supply remain unchanged. Developments which reduce the costs of production, such as an improvement in technology, a fall in the price of raw materials or a rise in the productivity of labour, will mean that the firms benefiting from these changes will be prepared to supply more at each price than previously. Although the price of the product has remained unchanged, the lower costs enable firms to produce what were previously unprofitable units of output. This produces a rightward shift of the supply curve in Fig. 7.20 from S_1 to S_2, so that at a price of OP_1, for example, the quantity supplied will be OQ_3 rather than OQ_1. Similarly, at the price OP_2 the quantity supplied will now be OQ_4 rather than OQ_2. A rise in the costs of production, however, will indicate that firms are now prepared to supply less at each price than previously, as shown in Fig. 7.21 where supply at OP_1 falls from OQ_1 to OQ_3, while supply at OP_2 falls from OQ_2 to OQ_4. It should be emphasised, however, that a change in the price of the product itself will cause a movement along the relevant supply curve, as the supply curve provides this information on how supply changes with the price of the product itself.

(iii) A change in relative profitability

A change in the prices of products will affect the relative profitability of firms operating in the respective markets for these products. A rise in the price of floor tiles, for example, perhaps caused by a change in tastes and preferences shifting the market demand curve to the right, will attract increased supplies from existing producers, and this will be shown by an upward movement along the existing market supply curve as these producers expand their output. After a period of time, however, firms engaged in other products and making lower—or even only normal—profits will see the manufacture of floor tiles as relatively more attractive. It may prove comparatively easy for firms engaged in similar products to move into tile production because their existing materials, items of plant and equipment and labour force may be flexible in this direction.

After a time lag, therefore, depending upon the nature of the product and the technical conditions governing production, the market supply schedule relating to floor tiles will shift to the right, as in Fig. 7.20. This indicates that more is supplied at each price than previously, as more firms are now involved in the product. If the price of floor tiles remains at a sufficiently high level, so continuing to make this a relatively more profitable line of output, firms engaged in perhaps totally different products may eventually diversify into the production of floor tiles and the supply schedule will shift further to the right. The result of this shift of resources into the manufacture of floor tiles will obviously be at the expense of other products. This will be reflected in a leftward shift of the supply curves relating to these products, as shown in Fig. 7.21, whereby less is now supplied at each price than previously. This is again an example of how resources are re-allocated according to changes in consumer demand, and this re-allocation will come to an end when relative profitability no longer makes such a transfer of resources worth while.

The elasticity of supply

This refers to the extent to which the quantity supplied responds to a change in price. Figs. 7.22 and 7.23 show that the same percentage rise in price from OP_1 to OP_2 and from OM_1 to OM_2 has produced a different response in the quantity supplied. Supply of product X in Fig. 7.22 (p. 146) is said to be elastic in that the percentage change in price has caused a larger percentage change in supply. Supply of product Y in Fig. 7.23 (p. 146) is said to be inelastic as the percentage change in price produces a smaller percentage change in the supply. The formula for the elasticity of supply (E^s) is as follows:

$$E^s = \frac{\text{percentage change in the quantity supplied}}{\text{percentage change in price}}$$

If, for example, when the price of wool is raised from £12 to £15 per unit, the supply is increased from 5 million to 6 million units per period of time, the change in price is 25 per cent and the percentage change in the supply of wool is 20 per cent.

Using the above formula, this produces an E^s of 0·8. Thus for every 1 per cent rise in the price of wool, there is a 0·8 per cent increase in the supply of wool and, since the value of the E^s is less than one, supply in this price range is inelastic. If the value of the E^s is greater than one, supply is elastic. It should be noted that as with all elasticities, the value of the E^s can also be established for a downward movement in the price level. The value of the E^s is important to firms, as they will wish to know how the supply of their inputs will be influenced by changes in the prices which they are willing to offer to attract additional quantities.

The factors that influence the E^s

(a) *The response of firms to an increase in the price of a product will depend upon the rate at which costs increase as output is expanded to take advantage of increased profitability afforded by the price rise.* If firms are currently maximising profits, where marginal revenue is equal to marginal costs, a rise in price as shown in Fig. 7.16 (page 142) will allow firms to expand output. A cost structure which displays rapidly rising marginal costs will not provide the firms with much more scope to increase output. This is because the rapidly rising marginal costs associated with increased units of output will soon meet the marginal revenue resulting from the sale of these extra units. If, however, marginal costs rise very slowly, firms will be able to expand output by a much larger amount before marginal revenue again equals marginal costs. Thus rapidly rising costs will tend to produce an inelastic supply, while costs that rise relatively slowly will produce an elastic supply. This is shown in Figs. 7.22 and 7.23. The cost structure involved in producing product X is such that a small percentage price rise will promote a large percentage increase in supply. But product Y requires a relatively large percentage rise in price even to call forth a small percentage increase in supply. At some point, however, as shown in Chapter 5 all costs will start to rise at an increasing rate and thus all supply curves will become increasingly inelastic at higher levels of output.

(b) *Chapter 5 demonstrated that the ability of firms to adjust to a change in their market demand for their product depended very heavily upon the length of the time period considered.* The longer the time period, the greater was the opportunity of firms to vary the employment of all factors of production in order to adjust more fully to the changed market conditions. The lower average total costs and marginal costs would then produce a greater response in supply, as firms were no longer operating within the constraints imposed by a capacity that was essentially designed for a lower level of output. Fig. 7.24 shows how supply will react according to the time period considered.

Fig. 7.22

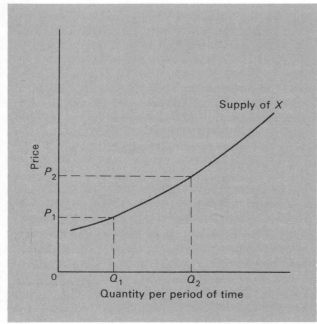

Fig. 7.23

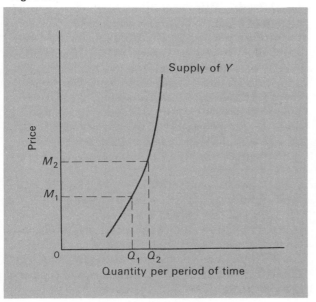

Fig. 7.24

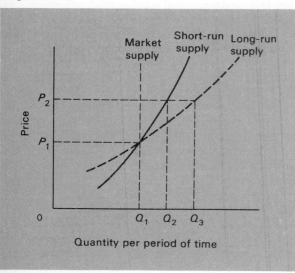

When the price is OP_1 the firms are prepared to supply OQ_1. When price rises to OP_2 there first exists what is known as a **market supply period,** and this is defined as a period of time during which the supply flowing on to the market cannot be increased and, as with all time periods, this depends upon the nature of the product and the technical conditions surrounding production. A sudden rise in the price of leather, for example, will not immediately lead to an increase in supply, and during this market supply period the quantity is said to be perfectly inelastic in that a percentage change in price has left supply unchanged, and thus $E^s = O$. In the short-run period, however, the firm is prepared to supply OQ_2 while in the long run it is prepared to supply OQ_3. Supply is thus more elastic the longer the time period considered, and this illustrates the economies of scale which firms can derive from a more complete adjustment to higher output.

Methods of distributing products

The selection of the most effective means of distribution is an essential part of the responsibilities of the marketing department of a company. Not only should the distribution costs be kept at a competitive level, but they should also encourage the consumer to re-purchase, not solely on the basis of price, but also because the selection of distributive outlet can increase the extent to which the

marketing department can become consumer orientated. This latter point is one of the reasons for the increased tendency for manufacturers to by-pass the wholesaler and deal direct with retail units or consumers themselves. This is because of the savings in costs which such a move may produce, and the closer connection with market trends. Four such channels of distribution will be examined.

(i) The wholesaler
Although often accused of simply taking his cut and contributing to higher prices, the wholesaler plays a vital role in many areas of distribution. Since the independent wholesaler still exists, it can be concluded that both manufacturers and retailers still see advantages in using his services. If either the manufacturer or retailer believe that they can perform these services, a wholesaler will be avoided in the interests of both profit and competitive sales. It is difficult to imagine manufacturers and retailers allowing wholesalers a mark-up if no benefits accrue to either of them. The advantages of wholesalers are as follows.

(a) The wholesaler is prepared to *buy in bulk* which allows the manufacturer to benefit from fewer but larger orders with resulting economies of scale for production, and the avoidance of what may be a high minimum outlay for sales and transport facilities. Producing a multitude of small and perhaps differentiated orders will not allow long production runs unless the producer is prepared to tie up capital in large stocks of finished goods and warehousing or storage facilities.

(b) *Less costly administrative work* in that fewer but larger accounts will have to be dealt with.

(c) An experienced and effective *sales force* takes time to build up and the advantages of a market trend will not be fully exploited if the firm is a newcomer to the market.

(d) The *delivery costs* of small consignments to a large number of retail outlets or consumers which are widely dispersed may weaken the product's competitive position.

(e) The wholesaler can assist the manufacturer in avoiding *seasonal fluctuations in output* which would otherwise involve the accumulation of stocks if capacity was to be utilised so that unit costs of production were to be kept to acceptable levels. If the manufacturer was obliged to install capacity to meet a peak demand, spare capacity would raise unit costs in the slack periods.

(f) From the retailer's point of view, by using a wholesaler he avoids the necessity of dealing with *a large number of widely dispersed manufacturers*, and he can also obtain supplies in more acceptable quantities which can readily be replenished. This is particularly important for the small retailer unable to hold large stocks and without premises for storage. If he dealt direct with the manufacturer, he would have to pay higher prices for small quantities.

(g) The retailer may also receive *credit* from the wholesaler as well as benefiting from advice on window displays and sales in other areas where a new product is involved. As will be seen later it is in the interest of the wholesaler that the small independent retailer does survive as the expansion of large-scale production and retailing is by-passing the independent wholesaler.

(h) The wholesaler may undertake *specialist activities* involving blending, processing or packaging which when conducted on behalf of many producers can be carried out on a more economic scale. As with many aspects of wholesaling, the facilities and staff are spread over a larger and wider range of products and these are opportunities not available to some small manufacturers.

(i) Large wholesalers may be willing to *purchase the product and market it under their own brand name*. This will reduce the need for promotional activities by the original producer as the wholesaler will then undertake this aspect of marketing.

(j) *Speed of distribution* may be vital with perishable products, such as fruit and vegetables, and the specialist activities of wholesale traders may be advantageous for reaching a scattered market.

(k) A new company with a very limited trading experience and financial resources may initially use a wholesaler who will have a greater *knowledge of local customers* in terms of creditworthiness and size and frequency of orders.

The independent wholesaler still survives, along with the small independent retail unit, particularly in the field of groceries and hardware, and where the blending and processing of commodities such as tea, coffee and wool, has produced specialist skills. The development of the **cash and carry** trade has led to the provision of facilities that allow both wholesalers and retailers to remain competitive in the face of rapidly changing market conditions.

(ii) The retailer

(a) The growth of both the size and scale of operations of retail units and the growth of consumer spending has brought about increased opportunities for both *retail units and manufacturers to deal direct* with each other. Large supermarkets and chain stores mean fewer retail units but they are prepared to buy in bulk as well as conducting their own blending, processing, packaging and in particular branding of foodstuffs. Direct contact with these retail units proves very attractive to manufacturers. The wholesaling function does not disappear but is absorbed by either the retailer or the manufacturer to whom such activities now become more economic.

(b) Manufacturers have also *diversified* so that the costs of dealing direct with a retailer are now spread over a wider range of products.

(c) Many of these products have achieved a hard won *brand image*. This will have created a degree of brand loyalty and thus a consistent demand, which is of primary concern to retailers as such a product will have a relatively short **shelf life.**

(d) The reputation for *freshness* associated with a brand of food will be better protected by avoiding the wholesaler, and dealing direct with retail units allows greater influence over the product.

(e) The appeal of *particular brands* is maintained by advertising on a national scale and the resulting demand must be met by an adequate shop distribution, whereas a wholesaler promoting his own brands will be in direct competition with such manufacturers.

(f) The sales staff of a wholesaler may be primarily concerned with maximising total sales, whereas the *manufacturers' representatives* will be pushing their own brand. These representatives, via the retailers, will have a more direct contact with the market, and trends that develop can be more effectively communicated to the manufacturer, which allows a better co-ordination of marketing activities.

(g) Where *new or re-styled products* are involved the wholesaler may prove to be rather conservative and prefer to deal in well-known lines until the product becomes established, by which time the producer will have developed an alternative means of distribution.

(h) Some products by their very nature are *distributed direct to retailers*. This includes relatively expensive products where distribution costs can be borne by the producer without a severe impact upon his competitive position or profit margins. It is not necessary for the retailer to deal in large and varied stocks of consumer durables and he is not expected to buy television sets or washing machines in bulk.

(i) The manufacturer may perhaps conduct his own wholesaling function in such products where *after-sales service* is required and close contact with retail units giving such services will be necessary.

(j) The increasing popularity of manufacturers dealing direct with retailers has been given added momentum by the *increased mobility of consumers*, allowing them to shop in cities and towns for the bulk of their purchases, and this has increased the turnover of fewer but larger retail units. Where congestion in city centres has created problems, these retail units have responded by taking sites in out-of-town shopping centres and establishing **hypermarkets.** This also assists in deliveries and increases warehousing facilities.

(k) Manufacturers have benefited from the building of *motorways* and the development of larger commercial vehicles, some of which are of a specialist nature, according to the product in question, such as frozen foods.

(iii) Mail order

In this case both the wholesaler and the retailer are by-passed and the manufacturer deals direct with the consumer. Methods of distribution change in accordance with social habits and pressures, and more recent years have seen a very rapid growth in the mail order business. Mail order would seem an obvious means of selling to a market where the consumers are widely dispersed and where access to urban shopping areas for a wide selection of products is not readily available. Such a description does not apply to many areas of the UK, yet mail order has still increased significantly over recent years. This growth can be attributed to several factors.

(a) An important element may be the *time and effort involved in travelling* to what may be crowded shopping centres and even then with no guarantee that a particular requirement can be satisfied.

(b) The growth of *branded products* with an established reputation provides the consumer with increased security concerning the quality of the product purchased via a mail order system.

(c) There may also be the possibility that a *lower price* can be paid as the manufacturer or dealer may be able to make significant savings in the marketing of the product. The warehouse and administrative centre can be sited outside an urban area and the lower property prices may permit a more extensive service to be provided.

(d) A large *sales force* is not required but this must be balanced against postal, advertising and delivery charges.

(e) The products selected for mail order must not incur large *transport costs*, particularly if a national market is being served.

(f) The costs of *packing* fragile goods would be an additional consideration.

(g) Some consumers are attracted by the sense of being regarded as a *personal customer*, especially where the product has an exclusive appeal, which is a common feature of mail order advertisement in the more expensive magazines.

(h) This latter point highlights one of the advantages of mail order in that a postal approach or an advertisement in a particular publication can concentrate upon *the sector of the market* where the bulk of the demand is expected to arise. If the product is not expected to have a wide popular appeal then neither a sales organisation nor widespread advertising will be justified, nor will either the wholesaler or retailer express a strong interest in the product.

(i) The actual *advertising cost* will be high if the product is to be adequately described, a colour picture may be important, and space must be available for instructions for purchasing and the order form itself.

There is a tendency to associate mail order with the well-established companies such as Great Universal Stores and Littlewood's, but in 1977 there were estimated to be over 2,000 firms dealing with consumers via mail order. Their products range from clothing, motor vehicle accessories, limited editions of prints and silverware to double glazing, DIY products and chest expanders. Virtually anything, it would seem, that is reasonably economic to transport lends itself to mail order, and this is witnessed by the range of such products that one can find in a newspaper or magazine containing mail order advertisements.

(iv) Marketing boards

Marketing boards are designed to strengthen the bargaining position of many widely dispersed producers by co-ordinating their marketing, administering price support schemes and standardising output. They play an important part in the marketing of milk, hops, potatoes and wool and have been used for pigs and bacon, tomatoes and eggs. Members sell their output to the relevant Marketing Board at a price fixed by the Board who then in turn sell to the market. If the price is set too high then this can lead to over-production and the creation of a surplus which may be both difficult and expensive to store.

With some products supported by schemes in the EEC this has led to the continued accumulation of surpluses which cannot be released within the EEC as this would defeat the object of guaranteed prices. High prices have been necessary in the EEC because farms there are, on the whole, much smaller and less efficient than those in the UK and the agricultural work force is larger in number and hence in political strength. As yet the Common Agricultural Policy has not managed to avoid the continual build-up of surpluses.

In the case of a Marketing Board it may restrict the output of a product on a **quota system.** This was done by the Potato Marketing Board during a severe shortage in 1975–6. The reason advanced was that the lifting of such restrictions on output would lead to a large surplus in the future involving an increased scale of financial support when the anticipated glut came on to the market.

Marketing boards have the unenviable task of adopting a system of marketing which, by reducing price competition, meets the needs of producers, consumers and is in the interests of the economy as a whole.

8. Market Forces and the Response of Organisations to Market Changes

Market Equilibrium

Having analysed the factors that influence both demand and supply, it is now possible to bring these forces together and discuss their interaction in a market, and the respective roles which they play in determining market prices. Fig. 8.1. illustrates the market for product X and includes both the demand and supply curves and their relationship to the price of product X.

A price of OP_2 in this market will not produce a market equilibrium, as this is defined as a condition when neither of the economic forces of demand and supply show any tendency to change.

Fig. 8.1

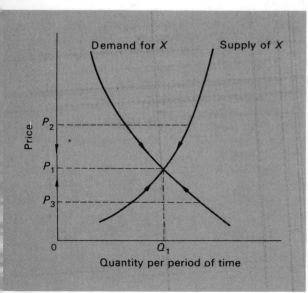

Quantity per period of time

At the price of OP_2 a situation of disequilibrium exists, in that the quantity which consumers are prepared to purchase is less than the quantity which firms are willing to supply at the price of OP_2. A surplus thus exists in this market, and the result will be a fall in price as consumers offer a lower price and firms reduce their price in order to sell this excess supply. This fall in price will rid the market of the excess supply, as not only will consumers be prepared to demand more as the price of X falls, but the fall in price will discourage some of the supply. Price will continue to fall until the excess supply has been removed from the market and this arises when the price is OP_1 as at this price the quantity which consumers are prepared to purchase will equal the quantity which producers are willing to supply. The price OP_1 has produced a market equilibrium in that neither demand nor supply will show any tendency to change and the quantity traded is OQ_1.

Similarly, OP_3 would not produce a market equilibrium because at this price the quantity which consumers are prepared to purchase is greater than the quantity which producers are willing to supply at this price of OP_3. Excess demand exists at OP_3 and this will cause the price to rise as some consumers are prepared to pay a higher price to obtain product X, and firms are prepared to supply more as the price of X increases. This rise in price will remove the excess demand by pricing some consumers out of the market and encouraging a greater supply. The price rise continues until the excess demand has been completely removed, and this occurs when price is OP_1, as once again demand is equal to supply and a market equilibrium exists. The way in which a market price changes, to produce a new equilibrium if any of the factors that influence demand and supply alter, can be seen in the following examples.

(i) A rightward shift of the demand curve

Fig. 8.2. depicts the market for product X which has produced an initial equilibrium at a price OP_1 and a quantity bought and sold of OQ_1. There is then a rightward shift of the demand curve, perhaps because of a rise in the price of a substitute, or a change in tastes and preferences in favour of the product. This market is now in a state of disequilibrium as the economic forces of demand and supply will show a tendency to change. At the initial price OP_1, demand now exceeds supply by Q_1Q_3 and the price of X will start to rise, which

Fig. 8.2

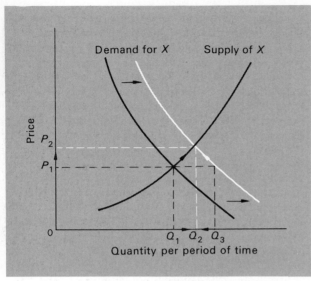

Fig. 8.3

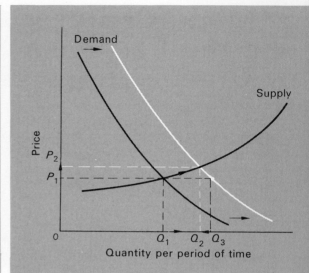

will help to produce a new market equilibrium. The path towards the new equilibrium can be traced by movements along the existing supply curve as they tell us how demand and supply can be expected to react to this increase in price. As the price increases, some of the excess demand is choked off while the higher price will at the same time encourage a greater supply. Eventually a new market equilibrium will be achieved at OP_2 where demand again equals supply at OQ_2. The end result is both an increase in price and an increase in the quantity bought and sold. The market has responded to the increased demand for product X and more resources will have been allocated to its production.

An interesting feature of this path towards a new equilibrium is that the excess demand of Q_1Q_3 was removed by an increase in supply of Q_1Q_2 and a fall of Q_3Q_2 in the initially higher demand as the price rose. The extent to which the shift of demand is met mainly by an increase in price that chokes off demand, or an increase in output that satisfies most of the demand, depends upon the E^s of the product. In Fig. 8.3 it is assumed that the supply of product X is elastic within the relevant price range, and thus only a small percentage price change is required to call forth a large percentage increase in supply from producers. The new equilibrium shows a small increase in price but a large increase in the quantity bought and sold.

This is in contrast to Fig. 8.4 where it is assumed that the supply of product X is inelastic. In this case, a large percentage increase in price is necessary to produce even a small percentage increase in supply, and the new equilibrium is established with a large price rise and a small increase in the quantity bought and sold.

The equilibrium situation produced by the increased demand for product X will also depend upon the time period considered, as the previous analysis has dealt essentially with the short-run reaction of firms. Although it is more difficult to predict the long-run reaction of a firm as the state of technology is never constant, it is possible to show in principle the long-run equilibrium to which the market will tend to move. Moreover, further change in the market demand and other factors governing production may, in the meantime, move producers on to a different path of expansion or contraction.

A rightward shift of the demand curve in Fig. 8.5 is first met solely by a rise in price to OP_2 during the market supply period when supply is totally inelastic. In the short run the type of supply curve dealt with in the previous analysis now operates, and shows how firms can expand output in response to this higher price, which then produces an equilibrium of OP_3 and OQ_3. In the long run supply becomes more elastic and the price falls further to OP_4 and the quantity bought would be OQ_4.

Fig. 8.4

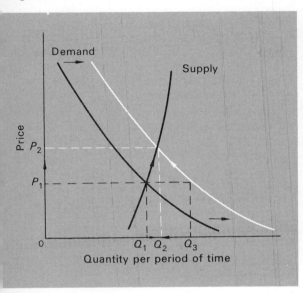

Fig. 8.5

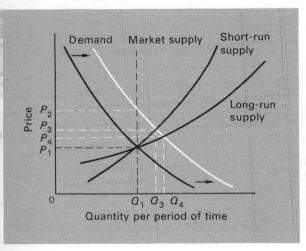

It is this gradual adjustment in the long run which enables firms to take advantage of economies of scale and to benefit from research and development by advances in technology, so that the relative prices of many products for which demand is expanding actually fall. This would be the case as shown in Fig. 8.6, where the firms in question must still be experiencing economies of scale as they expand, since the long-run supply curve is still falling. In this case the long-run price is even lower than the initial level and the increased quantity bought and sold decidedly higher.

Fig. 8.6

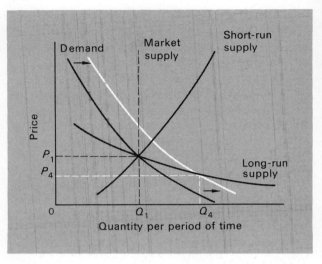

The question may then be asked as to why the firms which make up the market supply in Fig. 8.6 do not increase output beyond OQ_4. At first sight this would seem the logical development, as increased output that caused a further fall in average and marginal costs would be possible, even though the price would have to be lowered. However, the explanation as to why supply will not go beyond OQ_4 in Fig. 8.6 is that the fall in price necessary to sell the extra output, and the effect which this has upon suppliers' total revenues, does not make it worth while despite the fall in average and marginal costs in the long run. After all, firms will produce only when it is profitable to do so.

(ii) A leftward shift of the demand schedule

This fall in demand could be attributed perhaps to a fall in the price of a substitute or change in tastes and preferences away from the product in question. The analysis is similar to that in (i) (p. 151) except that the direction of the developments is reversed. In Fig. 8.7 (p. 154) the demand curve shifts to the left, which means that at the initial price of OP_1 a disequilibrium now exists in the market as at OP_1, supply now exceeds demand by Q_3Q_1 and the price will start to fall. As the price falls, the reaction of demand and supply is shown by movements along the new demand curve and the existing supply curve. The fall in price encourages greater demand, while reducing some supply until a new equilibrium price is reached at OP_2, while the quantity bought and sold is now at

OQ_2. The extent to which the increase in demand is met mainly by a fall in price or by a fall in quantity, will again depend upon the E^s relating to product X in this price range. In Fig. 8.8 it is assumed that the supply of product X is elastic, and the new equilibrium is characterised by a relatively small fall in price but a relatively large reduction in quantity. Only a small price fall means that a large part of the previous output now becomes unprofitable.

Fig. 8.7

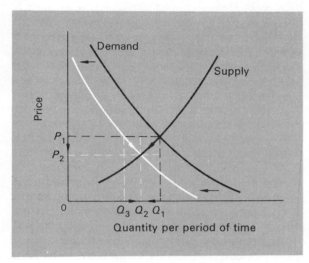

Fig. 8.8

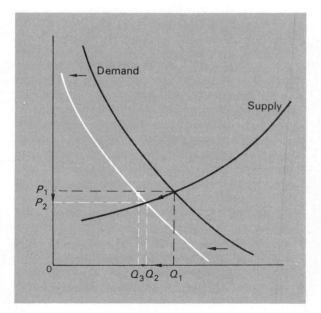

Fig. 8.9

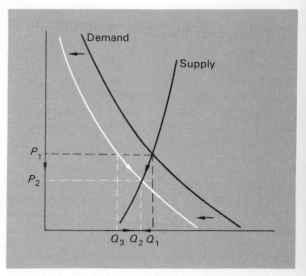

In the case of an inelastic supply in Fig. 8.9, however, the new equilibrium shows a relatively large fall in price compared with the reduction in quantity. If supply is inelastic, it means that very few extra units prove profitable despite a large price rise, and so the reverse of this is also true—that a large price fall makes relatively fewer units unprofitable.

The response of firms to a fall in demand and price may be more marked in the short run than in the long run, as the existing capacity will be designed for the previously higher level of output and hence unit costs will be increased if the fixed factors are spread over a smaller level of output. In the long run, however, the firms will be able to adapt the method of production so that it is more closely geared to this lower level of output, and any savings in unit costs which this adjustment permits will be reflected in the degree of recovery of output. In this case, supply will be less sensitive in the long run when compared with the short run.

(iii) A rightward shift in the supply curve
A change in any of the factors influencing supply, such as a fall in the costs of production because of improved production techniques, will cause the market supply curve to shift to the right. This is because not only will existing producers be prepared to supply more at each price than previously, but the supply will be added to by new firms entering the market because of the change in relative profitability which may result from

such a reduction in costs. The result of a rightward shift of the supply curve relating to product X in Fig. 8.10, is that at OP_1 supply now exceeds demand and the price will start to fall which, in turn, removes the excess supply by encouraging greater demand and discouraging some supply. This is shown by movements along the existing demand curve and the new supply curve. A new equilibrium is then established at a lower price of OP_2 and an increased quantity bought and sold at OQ_2. Elasticities are again important, but in this case it is the E^d which will dictate the relative price and quantity changes. If the demand for product X is elastic, as in Fig. 8.11, only a relatively small fall in price is necessary to encourage a relatively large increase in demand to absorb the increased supply. In Fig. 8.12 where demand is shown to be inelastic, a relatively large fall in price is necessary to promote even a relatively small increase in sales.

(iv) A leftward shift of the supply curve

A rise in production costs will mean that firms are now prepared to supply a smaller quantity at each price than previously, which will also be due to some firms leaving this market to seek more profitable lines elsewhere. When this occurs in the market for product X in Fig. 8.13 (p. 156) at OP_1, there is excess demand and the price starts to rise and encourages a recovery in supply while choking off some of the demand, again shown by movements along the relevant curves so that a new equilibrium is reached at OP_2 and OQ_2. The importance of the E^d within the relevant price range is shown in Figs. 8.14 and 8.15 (p. 156).

In the case of an elastic demand for product X in Fig. 8.14, only a relatively small increase is necessary to produce a new equilibrium as demand is very sensitive to the rise in price. In Fig. 8.15 demand for product X is assumed to be inelastic in which case a relatively large increase in price

Fig. 8.10

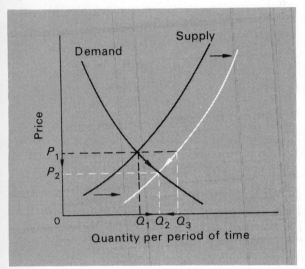

Fig. 8.11

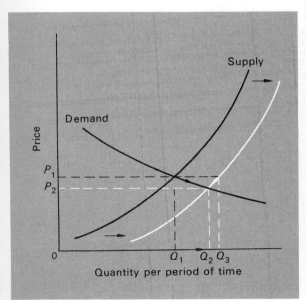

Fig. 8.12

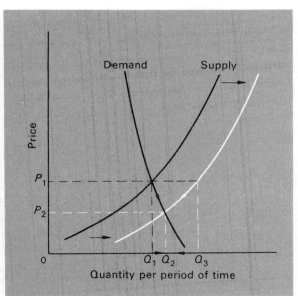

is necessary to restore an equilibrium situation with a correspondingly smaller reduction in the quantity bought and sold.

Another feature of these market adjustments is that the final position of price and quantity will be influenced by the time periods involved, not only from the point of view of supply but also demand. This is because demand will tend to be more elastic in the long run as prices change. The previous examples have served to illustrate not only how the economic forces of demand and supply interact in a market, but that both demand and supply are influenced by so many factors that many markets can be characterised by continual

Fig. 8.13

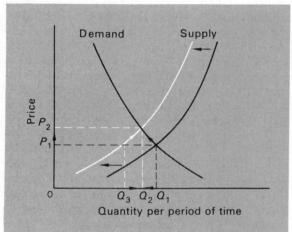

Quantity per period of time

Fig. 8.14

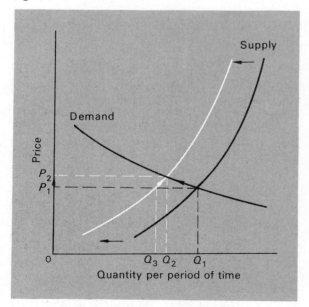

Quantity per period of time

Fig. 8.15

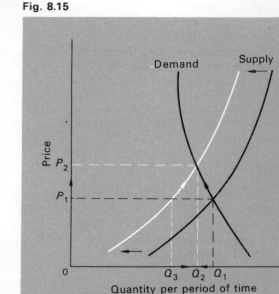

Quantity per period of time

changes. A market may move towards an equilibrium and for a while perhaps reach such a position, but firms will have to be continually aware of the need to adjust to both developments in demand and the conditions governing their supply.

Market forms

Having discussed how these prices and outputs are established in a market, it is now possible to describe the impact of changes in markets upon firms which are involved in them. The effect of market changes upon a firm will, however, depend very heavily upon the nature of the market as a whole, where it sells its product in terms of the degree of competition that it has to face. Changes in a highly competitive market will have repercussions upon the firms involved, which differ from those that arise out of a market where the forces of competition may be much weaker.

Imperfect Competition
This description is used to predict events in a market where there are many producers selling products which, although basically the same in their main characteristics and eventual usage, do display a degree of product differentiation. There may, for example, be a large number of firms producing biscuits and each of them will attempt to make their respective products particularly attractive to consumers by attention to ingredients, shape and

packaging.

The total market demand curve for biscuits will be downward, sloping from left to right, and the price E^d will depend upon how important biscuits are as a foodstuff. The overall price E^d for biscuits will be lower than the price E^d for the product of a single firm producing biscuits. The value of the price E^d facing a single producer will in fact depend upon the degree of product differentiation which the producer has managed to incorporate in his biscuits. The greater the product differentiation, the lower will be the E^d for his product and a rise in price will leave him with more consumers than would be the case if his product was less differentiated from some of his competitors. If, of course, his product was identical in every way, including packaging, and was equally convenient to purchase, then a rise in price would result in a total loss of demand.

A biscuit manufacturer is shown in Fig. 8.16 and is currently maximising profits at an output of OQ_1, where marginal cost is equal to marginal revenue. Since at this output OQ_1 the average total cost per unit is below the price received per unit sold, this firm is not just making profits but super-normal profits.

Imperfect competition is also characterised by the lack of any barriers that may exist to prevent firms moving into an industry. If the firm in Fig. 8.16 is typical of those in the biscuit industry, the existence of super-normal profits will be an incentive for existing firms to expand and new firms to enter the industry. The market supply curve will then shift to the right indicating that more biscuits will be supplied at each price than previ-

ously. Since there are now more firms in the industry the existing producers, as with the firm in Fig. 8.16, can expect to sell fewer biscuits at each price than previously. The demand curve facing this particular firm now starts to shift to the left. Not only will the firm sell fewer biscuits at each price but it can expect the demand for its particular product to become more elastic. This is because the increasing number of firms in the industry will mean a wider range of biscuits from which consumers can select their purchases, and as a result the demand for any particular brand will be more elastic. These developments will come to an end when there is no longer any incentive for new firms to enter the industry. This occurs when the typical firm is making only normal profits, which is the minimum return necessary to keep a firm interested in a particular line of output. Thus if the firm in Fig. 8.16 is typical of biscuit producers, the scale of the industry will cease expanding when the level of output produces a cost and revenue situation as exists in Fig. 8.17. At output OQ_2 total revenue is equal to total costs, as average total costs is equal to price, and since normal profit is included in costs then this firm is making normal profits.

In the long run each firm is pushed into the position where it has excess capacity, as any attempt by a firm to produce at the level of output where average total cost is at a minimum, would involve a range of output where marginal revenue was less than marginal costs. The firm can reduce average total costs in the long run by gearing itself more efficiently to produce OQ_2, but the super-normal profits that arise will again induce a further in-

Fig. 8.16

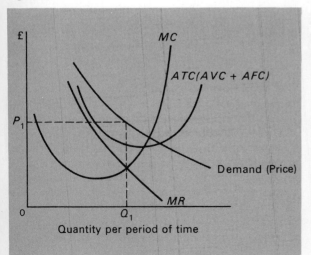

Fig. 8.17

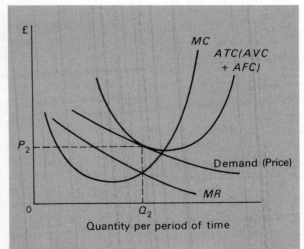

crease in the market supply, until finally a long-run equilibrium is reached where normal profits are again being made with a margin of unused capacity.

From the point of view of consumers, this type of competition raises several points. The greater the degree of product differentiation that exists in a market, the greater the real choice available to a consumer. In this case the value of the E^d for any single product will be lower than if there was less product differentiation. Fig. 8.17, however, implies that the steeper the demand schedule, the further the long-run output will be removed from the level of output where average total costs are at a minimum. The smaller the degree of product differentiation, the less steep is the demand schedule and the closer will be the long-run output to that at which average total costs are at a minimum. The choice confronting consumers, if they were ever in a position to exert such a choice, would be between a more markedly differentiated product at a certain price, or products which are less differentiated at a lower price.

Imperfect competition in markets will also see a great deal of **non-price competition** by firms in the form of advertising, packaging and other marketing activities, in an effort to persuade consumers that their particular product is superior. Large sums of money may be spent to attract consumers from competing brands, and this will prove successful to the extent that consumers feel a need can be better satisfied by switching brands. In fact a producer who does not maintain his promotional campaigns may soon lose ground to competitors. If the total market is virtually saturated, in that the income E^d is approaching zero, then such advertising does not increase the total market for the product but seeks to maintain or increase the **market share** of the firm involved. A larger market share may then strengthen the position of a single firm from the point of view of take-overs. If a firm gains an increasing share of the market, it loses many of the characteristics associated with imperfect competition. More significant economies of scale may be produced if the producer standardises the product to a greater extent, and this will then have to be judged according to the loss of choice available to the consumer. This loss of real choice, however, may already have occurred when the market was imperfectly competitive, as advertising campaigns and product development will seek to incorporate in the firm's product features almost identical to those attached to competing products. Thus consumers will believe that they perhaps lose nothing by switching brands in terms of these features, but rather gain from the additional qualities of the new purchase. Firms losing consumers will retaliate by adjustments in their product and marketing activities that include the new features of the more successful product and others of their own. This process is continuous and is reflected in the sudden emphasis by many producers on a common feature of the product once it has proved successful for another firm in the market.

Oligopoly

This is a market form about which it is far more difficult to make reliable predictions about the response of firms to changes in the market, or the extent to which they will initiate such changes. Oligopoly refers to a market in which there are very few producers of a product and is a strong characteristic of advanced manufacturing economies where growth has seen an increasing number of take-overs and mergers. This has resulted in the output of many products being heavily concentrated in relatively few but very large companies.

Where oligopoly exists, the policy of any one firm as far as pricing and output decisions are concerned will have a very significant effect upon the others. If the conditions influencing demand, for example, should change, the reaction of any single firm will be largely influenced by how the others are expected to react. But if all firms are considering their policies in this way, the results are very unpredictable. If Company A in considering the reactions of Companies B, C and D, the reaction of these other companies may then depend upon what they believe Company A thinks they will do. This of course is only one of many possibilities, but nevertheless generalisations can be made concerning the decisions of such companies and certain characteristics do exist to varying degrees in a market that is oligopolistic.

A very small number of firms with no real difference in strength in terms of profitability and market shares may produce a situation where they recognise their degree of interdependence, and this will be all the more obvious the less the degree of product differentiation. They will be aware that direct competition that provokes retaliatory reactions in a cumulative fashion will make them all worse off. Since they start from positions of equal strength, no single firm will be confident in its ability to survive a competitive battle or indeed in whether the victor can readily recover from what may be the excessive costs of such a competitive struggle.

There may be some form of tacit agreement on what pricing policies should be adopted, and this is likely to be the case if firms not only recognise their interdependence but a leader emerges in the form of a producer which is the largest and becomes the **price leader.** Despite its strength this leader may still believe direct competition is undesirable. The other firms then follow this price leader and their adherence to the set price will be more readily achieved if the market conditions have produced a stable price or an upward pressure because of demand. If this is the case, they can all expect to gain from such price leadership. Tacit agreements will also be strong when they have similar opinions regarding anticipated market trends and changes in costs, so that any price change would be advantageous to all the companies in the light of these expectations. However, in a rapidly changing market that produces a recession in demand, a tacit agreement on prices may prove increasingly difficult to hold, and a firm may be tempted to 'go it alone' in order to attract the demand that will be required to utilise spare capacity. A firm that makes this move first will achieve lower unit costs and will then be able to afford a further price reduction. The initial blow to the profits of other firms may place them at a disadvantage that then proves cumulative. This is because the firm instigating the move now succeeds in capturing an even larger share of the declining market as the greater utilisation of capacity allows further price reductions.

A tacit agreement on prices may also be motivated by a desire to keep out potential new competitors. This, however, can operate in either direction. If prices are kept too high the profits to be made make the costs of entering the market more acceptable to new firms who will be aware that a large capital investment will be required and a large share of the market necessary in order to be competitive. Obviously a risk will be involved, but if the prospects of a high return exist, it may more than compensate for this risk.

Similarly, there may be a common approach to a price reduction to forestall competition from firms displaying an interest in the market. The new firm, however, will then have to judge to what extent the existing producers can hold this price and whether it has sufficient financial resources to gain a foothold in the market. Non-price competition in the absence of barriers to entry may be evident, and may be seen as an effort to strengthen brand loyalty which a new entrant may find difficult to overcome with its new brand, even if it is competitively priced.

The larger the number of firms in an oligopolistic market, then perhaps the greater the degree of price competition, as this reduces the likelihood of many of them having equal strength, market shares, profitability, mutual interests and opinions regarding the future trends in their market. The possibility of a firm acting independently and engaging in direct competition thus increases. In particular, the most efficient firm may be less keen to assist other firms with a tacit agreement to raise prices, as this may hinder its plans for expanding its market share. Take-overs that reduce the number of independent firms in an industry would seem to suggest that tacit agreements are more difficult with a larger number of firms.

Markets that display oligopolistic features are monitored by government departments responsible for identifying **restrictive practices** and this provides limits to the extent to which firms can act in restraint of trade. The difficulty arises, however, in deciding the extent to which the government can promote competition on the basis of price. Many firms express a preference for non-price promotional activities which, although involving costs, do not initiate the substantial losses to revenue that would result from a more direct and fierce competitive struggle if one were ever to gather momentum. However, the end result of activities in an oligopolistic market may eventually be the creation of a monopoly.

Monopoly

This tends to be a very emotive word applied to the situation where there is only one producer of a product. There is, however, nothing inherently evil about this type of market form. A rational analysis of monopoly can show that, as with all market forms, there are both advantages and disadvantages from the point of view of the consumer, depending upon the way in which a monopolist conducts its business activities.

Since the monopolist is the only producer, the demand curve facing the firm is also the total market demand curve as this firm constitutes the whole of the industry. There may, for example, be just one producer of paint, ice-cream or car batteries, or one provider of a commercial service such as air freight. It should not be assumed, however, that a monopolist can charge whatever price he wishes for his output and that the demand for his product is perfectly inelastic with a price E^d of zero. The demand curve facing the monopolist will be downward sloping, and the value of the price E^d will depend largely upon the availability of substitutes.

Whatever the market form, a firm cannot dictate both price and quantity, since if it wishes to raise price then it must accept a fall in sales, while an increase in sales will require a reduction in price.

The eventual price and output combination will be arrived at on the assumption that the monopolist wishes to maximise profits, and it will be where marginal cost is equal to marginal revenue, as shown in the case of imperfect competition, since the underlying analysis of profit maximisation is identical. There is no guarantee, however, that a monopolist will always make super-normal profits, as this will depend upon the cost structure and revenue situations at various levels of output. The revenue and cost situations may be such that only normal profits are made, and there is no reason why a monopolist should not make a loss. The major difference, however, between monopoly and other market forms is that if super-normal profits are made, they will persist in the long run. A monopoly status exists because there are distinct barriers to entry whereby new firms cannot enter the industry. This means that super-normal profits will not allow the expansion of the industry to produce eventually a long-run increase in total supply and a fall in price. If this did occur through the entry of new firms, then by definition we would no longer have monopoly but some other market form. The barriers which restrict entry may take the form of a patent or franchise granted to the producer that prevents direct competition in a particular line of output. Barriers may also exist in the form of the costs of entry, where the capital expenditure involved, and the market sales to make such a move worth while, involve a risk not outweighed by the prospective return. This will be the case especially if the monopolist is likely to foul such competition with a price-cutting war.

It is often suggested that a monopolist has no incentive to indulge in cost-reducing innovations as profits are protected from competition by the barriers to entry and if they are introduced the consumer will not benefit from lower prices. Such a suggestion, however, assumes that the monopolist is a breed apart and is not interested in maximising profits.

As has been demonstrated in Fig. 7.19 (page 144), a fall in costs will permit additional units of output since if output is not raised then the firm, regardless of the market form, would be operating in an area where marginal revenue is greater than marginal costs. Similarly, the increased output by a monopolist will require a reduction in price, so the end result is higher profits and larger output at a lower price to consumers. There are, however, additional incentives to innovate in that if the costs of production rise and the monopolist is forced to a situation of lower output and a higher price, this can influence the availability of substitutes. Products that could compete with that of the monopolist were perhaps not justified as a commercial venture because of the price of the monopolist's product. These potential substitutes, however, then become a viable proposition because of their stronger competitive position. Even a rise in the price of car batteries, for example, may eventually provoke the development of a product that can fulfil many of the functions of the existing product. This will mean not only that the monopolist is faced with less demand at each price than previously, but the demand for the product becomes more elastic now that it has more substitutes. Similarly, a rise in the price of a particular type of energy under monopoly control will make the development of alternative sources a more viable proposition.

Innovations that reduce the necessity for a price rise can therefore weaken the threat from new substitutes. Indeed, one of the reasons for the granting of patent rights is that the profits derived from their application are made sufficiently secure to make research and development worth while. This bestows monopoly by creating a barrier to entry, and the absence of this barrier would erode profits as new firms entered a line of output utilising the same improved product or technology. Under these circumstances, the greater security of an adequate return on the capital expenditure involved may act as an incentive to innovate and from the point of view of the government can justify the provision of what amounts to monopoly power.

In highly competitive markets, the lack of any form of barrier to entry can result in lower prices and a higher output than would have existed under monopoly. If, however, output is spread between too many firms, there may be much duplication of effort and high unit costs as firms will be operating on a relatively small scale. This would then have to be compared with the possible economies of scale that may result from the concentration of output in fewer firms or even the creation of a monopoly. This is one of the economic motives behind nationalisation and the previous roles of the Industrial Reorganisation Corporation and the National Enterprise Board in promoting rationalisation to achieve economies of scale, particularly in the face of strong international competition.

Governments have to steer a difficult course between their desire to see the benefits of competition, and the potential disadvantages of a very strong monopoly, or a group of firms acting in such a way that they virtually constitute a monopoly. This is reflected in the legislation which exists to control monopolies, mergers, take-overs and restrictive trade practices. The growth of competition that results from the dismantling of import barriers that sought to restrict entry into a market can be beneficial from the point of view of prices, but it may also provoke the growth of tacit agreements between firms on an international scale. The growth of monopolies on a global scale in the form of the multi-national corporation is also a growing source of debate conerning their relative advantages and disadvantages.

Index

The Law is dealt with as follows:
Legislation *under* Acts of Parliament
Legal system *under* legislation and legal
system
Affecting business administration *under*
resources, legal implications of Litigation *under*
case law.
The letter-by-letter system has been adopted.